TEACHING AS INQUIRY

Rethinking Curriculum in Early Childhood Education

Lynn T. Hill

Virginia Polytechnic Institute and State University

Andrew J. Stremmel

Virginia Polytechnic Institute and State University

Victoria R. Fu

Virginia Polytechnic Institute and State University

PEARSON

Boston ■ New York ■ San Francisco
Mexico City ■ Montreal ■ Toronto ■ London ■ Madrid ■ Munich ■ Paris
Hong Kong ■ Singapore ■ Tokyo ■ Cape Town ■ Sydney

Series Editor: Traci Mueller
Editorial Assistant: Janice Hackenberg
Marketing Manager: Amy Cronin Jordan
Editorial-Production Service: Omegatype Typography, Inc.
Manufacturing Buyer: Andrew Turso
Composition and Prepress Buyer: Linda Cox
Cover Administrator: Kristina Mose-Libon
Electronic Composition: Omegatype Typography, Inc.

For related titles and support materials, visit our online catalog at www.ablongman.com.

Between the time Website information is gathered and then published, it is not unusual for some sites to have closed. Also, the transcription of URLs can result in typographical errors. The publisher would appreciate notification where these errors occur so that they may be corrected in subsequent editions.

Library of Congress Cataloging-in-Publication Data
Hill, Lynn T.
    Teaching as inquiry : rethinking curriculum in early childhood education / Lynn T. Hill, Andrew J. Stremmel, Victoria R. Fu.
        p.   cm.
    Includes bibliographical references and index.
    ISBN 0-205-41264-5
    1. Early childhood education.   2. Early childhood education—Curricula.   3. Inquiry-based learning.   I. Stremmel, Andrew J.   II. Fu, Victoria R.   III. Title.

    LB1139.23.H55   2005
    372.21—dc22   2004048316

Printed in the United States of America

10   9   8   7   6   5   4   3   09   08   07   06   05

Credits
All written and artistic works have been used by permission of the students, parents, and teachers who created them.
pp. 1, 75, 113, 145, photos by Julie Bryan; p. 3, photo by Martha Drinkard; p. 28, photo by Andrea Swepston; p. 43, photo by Sarah Smidl; pp. 44, 48, 61, 70, 80, 85, 116, 120, photos by Kate Mosher; pp. 52, 87, 97, 98, 99, 100, 101 (top), 102, 103, 105, 106, 108, 132, 134, 139 (bottom), 140, 152, 161, 171, 172, 201, 202, 205, 206, 207, 208, 209 (bottom), 210, 212, 213, 218, photos by Lynn Hill; p. 82, photo by Jennifer McCubbins; pp. 101 (bottom), 104, 109, 110, 138, 139 (top), 141, 153, 180, 181, 209 (top), photos by Kelly Wells; pp. 107, 190, 203, photos by Angela Primavera; p. 194, photos by Rebecca Rainey.

CONTENTS

PART TWO   The Child as Provocateur   75

5   The Child as Cultural Invention: Reconstructing Images of the Child   77

6   Creating an Environment for Children to be Known and Valued: Educational and Caring Spaces   93

PART FOUR   The Tools Of Teaching and Learning:
Life in the Classroom   **145**

FOREWORD

I'm the kind of early childhood teacher educator who rarely uses textbooks in my classes. I prefer the true voice of Vivien Paley to begin the conversation of narrative as a form of teacher reflection and inquiry. I often include books by Christine Chaille and Karen Gallas to discuss the meaning and pedagogical interpretation of the term *social constructivist curriculum*. Books from the early childhood programs of Reggio Emilia, such as *Making Learning Visible: Children as Individual and Group Learners* (Giudici, Rinaldi, & Krechevsky, 2001), bring the perspectives of teachers both experienced and novice to our conversation. Similarly, *Shoe and Meter* (1997) and *The Little Ones of the Silent Movies* (1996) offer us opportunities to study the process of documentation as it unfolds into increasingly complex yet expansive stories. I assign writings that have come out of our work here at the University of Vermont as well, to argue that a program's orientation, values, and theoretical underpinnings should be public and explicit.

But I may be forced to reconsider my choices.

This textbook, *Teaching as Inquiry: Rethinking Curriculum in Early Childhood Education*, is very unique in its efforts to accomplish in one book what I try to accomplish in many. The voices in this book are rich and multiple. I hear the voices of the authors, my friends and colleagues Lynn, Andy, and Vickie; of Kelly, a gifted mentor teacher; of engaged Virginia Tech graduate and undergraduate students; and throughout, the competent voices of the children and families of the Virginia Tech lab school. These many voices are expressed through personal narratives and metaphors and through stories about woozles and revolving doors and ducks named Love and Free. How extraordinary to find this range of perspective and experience between the covers of one book!

The authors' message is clear and unified from the outset: Teaching is "a highly moral profession that calls for us to see the students (children) as competent persons and allow them to learn in ways that bring out the best in them" (p. 5). This belief is personalized and transformed by the authors' students—students like Jessica, who identifies the goal of teaching as "the possibility of more authentic relationships" (p. 71), and by Kate who writes "teaching is an adventure" (p. 72).

Throughout this book the reader is invited to consider what it means to be a teacher. Chapter 9 tells a "long story" that offers an especially helpful portrait of the adventure of teaching and its attendant feelings of wonder, discovery, and confusion. I too have experienced the kind of pedagogical disorientation described by Kelly and Lynn as their "moment of reckoning," a moment when they realize that the children had a vision of creating something much more real, much more meaningful than a replica of a revolving door. They wanted one that was really going to go around by itself. The children's discovery that it is the door that revolves and not the floor is no simple accomplishment, and signifies the children's deep investment in understanding how their immediate world works and the willingness of their teachers to push their own boundaries as practitioners and researchers. The outcome, a "real" revolving door, would not have been possible if not for the strength of the relationships among all the members—children, teachers, students and families—in this committed learning community.

Yes, it's time to reconsider. I do believe next semester's reading list will be significantly shorter than those of the past.

Jeanne Goldhaber
University of Vermont

REFERENCES

Giudici, C., Rinaldi, C., & Krechevsky, M. (Eds.) (2001). *Making learning visible: Children as individual and group learners.* Reggio Emilia, Italy: Reggio Children.

The little ones of the silent movies. (1996). Reggio Emilia, Italy: Reggio Children.

Shoe and meter. (1997). Reggio Emilia, Italy: Reggio Children.

PREFACE

Dear Reader,

It is with an abundance of courage, a strong willingness to take a risk, and an enormous respect for children and their teachers that we write this forward-thinking textbook. We invite you to immerse yourself in its pages and prepare to begin to transform yourself as a teacher, friend, parent, thinker, and doer—whichever apply to you.

We have team-taught and directed the Virginia Tech Child Development Lab School for seven years. While living this experience we have come to understand what it takes to establish an environment in which all protagonists can thrive and develop. The road for us has been long, sometimes arduous, but always rewarding. We share our knowledge with you in these precious pages that we now offer as a guiding compass toward your own journey to becoming a teacher who can make a difference!

Each year we share the following words for reflection and consideration with our students. We hope they will be as visionary for you as they have been for our own community of learners.

> *"Come to the edge," she said.*
> *"We are afraid," they said.*
> *"Come to the edge," she said.*
> *"We are afraid," they said.*
> *"Come to the edge," she said.*
> *They came to the edge.*
> *She pushed them and*
> *They flew!*
> Apollinaire

Our book is divided into four sections that have been designed to help *you* fly. We begin each chapter with a story from the classroom, followed by a list of questions to be considered during the chapter. Next, we challenge you to consider the questions we pose in our "Think about It" boxes sprinkled throughout each chapter. And, finally, each chapter ends with suggestions for getting started, as well as a listing of helpful resources from the Web, books, and articles. In addition to these important components of our book, we have added many examples of both student teacher and child work. These artifacts from their own journeys to becoming inquiring thinkers contribute an authenticity that we feel enhances the powerful learning experience the reader will encounter and relish in this book.

Here is a section-by-section synopsis of our text:

■ The Journey to Becoming a Teacher offers the blossoming teacher the opportunity to take part in some deep and thoughtful self-reflection. First you will review historical theorists and their contribution to our field. Then, understanding that each teacher brings with himself or herself a strong background of experiences that have combined to influence the kind of teacher he or she will be in the classroom, we attempt to blend theory and practice. This part also includes a chapter on "The Teacher as Researcher," which opens another window into finding ways to think about and conduct inquiry-based learning in your classroom. As with other learning opportunities in this book, this chapter peels away a layer of what it means to be a teacher. The final chapter in this section, "The Preprofessional Portfolio: Documenting Self," offers a way to visualize and make tangible the teacher you are becoming and discusses styles for representing this important process.

■ The Child as Provocateur is a brief but highly influential section designed to examine the child. A historic retrospective is offered in Chapter 5, in which the reader is treated to a review of the child as a cultural invention. Here you will begin to formulate your own image of the child and consider how this image coincides with your earlier attempt to write a definition of "the image of the teacher." Are these definitions mutually exclusive, or dependent on one another? This is but one of the many thought-provoking and reflective questions offered for consideration throughout this book.

■ In Part Three, Families, Schools, and Communities: Learning from One Another, there is a strong emphasis on the willingness of the school to share and partner with families on behalf of the education of the children. Examples are offered of strategies for bringing communities together for a common cause. Also included is a detailed story of one school's attempt to define and build an amiable system of schooling in which all members are respected for what they bring to the whole.

■ And in the final section, The Tools of Teaching and Learning: Life in the Classroom, we bring the reader directly into our classrooms by describing in detail the means by which curriculum can be negotiated between teacher and child. Joyful, challenging, and inspiring learning is the goal of this brand of teaching as is the emphasis on children growing and developing as inquiring thinkers. We share several stories to express our belief that community projects can be the impetus for multiple styles of teaching and learning. Finally, four teachers who work in a public school system with a variety of age groups respond to interview questions that challenge them to elaborate on how this brand of teaching and learning can be successful in settings beyond those devoted to the youngest of learners.

The process of writing this book has been transformational for each of us. The experience of living and working together in just the way we have professed in this book has been exhilarating and moving. Using "inquiry and relationships" as the basis for rethinking curriculum causes the teacher to take a second (and third and fourth) look at the way he or she functions in the classroom. Building strong bonds as we question, wonder, and seek out the answers to our questions is a powerful way to teach and learn.

Here are a few thoughts from each of us regarding this experience of "learning to fly":

Lynn: It has been an honor to work with my friends and professional colleagues, Andy and Vickie, to make this dream book come true. During the course of writing and thinking together, I have been reminded again and again of how powerful the collaborative experience can be. I love the strong emphasis on community that weaves its way throughout the entire text. Thinking and working together in the classroom allows adults and children to take part in an exhilarating process that has strong and meaningful results. These are the same feelings I have experienced as a coauthor with my supportive colleagues as they have urged me to move beyond the ordinary and to truly rethink new possibilities for learning and teaching. It is my hope that our readers will catch this contagious way of being and will embrace the transformation that comes with the experience.

Andy: Last summer I read a book by Anne Lamott titled *Traveling Mercies,* in which she writes about her life experiences, good and bad, and how they have come to shape who she is and her relationships with others. Most of us do not have the challenge of writing a novel, short story, or memoir, but if we take our identity as teachers and teacher educators seriously, we do wonder how to speak meaningfully about our work and, in particular, how to describe our daily experiences in the classroom to others. We are, after all, authors of our own lives, and there is much to understand and tell about what we do and how we do it. I have found in my work with students that there is much I do not understand and much more that I have learned from these students, some of whose work is included in this text. When we begin by speaking of our relationship to our students and our common journey of inquiry into the mysteries of teaching and learning, we are freed from the restraints of old and, perhaps, outmoded ways of thinking about and understanding teaching and curriculum. Everyday experiences and relationships become front and center in the teaching–learning conversation.

The first rule of writing is, "Write what you know." This is equally good counsel when deciding how to invite other teachers and teacher educators into the community of inquirers who daily ponder, struggle with, and celebrate the challenge and mystery of becoming a teacher.

Vickie: Writing this book has been a nostalgic journey into the past as well as a way to experience the present with my eyes on the future. One of the greatest joys for me is to be able to collaborate with my dear friends and colleagues Lynn and Andy. Through the years, I have learned so much about teaching and learning from them and from my many students. It is a privilege to include many of the students' writings and artifacts in this book. I hope that readers will learn from these students' creations as much as I have. After all, we teachers are also students of our students. This fall, I attended the first football game of the season at my university. I was so happy to run into many of our former students and was moved by their stories of teaching. They are putting their learnings into practice, creating classrooms of inquiry, and continuing to find joy in teaching—they truly are agents of change! Yes, teaching relationships foster conversations and the discovery of possibilities that enrich our lives and the lives of others.

Acknowledgments

We would like to especially acknowledge and thank our families and friends whose support was indescribable during this venture. Thanks also to the children and families of the Virginia Tech Child Development Lab School and especially to the following contributing teachers: Kelly Wells, Angela Primavera, Angela Sumner, Sonia Mehta, Jenn Aschermann, Kathleen Wampler, Carla Liversedge, Nicki Nichols, Sara Smidl, Melinda Mottley, Christine McCartney, Kate Mosher, Jennifer Brugh, Elizabeth Bloomer, Gretchen Distler, Cindy Dowdy, and all the undergraduate student teachers who taught us so much about the compassion and courage to teach.

We would also like to thank the following reviewers: Dorothy W. Hewes, San Diego State University; Delores A. Stegelin, Clemson University; and Jill M. Uhlenberg, University of Northern Iowa.

We would like to express our deep gratitude and appreciation to the educators from Reggio Emilia for inspiring our work and for encouraging an inquiring way of living and learning.

So come along with us and share our adventure in learning. But don't forget to bring:

- A willingness to rethink your previous assumptions
- The bravery to risk falling or failing and the pluck to pick yourself up and try again
- The strength to transform and change yourself for the good of the children in your care
- The courage to "come to the edge"

Very sincerely, your partners in transforming education,

Lynn T. Hill
Andrew J. Stremmel
Victoria R. Fu

Lynn T. Hill lives on a farm in Giles County, Virginia, with her husband, two daughters, and several dogs, cats, and horses. Her love of nature contributed to her work as the studio teacher for the Virginia Tech Child Development Lab School, where she was also the director of curriculum. She has also served as an instructor in the Department of Human Development at Virginia Tech where she taught undergraduate and graduate courses in early childhood education. She has been inspired and provoked by the Reggio Emilia approach for over a decade and has been most profoundly affected by the concept of an education based on relationships. Her Ph.D. dissertation was an attempt to understand and live this concept with a dedicated group of middle school teachers who were attempting to transform the system of education in their school. She has also collaborated on projects, including books and articles, with several coauthors. She has contributed to several community projects that have introduced the concepts and principles of Reggio Emilia to her own hometown community and beyond. Besides writing, Hill is currently consulting for NAEYC as well as for regional and local organizations.

Lynn's Picks
- *Educating Esme: The Diary of a Teacher's First Year* by Esme Raji Codell
- *Educating Peter* (video), available on Amazon.com
- *The Art and Science of Portraiture* by Sara Lawrence-Lightfoot and Jessica Hoffman Davis
- *From Another Angle: Children's Strengths and School Standards: The Prospect Center's Descriptive Review of the Child*, edited by Margaret Himley and Patricia Carini

Andrew J. Stremmel is associate professor in human development and former director of the Child Development Laboratory School at Virginia Polytechnic Institute and State University. He received his B.A. in psychology from The Pennsylvania State University in 1978 and his M.S. and Ph.D. degrees in child development and early childhood education from Purdue University in 1981 and 1989, respectively. He is a member of the Academy of Teaching Excellence at Virginia Tech and has taught courses on curriculum and program planning in early childhood education, principles of working with children and parents, perspectives on multiculturalism, and child development theories. His research interests are in the areas of early childhood teacher education, particularly the formation of teacher identity. He has coedited two books, one with Vickie Fu titled *Affirming Diversity through Democratic Conversations* (1999, Merrill/Prentice-Hall), and another with Vickie Fu and Lynn Hill titled *Teaching and Learning: Collaborative Exploration of the Reggio Emilia Approach* (2001, Merrill/Prentice-Hall).

Andy's Favorites

- *To Teach: The Journey of a Teacher* by William Ayers
- *Awareness: The Perils and Opportunities of Reality* by Anthony de Mello
- *Let Your Life Speak: Listening for the Voice of Vocation* by Parker Palmer
- *The Tact of Teaching: The Meaning of Pedagogical Thoughtfulness* by Max van Manen

Victoria R. Fu is professor at the Virginia Polytechnic Institute and State University (Virginia Tech). She has taught undergraduate and graduate courses in child development and early childhood education for many years with her friends and colleagues Lynn Hill and Andy Stremmel. She also serves as director of the Virginia Tech Child Development Laboratory School. She values learning and teaching in an environment that fosters collaborative inquiry based on meaningful relationships among faculty and students. Her goal is to create a place where teachers and students learn from one another and together explore the multiple ways of knowing and the unlimited ways of learning. She is actively engaged in research that makes visible the role of teachers as inquirers, who in turn support their students' inquiry in the classroom. For Fu, teaching is a lifelong journey to revisit, revise, renew, and transform oneself as a teacher. She has published extensively in professional journals and books, including *Affirming Diversity through Democratic Conversations,* coedited with Andy Stremmel, and *Teaching and Learning: Collaborative Exploration of the Reggio Emilia Approach,* coedited with Lynn Hill and Andy Stremmel.

Vickie's Picks

- *Landscapes of Learning* by Maxine Greene
- *Teaching for Social Justice* edited by William Ayers, Jean Ann Hunt, and Therese Quinn
- *The Discipline of Hope: Learning from a Lifetime of Teaching* by Herbert Kohl
- *The Enlightened Eye: Qualitative Inquiry and the Enhancement of Educational Practice* by Elliot W. Eisner

The Journey to Becoming a Teacher

Part One offers the blossoming teacher the opportunity to take part in deep and thoughtful self-reflection. First you will review historical theorists and their contributions to our field. Then, as we attempt to blend theory and practice, the next goal of this section is to understand that each teacher brings with himself or herself a strong background of experiences that combine to affect the kind of teacher he or she will be in the classroom. This section also includes a chapter on "The Teacher as Researcher," which opens another window onto ways to think about and conduct inquiry-based learning in your classroom. As with other learning opportunities in this book, this chapter peels away a layer of what it means to be a teacher. The final chapter in this section, "The Preprofessional Portfolio: Documenting Self," offers a way to visualize and make tangible the teacher you are becoming and discusses styles for representing this important process.

Never in Full Bloom
I start as a seed, an idea then something starts growing. Before you know it I have a stem and leaves and a small bud. I gradually begin to open shaping to my destiny. I am a flower, I will never be in full bloom I will continue to grow until I die. And throughout that time I will share my life with others.
Julie Bryan, early childhood student teacher

CHAPTER 1

AN INVITATION TO LIFE
The Art of Teaching

. . . [T]eaching is an art guided by educational values, personal needs, and by a variety of beliefs or generalizations that the teacher holds to be true.

Elliot Eisner, *The Educational Imagination*

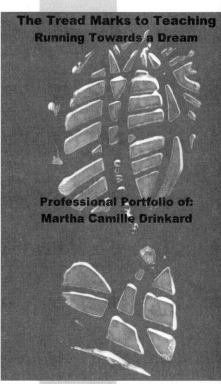

The Tread Marks to Teaching
Running Towards a Dream

Professional Portfolio of:
Martha Camille Drinkard

When I think back on my life, one activity always comes to mind. Running. Running has played a big role in my life and has taught me many life lessons. Long setting goals, having self-determination, and support from others. It is also important to keep your head up and use your arms. If things get tough, take a breather. No fear of getting messy is a must to run a good race. One also needs to be flexible to all unpredictable conditions and keep in mind that every race is different. All these factors are related to my image of a teacher!

Running a long distance race is no easy task. The right amount of training is required. Teaching is not an easy task, as well. To be a good teacher, proper education and experience are also required. Teachers need to understand how children develop, think, process, and learn. They also need to know many ways of teaching since no two children learn in the same manner.

When racing, the proper equipment is needed—running shoes, weather-appropriate clothing, a race number, a stopwatch, and plenty of water. Teaching requires equipment as well. Teachers need enthusiasm, patience, creativity, and smiles.

Setting goals is a must for runners. When completing a race, it is important to have a goal which one can strive to reach. Teachers also need to set goals. They need to establish goals for themselves, for their classroom, and for individual students.

Self-determination is needed throughout the race, and especially when things get tough. A runner must keep going on. However, when things get too tough, it is important to slow down the pace, take quick breathers to refresh themselves, allowing themselves to get a new start. Teachers also need self-determination to get through a school day, a school week, and a school year. Determination is especially needed when a day gets rough and the teachers feel overwhelmed. Teachers need to realize it is okay to take a quick breather for themselves and the students to gather themselves. This can help to start things off fresh.

Supportive teams cheer, encourage you, and push you further during a race and are there to celebrate the good times and to help you overcome the hard times. A teacher needs a strong supportive system he or she can go to for information or questions, encouragement and support. This support can be found from other teachers, co-workers, administration, and parents. . . .

. . . Teachers cannot fear getting messy either. A good teacher . . . does not hesitate to join in students' messy activities. Children learn through exploration and teacher guidance. That is why teachers, like runners, need to get down and dirty, to help their students explore and learn.

Runners need to be flexible in their racing surroundings, and to unpredictable factors, like weather—rain, sleet, or snow. The race must go on. Teachers also need to be flexible and mentally alert and physically prepared to overcome unpredictable events. . . .

. . . A successful teacher requires the proper equipment, training, and education, learns continuously, sets goals, gets messy, is flexible, and knows that every day is different.

Martha Drinkard, junior

From the first year that students are enrolled in our early childhood education program, they are challenged to continually reflect and revise their philosophy of teaching and their image of a teacher. Taking classes and participating in field studies in schools encourage the students to link theory to practice, which in turn leads them to change their personal philosophy of teaching and being a teacher—connecting the past, the present, and what could be. The preceding story reflects Martha Drinkard's image of a teacher and her notion of teaching at the beginning of her junior year.

QUESTIONS TO BE CONSIDERED
- What is teaching?
- How do theories inform teaching? How do theories and experience contribute to one's personal philosophy of teaching?
- Why is learning to teach a lifelong journey?

When you go on a journey or take a trip, you have a plan and an image of what you might experience. You might bring with you a map that charts your journey and an itinerary with plans of what you want to do and experience. But during the trip, your plans might change. You will then consult your map and, based on your interests, intentions, and new experiences, revise and rechart your itinerary. Similarly, on becoming a teacher, you enter the teacher education program with an idea or image of what teaching "looks like"—an image of being a teacher. You bring with you an idea—a plan or philosophy—of teaching to guide your journey. How willing are you to change and revise your plan? We invite you to be open to new ideas, new experiences, and the possibility of change.

We all have certain images of teaching that we have developed through our years in school. Knowingly or unknowingly, you have constructed a personal philosophy or theory of teaching that you bring with you when you enter a teacher education program—a journey charted on a "map" of teaching. Because you have carried this charted map with you for a long time, it has become a part of you, a part of your personality and disposition that is deeply ingrained in your psyche. What would it take for you to modify, revise, and rechart your map? Research in teacher education has shown repeatedly that changing one's beliefs and ways of teaching is a difficult task. It calls for us to be open to new ideas, knowledge, and ways of teaching and learning. It calls for us to critically evaluate our beliefs and sense of self in order to change and transform. Teaching is about change, and teachers are agents of change. As educators we have to believe that we have the capacity to change in order to recognize that a child also has the capacity to change (Garbarino, 1989, p. 30). The essence of education is hope and possibilities:

> The fundamental message of the teacher is this: you can change your life. Whoever you are, wherever you've been, whatever you've done, the teacher invites you to a second chance, another round, perhaps a different conclusion. The teacher posits possibility, openness, and alternatives; the teacher points to what could be, but is not yet. The teacher beckons you to change your path, and so the teacher's basic rule is to teach. . . . Education, of course, is an arena of hope and struggle—hope for a better life, and struggle over how to understand and enact and achieve that better life. (Ayers, 1998)

In the spirit expressed by Bill Ayers, we invite you to change, give yourself another chance, rechart your journey and form "perhaps a different conclusion" about teaching.

Teaching is the process of education that is "guided by educational values, personal needs, and by a variety of beliefs or generalizations that the teacher holds to be true" (Eisner, 1994, p. 154). Teaching is intentional and purposeful. It is a highly moral profession that calls for us to see the students (children) as competent persons and allow them to learn in ways that bring out the best in them. In this sense, teachers are in a position to constantly have to make real, meaningful decisions that affect the lives of students.

Teaching is both a science and an art. It is a science because it is guided by educational theories, especially personal theories that you will develop while living the life of a teacher interacting with students and other teachers, day in and day out.

All teaching is grounded in a philosophical, theoretical framework or approach, constructed by the teacher, that reflects the teacher's own knowledge, values, beliefs, choices, aspirations, intentions, and aims (Cuffaro, 1995, p. 1). Teaching is an art because it challenges us to practice our craft creatively, not by prescription but by attending to the quality of the process of the teaching–learning situations that are ever changing. Teachers are aware of emerging (teachable) moments in the classroom and have a repertoire of skills (tools) with which to improvise and invent ways to capture these potential moments of learning. Thus, the teacher has a philosophical framework or approach that serves as a map or a tool through which she or he makes sense of the world, coupled with a sense of teaching as an art that influences practices and relationships in the classroom.

All teachers have a general idea of the meaning of teaching—in other words, they have a perspective on what, how, and when to teach. That is, they have a general sense of what to consider in making decisions about teaching and the curriculum. For example, teachers have *beliefs* about development, motivation, how children learn, how to teach, and so on. These beliefs form a personal theory or philosophy of teaching that influences the way the teacher acts and what the teacher pays attention to in the classroom.

You may wonder, "Do I have a philosophy of teaching?"; "What is my image of teaching?"; "How does my philosophy or image of teaching guide my journey to becoming a teacher?" We begin to reevaluate our image of teaching and develop our individual philosophy or theory of teaching when we take teacher education courses and participate in practical experiences, observing and assessing children in the classroom. For example, in our teacher preparation program, the students begin to construct a portfolio when they are first-year students. A portfolio documents a student's journey in becoming a teacher. A portfolio, while documenting your work, also provides information that allows you to revisit, reflect on, and evaluate what you have learned and how you have changed over time; it is also a conduit through which to reconstruct your philosophy of teaching. You will learn more about portfolios in subsequent chapters. Here is a an example of one student's statement about her philosophy of teaching at the beginning of her junior year:

> **THINK ABOUT IT**
>
> What is my philosophy of teaching?
> What is my image of teaching?

> *My teaching philosophy is a very important part of my portfolio. This is a statement of my ideas and goals for being a teacher. My philosophy is something that will follow me from my first year as a teacher, to my last. It will go through revisions and changes, just as I will, but it will always reflect my love of teaching and my sincere dedication to influencing children's lives in a positive way.*
>
>   Kori

Kori's brief statement captures succinctly her philosophy at a particular point in time. She recognizes that both her teaching and her philosophy will change over time. It is a dynamic statement that reflects her dedication to children and her commitment to being a lifelong learner who is open to change. We encourage you to begin to think about and frame your own dynamic teaching philosophy.

OUR TEACHING PHILOSOPHY

This book on life in the classroom is based on our shared philosophy of teaching. This philosophy is based on *social constructivism* and *qualitative inquiry*. We believe that a teacher is always in the making, is empowered to make moral and ethical decisions, and has a desire to create communities for learning. For us, teaching is a lifelong project in the search for excellence. This project is most meaningful when it involves others and touches on others' lives (Ayers, 1995, p. 323). As Hannah Arendt (1958) said, "For excellence, the presence of others is always required." This calls for us to continually invite others to walk with us in constructing and living a pedagogy of relationship and possibility in what Maxine Greene calls a community in the making.

We want to share with you our notion of teaching. The philosophical underpinnings of this book are reflected in our teacher education program. Social constructivism is based on the idea that knowledge is socially constructed in a cultural setting. We view early childhood teacher education as the transformation of self and society. Our philosophy is expressed in the following statement regarding our early childhood teacher preparation program:

THINK ABOUT IT

What is your school's teaching philosophy?

Our teacher education program is social constructivist and views early childhood teacher education as the transformation of self and society. According to this philosophy, prospective teachers learn to see themselves as change agents, researchers, activists, and reflective thinkers. As teacher researchers, students develop the processes of inquiry and personal and professional renewal as a lifelong endeavor. First-year students are welcomed into a community of learners and co-mentored by early childhood education and elementary education faculty. Within this caring and safe community, they are instilled with the understanding that teachers, like their students, learn by carefully reflecting on their experiences. Through self-questioning and critical analysis of practice with young children, they have the opportunity to reinvent and reconstruct personal experience.

The notion of teacher as researcher is epitomized by students engaging in the ongoing and reflexive process of connecting what they do with children to the way they are guided and supported in their own developmental journeys. In particular, teachers and students from methods courses focusing on curriculum and assessment are engaged in the process of collaborative inquiry into the wonders, passions, and mysteries of young children and into how this critical pedagogy encourages the transformation of self.

THE ART OF TEACHING

This book challenges both preservice and in-service teachers to embrace *teaching as an art*—an art that it is creative, ever changing, and oriented toward student teachers as they begin to take on the responsibilities of teaching. It is an art of teaching that embraces a pedagogy of relationships and possibilities, that kindles in the students a sense of wonder, curiosity, and a desire to know—to ask questions, to look for answers, and to make sense in different ways. It is an art that supports the learner in representing and documenting his or her processes in multiple, aesthetic ways, using different tools that value individual orientation to "multiple intelligences" (Gardner, 1993) and "languages" (Edwards, Gandini, & Forman, 1998). The term *languages* is used in the Reggio Emilia approach to convey the idea that more than one way or one tool can be used to learn, communicate, and represent one's thinking and knowledge. For example, in addition to the prevalent use of spoken and written language to communicate, other "languages" could include the use of paint, clay, music, poetry, dance, drama, photography, and so on. Through these experiences, preservice and in-service teachers will begin to develop open and accepting dispositions toward teaching and learning in their classrooms. Teaching happens in relationships that encourage teachers to be imaginative and tune into students' diverse needs and ways of knowing; this pedagogy of relationships uses multiple tools (languages) that promote different ways of seeing, understanding, and demonstrating knowledge.

WHY DO WE NEED THEORIES AND PHILOSOPHY? HOW DO THEY INFORM TEACHING?

Why do we need theories? Every day we encounter many situations in which friends, family members, and people in the news voice their opinions on certain events they have experienced or heard about. They try to express their points of view and explain why people act in particular ways, why certain events happen, why children learn, why teachers teach, how parents rear their children, and so on. The common wisdom is that everyone is an "armchair philosopher" or theorist. Sometimes experts refer to these conjectures as "talking like a man or woman of the street," implying that these philosophies or theories are based on "gut instinct" or personal experience. Yet often enough you also hear experts espousing their opinions on news events voicing different perspectives. Why do both people in general and experts voice multiple opinions and see matters differently?

Let's begin by reviewing the dictionary definitions of the words *theory* and *philosophy*. *Theory* is "a coherent group of general propositions used as principles of explanations for a class of phenomena or a proposed explanation whose status is still conjectural, in contrast to well-established propositions that are regarded as reporting matters as actual fact." *Philosophy* is "the rational investigation of the truths and principles of being, knowledge, or conduct" (*The Random House Dictionary of the English Language*, 1979). The notion of a theory can be seen in the metaphor of "a window that opens to a reality." It frames and sets the perimeter of what we see. A philosophy might be referred to as the type of structure and design of the window we are looking through, for it determines how we see as well as what and how much we see. In short, both theory and philosophy are rationally constructed propositions that we use to investigate, inquire into, and make sense of events, behaviors, relationships, teaching, learning, and so on. Thus, a primary reason to have knowledge of theories and philosophy is that they help us ask questions and seek answers about the basic processes of growth, development, learning, and social interaction and how these processes help us understand what we have observed and experienced in the classroom. "Theories are useful because they help teachers understand why they do what they do and explain why something happens" (Bredekamp & Rosegrant, 1992, p. 12). Questioning and reflecting on what happens in teaching and learning help us make decisions about when, what, and how to teach students as a group while attending to and meeting the needs of individuals. Later in this chapter, we share with you the thinking of some theorists and philosophers we deem most relevant to teaching.

The metaphor of a window that opens to a reality makes us aware that a theory does not help us see the total picture of the classroom, but only a part of it. Holding on to only one theoretical perspective helps people make the error exemplified in the fable of the "Three Blind Men and the Elephant." Each man "sees" only a part of the elephant; although the description is true to that part, each man misses the whole concept of an elephant. Similarly, understanding teaching from only one or two perspectives may prevent us from seeing the whole concept of teaching. It is important to realize and appreciate the fact that there are different perspectives about teaching and not limit ourselves to a single point of view. We need to draw on knowledge from different theories in order to create a meaningful yet dynamic framework for teaching. Theories remind us to pay attention to what goes on in the classroom—all aspects of life in the classroom. Theories provide a framework for teachers to understand and interpret both their own and the children's intentions and actions. We find that the most useful theories are those that provide broad ideas or principles about development and learning and that have the potential to inform and interpret complex behaviors and experiences. Theories provide the basis for teachers to gain a breadth of knowledge, prompt different ways of seeing and knowing, and encourage teachers to be open to the possibilities of doing things differently. Theories remind us that our teaching decisions should be made based on our knowledge about child development and learning, individual children, and the social and cultural contexts. The metaphor of the structure and design of the window makes us realize that *how, what,* and *how much* we see is determined by the openness of a philosophical position. That is, the decision of how, what, and how much to teach—teaching itself—is not based on a rigid set of expectations but on an approach to or philosophy of working with children by attending

> **THINK ABOUT IT**
>
> How do you decide what, how, and when to teach?

to "*what* we know about how children develop and learn and *what we learn* about the individual needs and interests of each child in the group" (Bredekamp & Rosegrant, 1992, p. 4). Thus, by integrating and reconstructing our knowledge about theory and philosophy, we are prepared to reflect on our practice and make decisions regarding what, how, and when to teach.

CURRICULUM AND TEACHING

Curriculum and teaching go hand in hand. Let us consider the question "What is curriculum?" This question explores what to teach. *Curriculum* is the content or the subject matter to be considered in teaching and learning. In early childhood education, we take the stance that curriculum should be integrative. Integrated curriculum is an approach that reflects and supports how children learn and and how they learn by making connections across subject matter disciplines. Integrated curriculum has intellectual integrity when it is grounded in knowledge of subject matter disciplines. Curriculum emerges from children, their families, teachers, and current thinking on specific content areas. As a teacher of young children, you will make decisions about what and when to teach by being informed by child development knowledge and how children learn. For children, knowledge across disciplines becomes meaningful when teachers use an integrative approach such as projects. For further information regarding appropriate curriculum, consult, *Reaching Potentials: Appropriate Curriculum and Assessment for Young Children,* Volumes 1 and 2 (Bredekamp & Rosegrant, 1992, 1995).

As with teaching, knowledge about child development, learning, and the individual needs and interests of each child also factor into making decisions on why, when, and what to teach. The teacher must attend to and assess the children's interests in the context of the learning. That is, the teacher assesses what the children are thinking and what the children are learning (i.e., the contents) as they construct and represent their knowledge in multiple ways. The teacher observes, reflects, and attempts to discover the children's intentions and provide the appropriate action that scaffolds and guides them in the learning process as they solve real, relevant, authentic, and meaningful problems. The teacher is alert to how children form theories about objects and events in their daily encounters and how they make sense of and understand the world. The teacher and child are partners in learning. We call this a negotiated curriculum that is "child initiated and teacher framed." A negotiated curriculum is a system of interaction in which the curriculum originates from the children's interests as observed by the teacher. Through conversations with the children, the teacher reflects on their thinking and then reframes their interests into projects or follow-up activities that will extend the children's thinking on particular concepts (Forman & Fyfe, 1998). In this book, you will be exposed to many examples of negotiated curriculum. Following is one example of this process of negotiation and the many possibilities for teaching and learning that emerge in the process. This is the story of the Woozle, a fantasy character these three- and four-year-old children have created. The Woozle has been a part of their daily play. It is important to remember that fantasy and pretense play have that "as if" quality that opens up opportunities for children to explore many ideas. As teachers we want to be aware of the qualities of such play that lead us to think and reflect from a "what if? . . . what then?" question sequence. These questions, in accordance with our knowledge of theories and philosophies, will guide us in making decisions about the possibilities for the next steps in their play or other forms of exploration.

Where's That Woozle?

You will learn more about the Woozle in later chapters. Here is a segment that documents an early stage of the history of this play. While reading this segment, keep in mind the "as if" quality of pretense play and the "what if? . . . what then?" questions that will help you in your reflection.

The teacher recognized that the children were interested in "finding the Woozle." It was a rainy day, . . . the best time to go on a Woozle hunt because that is when the Woozles come inside. The children were preparing to go look for the Woozle in the building where the Lab School is located. . . . But first things first:

Teacher: What IS a Woozle?

Patrick: It only has one eye!

Isaac: I have the camera to find Woozles!

Jayna: It only has 2 legs.

Joel: I thought it had 4 legs?

Patrick: No, it has 4 legs.

Christopher: I think it has 2 eyes.

Jody: What color do you think it is?

Jayna: Brown and greenish.

Patrick: Blue.

Jade: Yellow.

Joel: Brown.

Caitlin: Red

Katie: Yeah, red!

Well, now that we know what we're looking for, our next issue was . . .

Teacher: What do we do if we find it?

Patrick: Punch him.

Jayna: Hug him and kiss him.

Patrick: Step on his feet!

Joel: We could step on him with our shoe and he's dead!

Alisha: Don't hurt her!

Christopher: I don't want to kill him!

Miller: I don't think we should catch it.

Jayna: Let it outside! Don't put a rock on it.

Finally it was time to go on our hunt. Which led us to ask . . .

Teacher: What should we take?

Jayna: A catcher! A butterfly net.

Christopher: I don't want a catcher, it will kill him!

Isaac: The camera!

Joel: A cup to put the Woozle in.

Christopher: I don't want to put the Woozle in a cup. I want it to be safe!

Miriam: I'm going to bring my glasses.

Caitlin: We need to bring a net!

Well, we all decided that we agreed with Christopher and we didn't want to kill the Woozle, but we did want to catch it and put it outside. So, we gathered up our supplies and off we went! We stopped at the foot of the stairwell to form a plan of action. . . .

Teacher: Where should we look now?

Patrick: Upstairs!

Miriam: I'm scared.

Christopher: Wait! I heard it!

Jayna: What does it sound like?

Christopher: I heard it walking around.

Isaac: I heard it too!

Miriam: I heard it too!

Off we went again, and we made some stops along the way to ask folks where they thought the Woozle might go. . . .

THINK ABOUT IT

After reading the documentation on the Woozle, reflect on the following questions:

What does this interaction tell you about teaching and learning?

What does it tell you about the teacher's understanding of children?

What does it tell you about children as learners?

What does it tell you about learning and problem solving?

What does it tell you about inquiry and the social construction of knowledge?

INFLUENTIAL THINKERS

An awareness of the history of early childhood education positions us to better understand our approach to teaching and learning in the context of how teaching has developed and changed over time in reaction to societal demands and the human quest for knowledge. The philosophies of influential thinkers help us construct our philosophy of teaching and ways to put this philosophy into practice. In this section, we highlight some of the philosophers and theorists who have influenced our teaching. All these thinkers have contributed to our understanding of teaching as inquiry in social contexts.

Jean-Jacques Rousseau (1712–1778)

Education, according to French philosopher Rousseau, should occur in a natural environment that is based on the children's experiences as they develop. Thus, education for young children should develop out of the children's daily experiences. Childhood is a distinct period of life with special needs and freedom. Because children are by nature "good," the educational process should be child centered and not teacher centered. Children's innate curiosity is a motivating source for learning. Teachers should limit their interference on the child's natural development. Instead, they should serve as guide or facilitator. Parents should be involved in their children's education. Rousseau's philosophy influenced the German educator Friedrich Froebel and Swiss educational reformer Johann Heinrich Pestalozzi and many modern education pioneers.

Johann Heinrich Pestalozzi (1746–1827)

Pestalozzi adopted many of the tenets of Rousseau's philosophy and put these ideas into practice based on research. His sense of social justice led him to promote education for the poor. Thus, he advocated for education for all children. His method of teaching is known as the object lesson, which engages children in active learning using their senses. Children should find answers for themselves while engaging in spontaneous activities. In these activities, children should be encouraged to develop their own powers of seeing, judging, and reasoning. The goal is to educate the whole child. Pestalozzi is recognized for setting the stage for early childhood education and the kindergarten movement. He was a reflective practitioner concerned with experimentation, research, and action as well as the importance of observation and reflection in order to make sense of experiences.

Friedrich Froebel (1782–1852)

Froebel studied with Pestalozzi and then conducted research to connect his philosophy to teaching. He studied biology and botany but became a teacher. He said that he found himself in teaching, "like a duck takes to water." He wrote in *Education by Development* that "[t]he human being is born for RESEARCH; and he is to practice it even as a child . . . to separate that which seems from that which is" (p. 199). He strongly supported the importance of family as the context in which love and respect are lived and experienced, calling the family the "sanctuary of humanity." To Froebel, education was a process for the child who is "becoming." Play is the highest expression of human development. Play is both creative and imaginative; through play the child transforms, learns, and grows. Play is the method of education and learning. Children learn through their own experiences, and the content of curriculum emerges in play. The teacher is the guide, the facilitator in children's learning, for "[i]f we begin to teach, if our words run ahead of her experience, all is lost, and her education will become hollow, dead and mechanical" (Froebel, in Corbett, 1990, p. 136).

John Dewey (1859–1952)

Teaching is based on relationships. It is a pedagogy of relationships. Dewey's philosophy (1897/1967) is a framework that guides teaching that details life in the classroom, a forerunner of what is known as a systems perspective to learning and development, in line with what is now known as social constructivism (Garrison, 1997). Dewey described the creation of a community for learning in which communication, shared interest, and activity are given purpose through social interaction. Dewey saw life as drama, according to Cuffaro (1995), and "as the work of an ensemble" (p. 27) of people coming together to create, share, and build in a caring, trusting community. There is room for growth, and there are "no absolute and final endings." A classroom is such a community for children and their teacher. This is what we strive for in our teacher education program (and at the lab school)—a community of learners working toward the construction of amiable classrooms.

Dewey's vision of the function of schooling was to

> extend, broaden, and improve the cultural construction of emerging minds begun at home and the community at large. Culture has us before we have it. The function of critical education is to make us aware of the contingency of this social construction of our minds and self, and to aid us in taking possession of ourselves through a long process of self-reflective recreation. (Garrision, 1997, p. 39)

Thus, relationships and community are crucial in education and teaching. He also saw teaching as moral, as reflected in his essay on teaching ethics (Dewey, 1932/1985). All inquiry begins and ends with a sensitivity for the quality of the situation, "the needs, desires, and interests of others" (Garrison, 1997, p. 33). Hence, caring is an important element in the classroom. Values and beliefs are reflected in our thinking, feeling, and actions (Dewey, 1925/1981). According to Dewey, all knowledge emerges from everyday practical experiences. Inquiry arises from doubt, or cognitive dissonance or conflict, and coupled with reflection leads to meaning making and understanding. The morality of teaching in sociocultural context is also central to our philosophy of teaching and can be found in the other perspectives, as described below.

Urie Bronfenbrenner (1917–)

Bronfenbrenner (1979, 1986) views the child as an active, developing individual engaging in reciprocal relationships with people in his or her environment. In this sense, the child, other people, and the environment all play a role in contributing to the child's development. The *environment* is conceived as broader than a single, immediate setting such as home or school. The *ecological environment* extends beyond these settings by taking into consideration interaction between these immediate settings (relationships in the home, between home and school, or between home and the workplace) and larger settings that include the culture, which has an effect on the various settings. Thus, teaching and learning in the classroom are influenced by social and political structures and the broad, overarching beliefs, values, and ideologies of a culture.

Jean Piaget (1896–1980)

Jean Piaget (1963) recognized that children actively explore and interpret the world. Thus, he focused on the importance of *action* and children's problem solving. Children explore the environment—manipulating objects, testing out ideas, and revising their understanding of concepts or theories—in ways not unlike those used by scientists. According to DeVries and Kohlberg (1987), Piaget's theory and research encourage practitioners to pay attention to the role of action in development; thus, teachers should devise approaches to teaching that capture children's spontaneous activity and interest through play, experimentation, and cooperation in adult–child and child–child relationships.

Lev Vygotsky (1896–1934)

Vygotsky's theory focuses on the sociocultural context of development—in other words, how development occurs in and cannot be separate from social and cultural activities. Of special interest to teachers are his writings on the development of mental processes, the use of cultural inventions or tools (such as language, mathematical systems, and technologies), and how children's development is best guided by people who are experienced in using these tools. Vygotsky's (1978) ideas help us understand the relationship between the individual and the culture, such as how children develop higher mental processes, as well as the tools and skills that are deemed important in their culture. His concept of the *zone of proximal development (ZPD)* has contributed significantly to our understanding and reconstruction of the role of the teacher, as well as of collaborative learning among children.

Jerome Bruner (1915–)

Bruner's (1986) thinking is influenced by both Piaget and Vygotsky, so you will see elements of both perspectives in his theoretical framework. In recent years, Bruner writes that Vygotsky's theory is one of an education that contributes to our understanding of the dynamic interactions among teacher, child, environment, and the cultural context. He has stated that Vygotsky's "educational theory is a theory of cultural transmission as well as a theory of development. For 'education' implies for Vygotsky not only the development of an individual's potential, but the historical expression and growth of the human culture from which Man springs" (1987, pp. 1–2).

Barbara Rogoff

Rogoff (1989) sees working in the zone of proximal development as the process of guided participation. Through interactions with mother, father, and others in daily routines, children are guided to develop skills and knowledge of the culture in which they live. In the process of guided participation, the adults or more experienced others build connections between what the children already know and new understanding and skills structuring and supporting children's participation (in the ZPD) until it is appropriate to transfer the responsibility for managing problem solving to the children. This description is congruent with Bruner's concept of "scaffolding," which describes the gradual withdrawal of adult guidance and support as children increase mastery of a problem or task (Wood, Bruner, & Ross, 1976). Guided participation or scaffolding within the ZPD, informed by Vygotsky's theory, helps us understand the importance of knowing the children and being sensitive to their ways of thinking and knowing. The child is not a passive recipient of knowledge from the teacher, nor is the teacher a model or expert of knowledge; together, they are participants in joint problem solving, sharing information and responsibility. The teacher or adult must create a level of "intersubjectivity," of shared understanding of the task "where the child redefines the problem situation in terms of the adult perspective" (Wertsch, 1984, p. 13). We believe that in this process, the teacher and child together redefine the problem for exploration, and the responsibility is gradually transferred to the child. We call this a process of negotiation. The curriculum based on this perspective is not solely emergent for the child or from the teacher but is negotiated—it is child initiated but teacher framed.

Howard Gardner (1943–)

Howard Gardner (1993, 1999) proposed in his theory of multiple intelligences (MI) that instead of the traditional perspective that only one or two intelligences exist, all human beings possess several or multiple intelligences. According to Gardner, there are at least eight intelligences: musical, bodily-kinesthetic, logical-mathematical, linguistic, spatial, interpersonal, intrapersonal, and naturalistic. He defines intelligence as one's ability to solve problems or to create "a *cultural* product" that transmits knowledge or expresses one's feelings and perspectives (1997, p. 15). The implication for teaching from an MI perspective is that there are many ways to teach and learn any content or skill. "Teachers have to help students use their combination of intelligences to be successful in school, to help them learn whatever it is they want to learn, as well as what the teachers and society believe they have to learn" (1997, p. 4). Teachers need to know each child and have

> a deep interest in children and how their minds are different from one another, and in helping them use their minds well. . . . We know people understand something when they can represent the knowledge in more than one way. We have to put understanding up front in school. Once we have that goal, multiple intelligences can be a terrific handmaiden because understandings involve a mix of mental representations, entailing different intelligences. (p. 5)

The Reggio Emilia Approach

Our philosophy of teaching, constructed in light of the works of the preceding philosophers, theorists, and practitioners and of our own experiences, is inspired in part by the approach to teaching in Reggio Emilia, Italy. In Reggio Emilia, educators have created a system of relationships that foster the implementation of a social constructivist, inquiry-based approach to teaching that takes into account the cultural transmission of learning and the transformation of self as teachers and learners. Following are the major principles of the Reggio Emilia approach (Gandini, 1997; Cadwell, 1997):

- Children as protagonists, collaborators, and communicators in the learning process
- Teachers as partners, nurturers, and guides in children's learning
- Teachers as researchers
- Parents as partners who take active roles in their children's learning
- Environments (as a third teacher) that support learning through social interaction and exploration
- Documentation as a means for negotiated learning through communication

Malaguzzi (1998) wrote that

> talk about education . . . cannot be confined to its literature. Such talk, which is also political, must continuously address the major social changes and transformations in the economy, sciences, arts, and human relationships and customs. All these larger forces influence how human beings—even young children—"read" and deal with the realities of life. They determine the emergence, on both general and local level, of new methods of educational content and practice, as well as new problems and soul-searching questions. (p. 60)

THINK ABOUT IT

How is the Reggio Emilia approach to teaching young children influenced by the thinkers discussed above?

Read Audrey's thoughts on her perception of a teacher researcher. After reading her writing, reflect on how theories and philosophies inform her practice in the classroom. In Chapter 3, you will study the role of teacher as researcher in more depth.

LIFE IN THE CLASSROOM

A teacher researcher is constantly requiring herself to learn more. She is a teacher who strives to improve her classroom environment. She asks herself questions. She asks, What do I want to know about my students/class? What do I not understand? What can I do to solve a particular problem? How can I help a student who needs help? How can I explain his behavior? The teacher researcher has certain roles.

A teacher researcher first observes and collects information about her class. She observes the behaviors and interests of children. She collects their work and records their learning processes. The teacher researcher makes certain that she takes into account all aspects of learning: social interactions, cognitive skills, and physical development. The teacher then organizes the information.

The teacher researcher applies the observations to her knowledge of child development and teaching. She makes connections between the information she collected and indicators of development. With all this information, the teacher finds some answers to her questions. She formulates strategies to change her approach in ways that will improve her classroom.

She tests her new strategies in the classroom. Through the same information-gathering process, the teacher can reflect and assess the results of the change. She learns from experience. She will revisit her strategies or continue to monitor the success. Either way, the process is ongoing. A teacher researcher is always studying her class and asking new questions. Over time, she uses the knowledge she has gained from being a teacher researcher and applies it to her current study.

Overall, the teacher constantly works to create the best learning environment for her students. She is faced with challenges of all types. She uses her philosophy of teaching and her personal ethical code to guide her through difficult situations. She may not always make the right choice, but she learns from her mistakes. The teacher researcher knows that she is not the source of all information. She takes advantage of resources—readings, theories, philosophies—and her own personal research to make the classroom the best learning environment.

Audrey Peikut, junior

OUR PHILOSOPHY OF TEACHING—REVISITED

As you review the theories discussed earlier in the chapter, we hope you have begun to understand that knowledge is socially constructed in cultural settings. We believe that teachers who are invested in a constructivist, expressive approach to teaching foster multiple ways of inquiry, discovery, and making sense and meaning. They are tuned into teachable moments when children encounter problems and seek to find answers. In our lab school, we call these moments "making a problem into a project." Teachers and children work together, negotiate, and create projects for exploration. In these situations, there is synchrony and rhythm between teachers and children and among the children themselves. These are moments of transcendence—*when teaching is being practiced as an art.* In this process, Eisner (1995) says, teachers help students "recognize that ideas can be expressed in different ways and that they can have a choice in the ways in which they choose to express what they know" (pp. 127–128).

This process of teaching and learning captures the essence of *progettazione* (Rinaldi, 1999) in a classroom. According to Bruner (1986), the classroom is "a forum for negotiating and renegotiating meaning" (p. 123) among teachers, children, and families. The classroom culture gives each participant opportunities to make and remake culture. Thus, in the classroom, children are "prepared for life as lived, [and] should also partake in the spirit of a forum, of negotiation, of the recreating of meaning" (Bruner, 1986, p. 123). The spirit of *progettazione* is dependent on relationships. In this process, according to Carolyn Edwards (Edwards, Gandini, & Forman, 1998), the teachers are involved in finding challenging, satisfying problems; identifying cognitive "knots," or cognitive conflicts; and deciding when to intervene. Vea Vecchi (1998), an atelierista, talked about identifying the "hot moment"—a teachable moment—that challenges the teacher to decide when to intervene and when to wait for the children to find their own answers and solutions. Edwards reported that Laura Ribizzi described teachers as working in a state of uncertainty but embarking eagerly on a voyage with the children. This tension reflects a "genuine commitment to progettazione," an openness, not knowing where a project will end up (pp. 183–184). Isn't this the essence of the art of teaching?

Here is the philosophy of teaching from one of our early childhood education students:

> *There is so much potential inside each child for greatness and amazing things; and it's just waiting to be found.*
>
> *I believe a teacher's job is to help a child discover this potential and to live up to it completely.*
>
> *I want my teaching to be merely an outline for the children to begin with, something to build off of, not to end with.*
>
> *I hope to have a classroom built on respect, not on strict rules.*
>
> *I want the classroom to have an open and honest atmosphere so that everyone feels comfortable there.*
>
> *I want my dedication and love of teaching to be evident every day.*
>
> *I am looking forward to all that I will get to teach children, and all that they will teach me.*
>
> Kori, early childhood education junior

THINK ABOUT IT

Can you identify the theories and philosophies that influence Kori's construction of teaching?

What is her idea about knowledge, skill, disposition, and feeling as related to teaching?

METAPHOR: TEACHING AS THEATER, OR PERFORMANCE

As this chapter comes to an end, we want to share with you one of our metaphors for teaching—teaching as theater, or performance. Imagine that you are sitting in a theater, the curtain is rising, and you see members of the cast posed, as in a tableau, in a classroom. As the curtain reaches the top of the stage, the people in the classroom come alive. If you were in the audience, how would you expect the drama to unfold? If you were the writer of the script, how would you present to the audience the drama of "Teaching as Inquiry" in an engaging, exciting way that captures their imagination? Who are the characters? What is the plot? What are the subplots? What human stories will unfold? What do you want the audience to experience? And, yes, even if you have a story to tell, with an intended meaning, it most likely will be presented in ways that reflect the interpretive minds and eyes of individual directors and actors. Likewise, the audience may have other interpretations of the drama that reflect and make sense of their own experiences and theories. The dramatic possibilities are unlimited.

> **THINK ABOUT IT**
>
> Imagine that you are engaged in a live, improvisational theater production of "Teaching as Inquiry"; what could happen? The possibilities are even more dynamic, ever changing and taking on the nuances brought to the stage by individual actors, in particular moments of time.

You may ask, what does theater have to do with teaching? As a metaphor for teaching, theater captures the relationships among teachers, students, parents, and the environment. Dramatic performances in theaters capture the essence of teaching as an art. It reflects the creativity, mysteries, and tensions of teaching. The main characters are the teachers and the students. The plot is teaching and learning, with many subplots (stories) of curriculum experiences. The richness of a theatrical production relies on understanding the characters—the teachers, students, and families—and what happens in the classroom. These are insights gained through observing, recording, documenting, reflecting, and interpreting. The setting is the classroom, the physical environment created by the set designer.

Some of the most memorable learning moments of college life are times spent with friends after seeing a play or a movie—dissecting, arguing, sharing different interpretations of what we experienced, and trying to understand different points of view. Often we reached no agreed-upon meaning in the wee hours of the morning. We left one another knowing that the story, if it reflects life, has multiple meanings. Sometimes, when we see the same play or movie again years later, with a different director, a new cast, a new set designer, and in the company of other friends, new meanings are created, and some of the earlier interpretations argued strongly by some friends may become meaningful.

In the same manner, we share stories of our teaching with one another and with our students. Teachers love to tell stories of their teaching. This telling and retelling of teaching stories began long before we were teachers. Think back to your own childhood and you will remember the stories you shared with your friends about your teachers and about the curricula. In this manner, we encourage you to engage actively in reflecting on the teaching stories shared in this book, as well as to share with one another your own stories of teaching and learning to teach. In telling and reflecting on these stories, you will better understand yourself and your unique ways of making sense of your values and knowledge. You will be challenged to ask tough questions and to reflect on what you have observed and on your own practice. That is, you will be engaged in constructing and reconstructing your sense of self as a teacher who is on a journey of becoming.

AS YOU EMBARK ON THIS JOURNEY TO PERFORM IN THE CLASSROOM . . .

As you prepare for the ever-changing production of "Teaching as Inquiry," read, reflect, and revisit this book. True to our beliefs and dispositions toward teaching, this book is presented in a format that approaches teaching as an art. In addition to stories of teaching and questions to engage you in reflection, we've included artifacts of our own students' representations of their multiple ways of learning to teach. These artifacts document their developing notions of the art of teaching that capture the Reggio Emilia idea of *progettazione*. You will become aware of and appreciate the linkages between theories and philosophies espoused earlier and as we put them into practice through insights we have gained from Reggio Emilia and in working and living with our students.

> *Working at the Lab School at Virginia Tech has been perhaps the greatest contributor to my understanding of children. With the opportunity to reflect daily on observations in the classroom I feel that my overall thinking and understanding of children has been greatly enhanced. One thing that working there has taught me so far is that learning is highly individual, understanding is highly individual, and communication is highly individual. In fact, I should rephrase the above saying that my understanding of how to understand children and their process of discovering has been enhanced. There is no universal understanding of children. The words of William Ayers have been solidified in my mind. He says, "Just when we have gained some worthwhile insight, just when we have captured some interesting essence, the children change, the kaleidoscope turns, and we must look again, even more deeply."*
> Lora, early childhood education junior

On your journey of exploring and experiencing this manifestation of our philosophy, the various theories and positions introduced earlier, and how all of these are tied together in a classroom, will become clearer. We hope you will begin to build a community with your fellow students, just as a cast is a community, as you embark on this journey to learn to teach, using this text as a new map to help you rethink and rechart your route of possibilities, or perhaps as a script to be reconstructed. Traveling together with your professors and fellow students can be a provocative experience as you learn together and discover the meaning of life and teaching!

> We do not learn a way of life in ways of deploying mind unassisted, unscaffolded, naked before the world. Rather, it is through the give and take of talk, the active discourse with other minds, that we come to know about the world and about ourselves. (Bruner, 1996)

THINK ABOUT IT

What is your current road map on your journey to becoming a teacher?
How would experiences prompt you to rechart your map?

GETTING STARTED ACTIVITIES

Personal Philosophy of Teaching: First Draft

1. Who is the most memorable teacher you had in your childhood? Why?

2. Make an appointment to visit and interview this teacher. Ask the teacher:
   a. What are her or his ideas on being a teacher and on teaching?
   b. What is her or his current personal theory or philosophy of teaching young children? What principles underpin his or her practice?
   Write a brief description of this teacher, including what you remember about her or him and what you have found out from the interview; reflect on what you have learned about teaching and learning.

3. Write a paper about your current personal philosophy of teaching. In writing your philosophy, reflect on what you have read in this chapter, classroom discussions, your teaching experience, and the interview with your childhood teacher.

4. Share your personal philosophy with others in your class.

5. Keep this paper as a first draft of your philosophy of teaching. Revisit, review, and revise your philosophy of teaching once a year. Keep these revisions in your portfolio. You will be able to evaluate you own development over time.

RESOURCES

On the Web
www.educationarena.com/educationarena/index.html

Readings

Clandinin, D. J., Davis, A., Hogan, P., & Kennard, B. (1993). *Learning to teach, teaching to learn: Stories of collaboration in teacher education.* New York: Teachers College Press.

Moyles, J. (2001). Passion, paradox and professionalism in early years education. *Early Years, 21*(2), 81–95.

Pradwat, R. S. (1992). Teachers' beliefs about teaching and learning: A constructive perspective. *American Journal of Education, 100*(3), 354–395.

Raths, J. (2001). Teachers' beliefs and teaching beliefs. *Early Childhood Research and Practice, 3*(1), Available http://ecrp.uiuc.edu/v3n1/raths.html

REFERENCES

Arendt, H. (1958). *The human condition.* Chicago: University of Chicago Press.

Ayers, W. (1995). Interview with Maxine Greene. *Qualitative Studies in Education, 3*(4), 319–328.

Ayers, W. (Ed.) (1998). *Teaching for social justice.* New York: Free Press.

Bredekamp, S., & Rosegrant, T. (Eds.) (1992*). Reaching potentials: Appropriate curriculum and assessment for young children* (Vol. 1). Washington, DC: National Association for the Education of Young Children.

Bredekamp, S., & Rosegrant, T. (Eds.) (1995*). Reaching potentials: Appropriate curriculum and assessment for young children* (Vol. 2). Washington, DC: National Association for the Education of Young Children.

Bronfenbrenner, U. (1979). *The ecology of human development: Experiments by nature and design.* Cambridge, MA: Harvard University Press.

Bronfenbrenner, U. (1986). The ecology of the family as a context for human development: Prospects and problems. *Developmental Psychology, 22,* 723–742.

Bruner, J. (1986). *Actual minds, possible worlds.* Cambridge, MA: Harvard University Press.

Bruner, J. (1987). Prologue to the English edition. In L. S. Vygotsky, *Collected works* (Vol. 1, pp. 1–16) (R. Rieber & A. Carton, Eds.; N. Milnick, Trans.). New York: Plenum.

Cadwell, L. B. (1997). *Bringing Reggio Emilia home.* New York: Teachers College Press.

Cuffaro, H. K. (1995). *Experimenting with the world: John Dewey and the early childhood classroom.* New York: Teachers College Press.

DeVries, R., & Kohlberg, L. (Eds.) (1987). *Programs in early education: The constructivist view.* New York: Longman.

Dewey, J. (1981). Experience and nature. In J. A. Boydston (Ed.), *The collected works of John Dewey: The later works* (Vol. 1). Carbondale: Southern Illinois University Press. (Original work published 1925)

Dewey, J. (1985). Ethics. In J. A. Boydston (Ed.), *The collected works of John Dewey: The later works* (Vol. 7). Carbondale: Southern Illinois University Press. (Original work published 1932)

Edwards, C., Gandini, L., & Forman, G. (Eds.) (1998). *The hundred languages of children: The Reggio Emilia approach—advanced reflections* (2nd ed.). Greenwich, CT: Ablex.

Eisner, E. W. (1994). *The educational imagination: On the design and evaluation of school programs* (3rd ed.). Upper Saddle River, NJ: Prentice-Hall.

Eisner, E. W. (1995). *The enlightened eye: Qualitative inquiry and the enhancement of educational practice.* Upper Saddle River, NJ: Merrill/Prentice-Hall.

Forman, G., & Fyfe, B. (1998). Negotiated learning through design, documentation, and discourse. In C. Edwards, L. Gandini, & G. Forman (Eds.), *The hundred languages of children: The Reggio Emilia approach—advanced reflections* (2nd ed., pp. 239–260). Greenwich, CT: Ablex.

Gandini, L. (1997). Foundations of the Reggio Emilia approach. In J. Hendrick (Ed.), *First steps toward teaching the Reggio Way* (pp. 14–25). Upper Saddle River, NJ: Merrill/Prentice-Hall.

Garbarino, J. (1989). *What children can tell us.* San Francisco: Jossey-Bass.

Gardner, H. (1993). *Multiple intelligences: The theory in practice.* New York: Basic Books.

Gardner, H. (1999). *The disciplined mind.* New York: Simon and Schuster.

Malaguzzi, L. (1998). History, Ideas, and Basic Philosophies: An Interview with Lella Gandini. In C. Edwards, L. Gandini, & G. Forman (Eds.), *The hundred languages of children: The Reggio Emilia approach—advanced reflections* (pp. 49–97). Greenwich, CT: Ablex.

Piaget, J. (1963). *The origin of intelligence in children.* (M. C. Cook, Trans.). New York: Norton. (Original work published 1936)

Rinaldi, C. (1998). Projected Curriculum through Documentation—*Progettazione*: An Interview with Lella Gandini. In C. Edwards, L. Gandini, & G. Forman (Eds.), *The hundred languages of children: The Reggio Emelia Approach—advanced reflections* (pp. 113–125). Greenwich, CT: Ablex.

Rogoff, B. (1989). *Apprenticeship in thinking: Cognitive development in social context.* New York: Oxford University Press.

Vecchi, V. (1998). The Role of the *Atelierista*: An Interview with Lella Gandini. In C. Edwards, L. Gandini, & G. Forman (Eds.), *The hundred languages of children: The Reggio Emilia approach—advanced reflections* (pp. 139–147). Greenwich, CT: Ablex.

Vygotsky, L. (1978). *Mind in society.* Cambridge, MA: Harvard University Press.

Wertsch, J. V. (1984). The zone of proximal development: Some conceptual issues. In B. Rogoff & J. V. Wertsch (Eds.), *Children's learning in the "zone of proximal development"* (pp. 7–18), *New Directions for Child Development, No. 23.* San Francisco: Jossey-Bass.

Wood, D. J., Bruner, J. S., & Ross, G. (1976). The role of tutoring in problem solving. *Journal of Child Psychology and Psychiatry, 17*(2), 89–100.

CHAPTER 2

HOW YOU TEACH
IS WHO YOU ARE

The desire to teach in a certain way does not magically erase all of my own negative experiences. We are a product of experiences. We tend to teach the ways we were taught. Struggling against this tendency is an exhausting and yet exhilarating effort. It means, on my part, a long-term commitment to reworking me.

Freidus, 1998, p. 51

It was midsemester; the early childhood education students were asked to create a metaphor that symbolized their personal image of teaching. This metaphor of teaching could also be represented in an artifact such as poetry, painting, sculpture, or photography. A written description of the metaphor reflects a student's personal notion of the art of teaching. In small groups, the students shared their metaphors and listened to one another's comments. Martha saw teaching as long-distance running; Amanda, as playing a flute in a marching band; John, as an explorer; Lauren, as a dancer; and many, many more. Everyone was deeply engaged in this activity, complimenting one another's creativity and extending the meanings of these metaphors from their respective points of view. It was interesting to watch and listen to the student teachers, who also pointed out that many of the metaphors reflected their creators: "Oh, yeah! That's you!"

We all have certain images of teaching that are woven together in the stories of life in the classroom. Think back to your childhood and you will remember special stories that have influenced your notions and images of teaching. As you begin to teach, you will have stories of your own teaching experiences. These stories will become a part of you as you create, re-create, and rework your image and personal theory of teaching. In this chapter, you will read a number of personal stories, autobiographies, and images of teaching written by students in an early childhood education program. Each student created a metaphor to capture the essence of her or his story.

A metaphor is a tool for reflection as we revisit our discoveries in teaching and imagine what lies ahead. Each story provides insight into the author as he or she "reworks" himself or herself on the journey to becoming a teacher, "choosing a past and inventing a future" (Greene, 1995a, p. 65). We invite you to reflect on these stories to find meaning and understanding about teaching.

Q U E S T I O N S   T O   B E   C O N S I D E R E D

- How is teaching a self-transforming experience?
- What are the tools for understanding self in the context of teaching and learning?
- Why is the art of teaching both aesthetic and intellectual?

In her junior year, Jennifer "Nicki" Nichols wrote the following autobiography, which reflects her journey to becoming a teacher. She created an artifact that consists of covers of favorite books, a poem, and a metaphor of her story "A Place to Ponder."

The moon casts its glow
On the peaks of mountains
And beneath it
The ridges throw out their shadow,
Falling into the valley
The clouds stretch heavily across the sky
A cushion for the moon to lay upon
Shimmerings of civilization
Appear in the distance,
But I am alone
Here,
I am left alone in my fluorescent world
To ponder and dream
As the moon takes a swim
In the branches of swaying trees.

Here is an excerpt of Nicki's story:

A PLACE TO PONDER
Jennifer "Nicki" Nichols

My artifact is a poem that I wrote, surrounded by a collage of books that have profoundly influenced my writing, my perspective, my interests, and essentially, the person I am today. In a deeper way, the poem reflects the sense of time and emotion that I experience when I read a story.

From an early age books influenced my life. My mother read to me on a daily basis from infancy. . . . As I got older books became an escape for me. I would become lost in them with no concept of the passing time as I read. I wrote my poem about the moon in one of my places to go when I don't want to be found. From there, . . . I am left alone "to ponder and dream." For me, reading a book isolates me from my surroundings, just as being in my secluded spot isolates me from the world. . . . Books are how I learned about other people. . . . As a child I can remember lying in bed at night and imagining that I was Georgie, an abused boy who was abandoned by his mother, in The Lottery Rose. *I tried to walk through the world in which he lived. . . . I can remember trying to feel what he felt. . . . I'd get angry at the characters he hated. I'd feel affection for the ones he most loved. I learned about other people's feelings through books. I lived vicariously through the characters. Books helped me to feel for people who had experiences different from my own.*

As I grew up, reading continues to provide an escape for me. Only my focus turned from people to places. I took a 4th year Spanish course in high school, which focused on Spanish literature. . . . This began my fascination with that heritage. I poured over books about South American life and culture. . . .

In the chaos of everyday life, the intensity of my dreams becomes dim. Yet, there are times when on my way home from school I find myself driving to that special spot where I was inspired by the moon. And there, my dreams are enlightened as I remember how wonderful it is to have a place where I can go to "ponder and dream." The most wonderful thing is that it is not merely a physical space. I can go there in my mind. . . .

In my classroom, I hope to foster an environment where children can discover themselves and their world through the power of story, whether it be their own or someone else's. I hope to enhance one of the greatest joys of literature that is found in the world that we create when we read a story and the exchange of our passion and excitement with others. I hope to help children cultivate their interests through stories and books, because from interests, dreams emerge. And dreams become a force inside of us that sustain us. Through a love of reading children can journey through a world that intrigues, enlightens, and sometimes startles them. Perhaps the most startling thing of all is what they will discover about themselves.

THINK ABOUT IT

After reading Nicki's story, do you have a sense of the kind of teacher she is?
How does her past influence her image of a teacher-to-be?
How does the power of story influence Nicki's image of teaching?

THE TENSIONS OF TEACHING AND LEARNING TO TEACH

The life of a teacher is an adventurous one. Bill Ayers (1993) wrote, "Teaching is highly personal—an intimate encounter. The rhythm of teaching involves a complex journey, a journey of discovery and surprise, disappointment and fulfillment" (p. 127). Your journey to teach began at the beginning of your life. Through the years, you had and continue to have encounters with many teachers, formally and informally. Parents, other parental figures, and significant caregivers are our first teachers. The quality of these relationships is the foundation on which we experience the world, predisposes us to future relationships with people, influences the kind of perspectives we take on the world, and helps form the kind of teacher we may become. Life, from its very beginning, is involved in finding a balance between freedom and control. This balance continues in the life in the classroom. Max van Manen (1991) wrote:

> One of the most fundamental conflicts in the pedagogical world consists of the tension between freedom and control. Associated with freedom are notions such as autonomy, independence, choice, license, liberty, room, latitude. In contrast, the language of control is associated with ideas such as order, system, discipline, rule, regulation, precept, organization. All parents and teachers know something of the tensions and pulls associated with the antinomy of freedom and control. (p. 61)

Studies of early attachment and parenting styles have provided us with many lessons regarding the quality of attachment and its possible effects on parent–child, teacher–child, and adult–adult relationships throughout life. *Quality of attachment* reflects the negotiation of tensions between parents and children and, consequently, our disposition to teach in particular ways. However, if we see teaching as a *journey of becoming,* then we believe in change and transformation. For teaching "is

Teacher as a Road

bold, adventurous, creative, vivid, illuminating—in other words, education is for self-activating explorers of life" (van Manen, p. 138).

Andrea wrote about her image of teaching through the metaphor of teaching as a road:

TEACHING AS A ROAD
Andrea Swepston

Teaching can be viewed as a curvy road, a straight road, a road that is uphill, and/or a road that is down hill. Teaching can go in many directions and many places. . . . Teachers who are happy doing their jobs have chosen an exciting road. A road full of curves, hills, bumps, and a path that is unpredictable. Children . . . who throw things at you that may be least expected. Happy teachers expect these things and enjoy the challenge of dealing with them. Those teachers who are not happy with their jobs . . . have chosen, however, the straight, boring road of not challenging themselves to be lifelong learners and not challenging their students. They view the curves and the bumps that the children are willing to go through as a vexation or a bother.

During my schooling, I have had both kinds of teachers . . . ; those teachers who wanted the challenge of the rough, curvy road, that were willing to let me take risks as well as take risks themselves . . . are the teachers who I have learned the most from. These teachers are also the teachers that have impacted my life in such a way that I carry the memory of them and the experiences they allowed me to this day in my life.

As I continue to develop into a teacher, I want to vow to be a teacher who stays on the exciting road and who is always willing to accept the challenges or bumps in the road from the children. I want to learn with the children and make their trip through the school year and their life a little more meaningful.

THINK ABOUT IT

What have you learned about Andrea on her journey to becoming a teacher? What tensions had she experienced in the classrooms of different teachers? Have you experienced the same?

Is it possible to imagine all the questions she has asked and reflected on throughout the years about why certain teachers are the way they are?

How does her writing reflect the road she will take to becoming a teacher?

AUTOBIOGRAPHY, REFLECTION, AND TRANSFORMATION OF SELF

Research has shown that most teachers' images of teaching are based on what they have observed and experienced in school. These ideas and practices, once formed, are difficult to change: *"We are a product of experiences. We tend to teach the ways we were taught."* How have positive and negative experiences influenced your image of teaching? *"The desire to teach in a certain way does not magically erase all of my own negative experiences."* Change comes when we gain self-awareness as a person and as a teacher, "because we teach who we are" (Stremmel, Fu, & Hill, 2002, p. 144). Thus, autobiographies and teaching stories can be used to construct knowledge, ideas, and understandings through reflection. These stories encourage us to inquire into our own believes, values, and images of teaching.

A teacher struggles to understand her teaching. The teacher is an inquirer of herself and of her practice. "Why do I embrace certain beliefs?"; "How might these beliefs influence how I teach?"; "What are the roots of the tensions in teaching?" The teacher continually reflects on questions such as these when she is teaching. The teacher is a researcher, an inquirer into her practice—posing questions, reflecting, looking for understanding and self-awareness—in order to *transform* it. That is, you must reflect on your experiences in order to make sense of them, understand the way you teach, and choose the way you want to teach.

We ask our students to write their autobiographies and notions of teaching using as many different forms and styles of writing as possible: poetry, stories, anecdotes, and so forth. Through writing they learn to make connections and make sense of their experiences. The importance of reflection on one's practice and experiences is one of the attributes Elizabeth Halter included in her description of her image of a teacher:

> *Good teachers never stop learning. They learn just as much from their students as their students learn from them. Good teachers reflect on various situations and recognize where they may have been wrong. They acknowledge their mistakes and come up with ways to improve their teaching. This takes place through deep reflection on what takes place in the classroom daily.*

Stacie Housel's autobiography reflects how her past makes her keenly aware of differences in ways of learning and reflects the kind of teacher she would like to be:

TYPES OF LEARNING
Stacie Housel

For as long as I remember, whenever I asked why my sister did things to get her in trouble, my parents replied, "that's how she learns." To me that seemed silly—I always played the scenario out in my mind to determine the probable outcome before I did anything. . . . My sister, however, had to get burned before she'd learn just how hot the fire was.

It amazes me now to realize how different my sister and I learned things. After all, we were raised by the same parents, and in the same life situation. But we are not the same. Our personalities set us apart.

Reflecting on my sister's learning style led me to discover what my learning style is. As a child (and adult) I read voraciously. Not only did I read the books, but I became so involved in them that I felt like the boy from The

Never Ending Story. . . . *I carried the main character's emotions into my
life. Anger, fear, hate and worry played themselves out in me. My mother
worried about the way I became so emotional over fiction, and was always
trying to get me to go outside and play. Reflecting on this, I see now that I
learned a lot from the stories . . . about human nature, science, politics, and
logic. . . . While this learning style may have made me rather worldly at an
early age, . . . now, I can see that because I have always learned through
reflection, I have difficulty learning and analyzing in the spur of the
moment. . . . Working with children, this could present a problem, as there
is rarely time to ponder before making decisions that affect others.*

*Thus, I have created a "plan." I try to take a few moments to play
out cause and effect relationships in my mind before making decisions, but
when that is not possible, I act on my gut instinct and reflect on that action
later. . . . In addition, recognizing the weaknesses that result from my
learning style proves that I still need to encourage the introspective child to
engage in activities that require her to "think on her feet" . . . I should keep
in mind, though, that just as my learning style created weaknesses in me,
other styles might do the same for other children. Thus, as a teacher I should
provide opportunities for and encourage children to learn in styles other than
what they are accustomed to.*

THINK ABOUT IT

Reflecting on her past, Stacie has gained insight into her personality, both the
strengths and the challenges. Stacie's self-awareness, based on reflections on
her own experiences, encourages her to take steps to change, to transform as a
teacher. How does her story inform you about teaching as transformation?

METAPHORS AND THE ART OF TEACHING

We challenge students to use metaphor as a means of organizing their stories and
notions of teaching. A *metaphor* is "the application of a word or phrase to an object
or concept which it does not literally denote, in order to suggest comparison with
another object or concept" (Stein, 1979). A metaphor represents lived experiences
in the form of unexpected relationships that bring a new perspective to the writer
and the reader. Metaphor can be used to capture the essence of teaching in a creative, expressive manner that challenges us to be imaginative, to think, to reflect,
and to find deeper meanings and understanding. Metaphor releases the imagination, which can lead to transforming and representing our thoughts and beliefs in
other languages of the arts. So we also ask our students to create artifacts, expressive representations, of their images of teaching using different art forms—poetry,
painting, sculpture, music, dance, drama, photography, and so on—that further

challenge them to be self-critical, reflective, and open in telling their stories. "Break with the taken-for-granted, with the ordinary and the mundane . . . to achieve the reconstruction of experience" (Greene, 1988, p. 173) in order to realize that *teaching is transformation of self.* The stories, metaphors, and artifacts of Nicki and Andrea demonstrate how these three ways of thinking and representing intersect to create a three-dimensional whole of *who* they are as developing teachers.

Leah Slade's metaphor of a teacher as a gardener and her artifact, a drawing of a rich, vibrant garden, reflect the notion of teaching as transformation of self:

A TEACHER IS A GARDENER
Leah Slade

A teacher is a gardener. A teacher tends to the needs of each individual child as a gardener tends to the needs of each flower in the garden. Each child is unique, at a different level of development, with a specific set of needs, which are uncommon to the other children. Individual kinds of flowers have specific needs, which help them grow. A teacher must research the children in order to discover their needs so she can be able to tend to those needs. A gardener knows the flowers within his garden so he can tend to each one specifically. A gardener knows the type of environment his flowers need so that they can grow and live. A teacher too must create the best environment for her children so they can learn and grow mentally. Both must be prepared for harmful circumstances, which will come, and be able to rebuild the safety of the environment.

Leah's writing reflects the role of inquiry and reflection in the life of a transforming teacher who teaches and learns with and among the children she teaches. The reciprocity of teaching and learning between these protagonists is clearly visible as she envisions a pedagogy based on relationships, one that balances freedom and control.

In summary, the underlying assumptions of using autobiography, stories, metaphors, and expressive, representational artifacts as tools of inquiry into how you teach are as follows:

- Autobiography and teaching stories are tools for understanding the self as teacher in relation to others—teaching happens in relationships.
- Teaching stories are a basis for understanding praxis.
- Reflection on experience is crucial to understanding self and others and one's evolving theory of practice.
- Metaphor and expressive representation (artifacts) of experiences open up new ways of seeing and knowing.

THINK ABOUT IT

What is your metaphor for teaching?

TEACHING HAPPENS IN RELATIONSHIPS: TEACHER AS PARTNER, NURTURER, AND GUIDE

Teaching happens in relationships of caring, thoughtfulness, and mutual respect. Reflecting on stories in your classroom helps you become aware of and understand your values, beliefs, and theories of teaching and why you teach the way you do and helps you find answers to the fundamental questions of teaching: What is teaching? What is learning? How should I teach? What does teaching mean? We have found that reflection using self-criticism encourages us to change and reconstruct our practice when we encounter new challenges.

> The teacher meets the children when they show up in class. But, this encounter, too, contains the possibility of a certain pedagogical eros that transforms the teacher into a real educator. The glance of the educator embraces them all and takes them all in. The pedagogical love of the educator for these children becomes the precondition for the pedagogical relations to grow. (van Manen, 1991, p. 66)

The very essence of teaching is knowing the student, seeing through the eyes of the student, up close and personal. "The caring teacher tries to look through students' eyes, to struggle with them as subjects in search of their own projects, their own ways of making sense of the world" (Greene, 1988, p. 120). The caring teacher finds ways to build pedagogical relationships with his students. Reflecting on what he learns about the students through detailed observations enables the teacher "to interpret from as many vantage points as possible lived experience, the ways there are of being in the world" (Greene, 1988, p. 120). The teacher learns about and from the children through observing, listening, and interpreting their ways of knowing, which enables him to be a *partner, nurturer,* and *guide* in creating multiple opportunities for learning based on relationships. The goal of observation and listening is to understand the child and how best to teach the child. The goal of interpretation is to understand oneself (have self-awareness) as a teacher. Self-awareness and knowing the students go hand in hand in the teaching–learning enterprise. The teacher is in effect a partner, nurturer, and guide to the students on their journey to learn and grow. His students in turn, year after year, are fellow travelers on legs of his journey to becoming a teacher.

Read Audrey's observation of and reflection on her life in the classroom before reading the next section of this chapter. While reading the next section, reflect on how Audrey's image of the child and understanding of children facilitates her practice as a teacher.

LIFE IN THE CLASSROOM
I wanted to see how interested and skilled the children were at classifying things. I began lining up animals that were the same. After completing only one row, Kika wanted to join in. She helped me find the matching animals and carefully put them in a row. When the row was finished, she counted up the total of that particular animal. A couple other children joined in periodically.

*They really enjoyed finding animals that matched. I was surprised that this
was so entertaining for them. The activity was very relevant to future studies:
graph making, classification, counting . . . etc. I think the fact that it was
animals, something the children have shown a lot of interest in, helped
immensely. This activity taught me a lot about tying interests to learning.*
                                              Audrey Piekurt, junior

KNOWING THE CHILD: IMAGE OF A PARTICULAR CHILD

Teaching begins with knowing the students intimately as individuals and as members of the community—the image of a particular child. Understanding each child as an individual is a step toward creating a curriculum in a learning environment that affords a variety of opportunities to meet the varied needs of the children.

Following are two early childhood education students' metaphors and descriptions of their respective "image of a particular child." These images reflect the writers' depth of understanding of the physical, social, emotional, and intellectual dispositions of each child.

AMANDA JAMES ON OCEAN (METAPHOR—A SUNSET)

*If I had to represent Ocean's temperament and disposition through one thing,
I would use the metaphor of a sunset. Ocean's calm manner, steady and persistent emotional balance, and "normality" remind me of the reassuring and
expected horizon that stretches across the sky. Ocean is a happy child who
seems content with his life. He seems to always greet the day smiling, somehow
knowing that, whatever the circumstances may be, he will find it positive.*

*However, just as Ocean's disposition is as normal as the gentle horizon,
his personality is as bright and interesting as the colors that fill the sky,
reflecting from the setting sun. Ocean is a very lively, entertaining, thoughtful, and culturally inspired and aware person. Although I would agree that he
has a very constant balance in attitude, sometimes he seems somewhat subdued, as when the sun is just starting to set and only a few colored clouds are
visible in the sky. At other times, he seems to burst with character when he
becomes excited about something he cares about, just as the sunset is most
brilliant when all the bright colors flood the sky.*

*Ocean's warm heart, eagerness to help other children and adults, and
love for his family reminded me of the sun, shining boldly and reflecting
colors as it sets. Ocean tends to "warm up" as you spend more time with him
and get to know him. Also like the sun's warm rays, Ocean's generous and
kind nature tends to stretch out to all the other children. He is happy to play
with almost any child and seems talented in finding something to enjoy and
have in common.*

*Ocean needs space. Less frequently, he will withdraw from a situation,
depending on his mood at the moment. However, I would never describe him*

as a moody child. It just seems that he needs his "quiet time" once in a while to maintain his outgoing personality.

THINK ABOUT IT

In reading this caring and thoughtful description of Ocean, what is your image of Amanda as a teacher?

What have you learned about Ocean's temperament, disposition, and status as a member of the classroom?

If you were the teacher, how would you use this information to create learning opportunities for Ocean?

LINDA BRUCE ON CALEB (METAPHOR—A NASCAR DRIVER)

If you have ever watched a NASCAR race you will understand right away how similar Caleb's temperament is to that of a NASCAR driver. When Caleb first enters the classroom he is extremely reserved and just beginning to warm up much like the first few laps of a race. The drivers don't immediately go from a dead stop to racing at 200 mph. Instead they take several pace laps allowing [them] to familiarize themselves with their cars' handling and track conditions. They are essentially warming up and preparing for the race ahead much like Caleb is preparing for the day ahead. He wanders around the room examining the activities of the day and seeing who has arrived and who hasn't. He may find an area to himself and engage in some personal time before the rest of the children arrive. He seems to be in a state of serenity and calmness.

As the pace laps wind down and the beginning of the race nears, the excitement and anticipation of the race takes over. The crowd cheers, the engines rev up and then the green flag drops and the racing begins. This is similar to the arrival of the other children. As soon as Dylan, Nick, or Ocean arrives, Caleb immediately engages in a whirlwind of emotions. He goes from excitement to disappointment back to excitement to frustration and so on. He seems to experience so many emotions throughout the day, just as a driver experiences through the course of a race. When Caleb is guiding a game or fully involved in an enjoyable activity, his emotional state is similar to that of a driver who is leading a race. Both are totally having fun at what they are doing. Then suddenly Caleb's toy may be taken away or his feelings may be hurt by the unkind words of a friend. He would immediately go from an emotional high to an emotional low. Just as a driver leading the race does when suddenly he blows a tire or loses control, slamming into the outside retaining wall. Yet both recover quickly, the driver visits his pit stall where his crew quickly fixes the tire, straightens the fender, refuels the car and sends him out on the track to complete the race. Many times when Caleb has become disappointed, he goes off by himself for a chance to regroup. Sometimes he needs his own pit stop where he can refuel himself emotionally and recover from the morning's events. Then it's right back to the excitement of the next activity. He is back in control and [raring] to go.

As the day proceeds, Caleb is forced to work his way through many emotional situations. Some irritating, others exhilarating, and some even discouraging. Yet at the end of each day Caleb always seems to be in a good mood. His daily struggles with emotions are very similar to a driver trying to work his way through the pack and on to victory. He may be rubbed into the wall or spun from behind. Yet both seem to have the perseverance necessary to work through whatever situation arises and come out on top.

A day in a child's life is not an easy one and neither is that of a race driver. Both involve emotional highs as well as lows and require the ability to deal with a variety of situations and obstacles being thrown at them from all directions. However, Caleb appears to have the temperament needed to remain in control of the most important race . . . Life.

Caleb appears to be an "easy" child. He adapts to new situations easily and is generally in a positive mood. He rarely, if ever, seems anxious about a situation; [he] maintains a sense of control and adapts in a manner in which he feels comfortable.

THINK ABOUT IT

After reading Linda's thoughtful description of Caleb, what is your image of Linda as a teacher?

What do you know about Caleb as a learner and as a member of the classroom?

How would you use this information to create learning opportunities for Caleb?

How would you provide balance and control in his life of learning?

KNOWING THE CHILDREN: IMAGE OF *THE* CHILD

In the process of knowing each child as an individual and as a member of the community, the teacher begins to construct her image of children in general—an image of *the* child. An image of *the* child is a complex construction of what one knows about diverse children's personalities, dispositions, capabilities, needs, and interests intermingled with one's knowledge of child development. This image provides a blueprint for teachers to understand the ways children interact, learn, and make sense of their world. With this blueprint, the teacher can plan for a group of children while editing and making changes to accommodate individual children's needs, interests, expertise, and ways of knowing.

Elizabeth Halter created an artifact, a collage of children, to reflect her image of *the* child. Here is an excerpt from her written caption for the artifact:

Each child is unique . . . [in ways] that set him or her apart from others. All children have special sets of genetic materials that give them distinct personalities. This makes [for] a wide variety of children in the classroom. . . . Children come from different socioeconomic statuses, family structures, ethnic groups, religions, and a host of other variations. . . . I immediately think of faces when I think of children. . . . The expressions on the children's faces in my collage show faces filled with happiness, fear, surprise, excitement, sadness, neediness, love, and many other [emotions]. . . . It is easy to feel a connection with children when one realizes that children experience the same emotions that adults experience. . . . This helps me to empathize with children and respect their feelings. . . .

Children have many of the same desires as adults. They want to be treated with respect. They want their ideas to be heard and considered. Children need to show off their hard work. They need to know that their work is recognized and appreciated. . . . Children want to be loved and to know that people care about them. They want to feel as if they are a part of something important.

My image of the child is very important to me as a future teacher. It will ultimately shape the type of classroom that I construct with my students. . . . [T]he most important [element] is respect for each child. This requires listening carefully to children's thoughts and feelings. . . . I want my classroom to be a place where everyone's feelings are respected even if they are not understood. . . . [E]ach child's opinion will be heard and taken into consideration. . . . This will be represented through documentation and displays of children's work. Since I realize the importance of a child's sense of control, my classroom will give children the chance to explore their dreams and interests and hopefully be a positive experience for everyone involved.

THINK ABOUT IT

How does Elizabeth's image of *the* child recognize and value individual differences and the group?

How does her image of *the* child influence her construction of teaching?

What is her image of a teacher?

Andrea Mahoney's image of the child is reflected in the metaphor of children as life gifts:

The image of a child is an ongoing, developing process that teachers and parents alike are constantly refining. . . . As long as the person developing the image has an open mind, the possibilities are endless but once we think our image is complete, that is when we miss out. The amazing thing about children is that every single one of them is different, like snowflakes, no two are alike. . . . My own image of the child reflects my personal and teaching values in that children are like gifts. They come wrapped in different shapes and sizes, each having their own unique wrapping. . . . [T]he gifts are beckoning to be opened is how the first day of school is to a teacher. So many gifts walk in wrapped differently. . . . [S]ometimes the packages come with a card of warnings from other teachers or a tear in the paper from a rough family life but I know that is exterior. But the job of a teacher . . . is to view the gift as new to them. Each child must be unwrapped layer by layer not all at once. . . . [T]he time spent in unwrapping can be as valuable as the time spent enjoying the gift. Each gift is given with the utmost hope . . . ; each gift is received by someone who sees the beauty in each one. . . . [O]ver time each gift changes and becomes a part of the collection of gifts that all blend in together to make a perfect menagerie of presents.

This artifact represents . . . the idea that children are teachers, and that we learn from them is an important fact. . . . [S]eeing the child as a gift can help us remember . . . to respect children and their learning interests . . . and [to] encourage children as inventors and lesson planners.

My learning from this artifact comes from an example of when I was a camp counselor. One of the little girls . . . gave me a potholder that she made by herself. She came from a broken home and had no money. . . . The gift she gave wasn't the potholder, it was her simple, childish ways about her. That is the basis for any teacher in their career. This artifact represents my image of the child and my utmost respect for each one of them.

THINK ABOUT IT

How does Andrea's description capture her image of children as unique, competent individuals?

How does her caption reflect her belief that teachers are also students of their students?

How does a simple encounter in the past influence her images of the child and the teacher?

KNOWING THE SELF AS TEACHER: IMAGE OF THE TEACHER

All the preceding stories, artifacts, and texts are either large or small fragments of images of how the past is connected to the present and to the future of developing teachers. A web of understandings, created by weaving together different perspectives, provides food for thought and insights into the complexity of being a teacher. The thread that runs through these perspectives and holds the web together is the teacher in the making—the teacher who is a guide, nurturer, and partner with her or his students in the teaching and learning endeavor. This sense of community permeates all the experiences and interactions in the life of a classroom. In this community, "a disposition and habit of mind that is one of great curiosity and interest in what is possible to do together is essential, as is trust in the child to lead the way" (see Chapter 10).

In each of the artifacts of the images of teachers and children documented in this chapter, you can feel a shared "disposition and habit of mind" among the protagonists of learning. You will find this disposition in the following pieces by Jessica and Kate. First, Jessica's image of the teacher who values teaching in relationships is reflected in the metaphor of combined action, and in a painting of children and adults joining hands and standing on a globe.

TEACHING AS COMBINED ACTION
Jessica Scotko

. . . Teaching is a combined action between the teacher and students where a detailed connection is achieved. It not only requires the energy of the teacher, but also that of the children. If a teacher is not aware of the needs and interests of each individual student, true success and improvement will never be reached. As a teacher, I have a mind set about children that reveals curiosity and delight in who they are and what they do.

. . . The goal of a teacher should not be instant results but the possibility for more authentic relationships. Teachers who learn the individual needs of the students know when to step in and when to step back. Every child may require a different strategy of teaching. There is no one way. It is the responsibility of a teacher to help his or her students find acceptable ways to gain their knowledge experience. When a teacher tells children what to do, their ability to do things is diminished. A teacher should always be in the middle, but not in the way. The more choices available, the more tasks accomplished and increased self-esteem. Teachers are helpers for their students. They should allow them to make their own decisions and fix their own conflicts. The more freedom children have, the more teachers will discover what is happening in their little minds.

Students should feel comfortable, respected, and motivated in their learning environment. . . . [C]hildren need to feel powerful and content, and all must be fair as well. . . . The fundamental challenge of teaching is to recognize that everyone who comes before you has capacity. . . . Teachers who work together with their students . . . remember that children possess effective theories too. Every student is a teacher and every teacher is a student.

Jessica is attuned to the reciprocity and partnership between teacher and students in a learning community in which "every student is a teacher and every teacher is a student." The teacher provides a nurturing, trusting environment in which children have freedom to learn, with guidance from the teacher.

To Kate, teaching is an adventure, as represented by her metaphor and collage of teaching as an adventure:

> *. . . When I think of a teacher, I see many ideas and faces. . . . [A teacher needs] to be many things to many unique individuals. . . . [T]eaching is an adventure. Each day brings something new, and it is sometimes hard to tell what the children have in store for you. The teacher becomes "full of wonder" by the children themselves, and the demands of teaching.*

In Kate's description of teaching, we find a teacher who is always looking forward to being and waiting to be challenged by the students. There is a deep feeling of joy, and a love of learning and teaching in a trusting environment. This is a teacher who chooses to take the exciting, curving road that inspired Andrea Swepston in her metaphor of teaching as a road.

WHO AM I? HOW WILL I TEACH?

After reading and reflecting on the stories and text offered in this chapter, you should be able to recognize the value of autobiographies and teaching stories in a teacher's journey to teach. These are narrative studies of lives. Ayers (1989) wrote, "Autobiography is an act of self-understanding, . . . the way in which memories and recollections must have meaning for now, and how that meaning can help shape intentionally and wide-awakeness for the future" (p. 19). Embedded in teaching stories (biographies and autobiographies) are the teachers' beliefs, passions, actions, and hope. Reflecting on these stories helps us understand where we have been and where we would like to go in our constantly changing life course.

We ask our students to write and reflect on their lived stories at different times during their teacher education program. These stories are selections in their portfolios. A portfolio is an artifact of a teacher's professional autobiography, and teaching stories are embedded in it. As discussed in Chapter 3, a portfolio is a means of making visible the work, the intentions, and the growth of a teacher; it has the power to illuminate teacher practice and foster the development of self-awareness. As a documentation of self, portfolios represent the notion that the past has the power to influence the future. Writing and revising their stories help the students chart their journey to becoming teachers. Revisiting the stories makes visible the bridges they have built, connecting the past with the present and their hopes for the future. The meaning of "how you teach is who you are" becomes increasingly clear to them. Peter Abbs (1974) wrote:

> How better to explore the infinite web of connections which draws self and world together in one evolving gestalt than through the act of autobiography in which the student will recreate his [sic] past and trace the growth of his experiences through

lived time and felt relationships? What better way to assert the nature of true knowledge than to set the student ploughing the field of his own experience? . . . May he not discover that "education" [is] that action of the inward spirit, by which . . . one discovers who one is? (p. 6)

We invite you to write your stories and autobiography as you continue on your journey to teach. As a beginning teacher researcher, you will begin to ask the following questions: Who am I as a learner? How was I taught? Who am I as a teacher? Why do I want to teach? What is my role in relation to children and parents? What is appropriate and possible? (Stremmel, Fu, & Hill, 2002). In revisiting your past, you may discover who you are today and what you did to get here. The questions to guide you on the next leg of your journey to teach may be: What kind of teacher will I be? How will I get there? Will I get there?

> Michele conveys a sense of incompleteness, a sense of reaching, of going beyond. . . . [A]s a teacher, Michele is nurturing, stimulating, calm, quiet, unsatisfied. She strives for something more. When creating an image of her teaching with clay, she shaped and reshaped the clay, never stopping; when asked to describe it, she said, "Well, it's flat now with little bumps, and it's changing and growing, now it's round and getting longer." Her hands kept working; she never settles on a single object to hold up her image. Michele's teaching, beautiful in itself, is also inspiring for what it is not yet. (Ayers, 1989, p. 95)

THINK ABOUT IT

What kind of teacher would you be?

How would you get there?

What are you current thoughts about your map that will guide you on your journey to becoming a teacher?

GETTING STARTED ACTIVITIES

Create Your Teaching Metaphor

1. Review the examples of teaching metaphors in this chapter and then create a metaphor that best reflects your personal idea of teaching.

2. Create a physical representation—an artifact—of your metaphor using paint, clay, paper, wire, poetry, music, photograph, and/or other mediums.

3. Write a description of how the metaphor reflects your image of teaching.

4. Share your metaphor and its representation with others in your class. Listen to their questions, ideas, and comments about your metaphor. Are there other interpretations?

RESOURCES

On the Web
http://ecrp.uiuc.edu/v3n1/raths.html
Early Childhood Research and Practice (An online journal)
http://pbs.org/teachersource
PBS TeacherSource

Readings
Cartwright, S. (1999). What makes good preschool teachers? *Young Children, 54*(4), 4–7.
Duff, R. E., Brown, M. H., & Van Scoy, I. J. (1995). Reflection and self-evaluation: Keys to professional development. *Young Children, 50*(4), 81–88.
Fu, V. R., Stremmel, A. J., & Hill, L. T. (2002). *Teaching and learning: Collaborative exploration of the Reggio Emilia approach.* Upper Saddle River, NJ: Merrill/Prentice-Hall.
Henry, J. (1994). A letter to my students (from a college teacher). *Young Children, 49*(5), 84–88.
Jacobs, N. L., & Eskridge, B. J. (1999). Teacher memories: Support or hindrance to good practice? *Young Children, 54*(5), 64–67.
Tertell, E. A., Klein, S. M., & Jewett, J. L. (1998). *When teachers reflect: Journeys toward effective, inclusive practice.* Washington, DC: NAEYC.

REFERENCES

Abbs, P. (1974). *Autobiography in education.* London: Heinemann Education Books.
Ayers, W. (1989). *The good preschool teacher: Six teachers reflect on their lives.* New York: Teachers College Press.
Ayers, W. (1993). *To teach: The journey of a teacher.* New York: Teachers College Press.
Freidus, H. (1998). Mentoring portfolio development. In M. Lyons (Ed.), *With portfolio in hand* (pp. 51–68). New York: Teachers College Press.
Greene, M. (1988). *The dialectic of freedom.* New York: Teachers College Press.
Greene, M. (1995). Choosing a past and inventing a future: The becoming of a teacher. In W. Ayers (Ed.), *To become a teacher: Making a difference in children's lives* (pp. 65–77). New York: Teachers College Press.
Stein, J. (Ed.) (1979). *The Random House dictionary of the English language.* New York: Random House.
Stremmel, A. J., Fu, V. R., & Hill, L. T. (2002). The transformation of self in early childhood education: Connections to the Reggio Emilia approach. In V. R. Fu, A. J. Stremmel, & L. T. Hill (Eds.), *Teaching and learning: Collaborative exploration of the Reggio Emilia approach* (pp. 135–145). Upper Saddle River, NJ: Merrill/Prentice-Hall.
van Manen, M. (1991). *The tact of teaching: The meaning of pedagogical thoughtfulness.* Albany: State University of New York Press.

CHAPTER 3

THE TEACHER AS RESEARCHER
Asking Questions, Discovering Answers

Be patient toward all that is unsolved in your heart and try to love the questions themselves. . . .

Rainer Maria Rilke,
Letters to a Young Poet

Teachers carefully and thoughtfully observe and reflect on life in the classroom in order to build an inquiring curriculum.

A few weeks into the semester, some children were asking, "What's up those stairs?" referring to the stairway they pass every day on their way into the lab school from the parking lot. Unlike our students, and probably most parents, who take for granted this particular stairway, which leads to the second, third, and fourth floors of offices, laboratories, and classrooms of the many faculty and students who teach and learn in the same building, our preschoolers are fascinated by this stairway to the unknown. One particular classroom teacher and her students noticed this interest and the children's repeated questions. As a result, they questioned children further about their ideas and hypotheses related to the primary question of "What's up those stairs?" Before long, children were drawing and painting pictures, using blocks to represent their ideas, and planning ways to explore this and related questions. Thus, a curriculum emerged and an inquiry began that will occupy the wonderings and curiosities of children and their teachers over many weeks.

In the lab school where we prepare students to be teachers, children, students, teachers, and even parents routinely engage in curriculum activities (i.e., projects) that include the meaningful investigation of issues emerging within the classroom and school. This collaborative activity, in which teaching and learning partners work together to design and carry out investigations on things that matter, forms the foundation of *teacher research.*

QUESTIONS TO BE CONSIDERED

- What is teacher research? How are teachers also researchers?
- What dispositions and understandings are necessary to becoming a teacher researcher?
- How is teacher research carried out in the classroom?

When teachers work together with children to pursue their questions and ideas, with their own sense of wonder and awe, teachers encourage discovery and learning

When teachers see themselves as researchers in the classroom they have the opportunity to consider hypotheses and to test theories. These highly reflective experiences are important professional development moments.

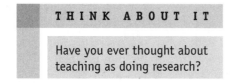

THINK ABOUT IT

Have you ever thought about teaching as doing research?

while connecting to children in ways that are meaningful and enduring. Further, teachers develop their own questions based on their curiosity about children's learning. Investigating these questions together with children while systematically documenting what happens is no less than authentic and collaborative teacher research.

THE MEANING OF TEACHER AS RESEARCHER

Although *teacher research* means different things to different people, it is a routine and expected function of teachers' lives in the classroom to learn and relearn with children through observation, reflection, speculation, questioning, and theorizing (Malaguzzi, 1998). Whether it involves simply observing children and writing reflections on what happens in the classroom, or the purposeful and solution-oriented investigation of particular classroom issues or problems, teacher research stems from questions about and reflections on everyday practice and a desire to improve teaching and learning (Hansen, 1997).

Like the children they teach, students, in their quests to become teachers, must have opportunities to pursue their deepest interests and passions if they are to transform their attitudes toward teaching and discover that teaching is not simply about the conveyance and receiving of information. Too often, students of teaching hold fast to the image of teachers as disseminators of information, as performers who stand before a class of willing and eager students, ready to dispense the wisdom of the ages (Stremmel, Fu, Patet, & Shah, 1995). But teaching is more than that; it is more challenging and intellectually demanding; it is more uncertain and ambiguous; and, if done well, it is more rewarding, more joyful, and ultimately more satisfying. Like learning, teaching is a serious encounter with life's most meaningful and mysterious questions. A teacher, among other things, is first and foremost a questioner (Hansen, 1997).

It is our hope that you, as a student of teaching, will be enlightened and transformed after reading this chapter. So read on, and prepare to be challenged!

DEVELOPING THE DISPOSITION OF INQUIRY

William Ayers (1993) has stated that teachers need to be part detective, searching for children's clues and following their leads, and part researcher, gathering data, analyzing the information, and testing hypotheses. But, in moving from the perspective of teacher as consumer and deliverer of facts toward that of teacher as *protagonist,* one who generates new knowledge and understanding of children and teaching, we have to think differently about the meaning of teacher as researcher.

To begin with, the act of research must be redefined as something teachers do as part of their teaching. Thus, teaching must be viewed as more than action and activity; it must also be seen as reflection and speculation. Science, after all, is a systematic form of reflective thinking and inquiry (see Dewey, 1933), and teachers, like scientists, encounter *problems,* experience obstacles to understanding, and ponder daily why something is the way it is. Note that problems in teaching are not the same as those that seek solutions or correct answers. To be more precise, problems in teaching are problems of meaning or substance; they are situations, predicaments, or dilemmas to be pondered, discussed, analyzed, interpreted, and understood so that we can act more thoughtfully.

Therefore, an important first step in teaching and research is to articulate the problem, even if it is rudimentary and tentative. After expressing a problem, a teacher typically draws on a combination of theory and intuition, experience and knowledge of children, observation and reflection, and perhaps the experiences of valued colleagues, to develop questions and assumptions (*hypotheses*) relevant to a given problem. This is no easy task, and the process often occurs without awareness, but it does occur. These assumptions form the basis of important decision making and action that will have subsequent influence on children and teaching practice. Actions are taken; information is collected through observation, formally or informally; and assumptions may be reformed or reconstructed with the gathering of evidence. Ultimately, our discoveries are used to reflect on and address the original problem, and the cycle continues as we live out our questions in the classroom. This process, often messier and more disorderly than may be implied here, is nonetheless a process of reflective inquiry, the so-called scientific approach to inquiry (Dewey, 1933; Kerlinger, 1973). For as often as teachers have engaged in this process, how often have they thought about their work as research?

Research must be seen as an orientation toward one's practice, a questioning disposition toward the world leading to inquiry conducted in the classroom. And the classroom, therefore, must be seen as the teacher's laboratory. Teachers must think of themselves as generating knowledge, not just using it. Otherwise, we leave it to others to define the knowledge that is of most worth, the questions that are most worth asking, and the knowledge that forms the basis of teaching, a dilemma with which the teaching profession arduously wrestles.

THINK   ABOUT   IT

What are the questions worth asking?

What knowledge is most worthwhile?

These questions, fundamental to curriculum planning and good teaching, are at the heart of the notion of teacher as researcher.

In this chapter, then, we suggest that *inquiry* is the basis of teacher research. Here we mean that inquiry, as a routine and expected function of teachers' daily lives in the classroom, is about wondering what, how, and why they do what they do. In what follows, we outline various ways in which we have explored and implemented the notion of teacher as researcher in our own work as teacher educators and researchers. Keep in mind that the notion of teacher as researcher is one of the basic principles of the Reggio Emilia approach, which views teachers as partners with children and parents in the learning process. In Reggio, and in our child development laboratory school, teachers are seen as active initiators of research in their own classrooms, as expert knowers of their children, and as creators of curriculum and knowledge.

BECOMING A TEACHER RESEARCHER

We believe there are three major understandings that students of teaching should develop as a result of their teacher preparation experiences. These represent critical elements of what it means to be a teacher researcher.

- An understanding that teachers and children are active learners, collaborators, and coconspirators in the negotiation of curriculum
- An understanding of the importance of observation, reflection, self-awareness, and interpretation as the foundation of learning in the classroom
- An understanding of the *documentation process* as a cycle of inquiry involving questioning; observation; organization of data; analysis, interpretation and theory building; reframing of questions and assumptions; planning; and evaluation (cf. Gandini & Goldhaber, 2001)

ACTIVE LEARNERS IN THE CLASSROOM

We are active agents in our own lives. In Reggio, educators like to say that we are protagonists in our own development—that is, we have agency and an inherent motivation to act in ways that contribute to our own learning and understanding. From the first year they enter our program, students are instilled with the notion that they are active learners with their students and that together they negotiate learning opportunities in the classroom. The idea that all students are teachers and all teachers are students permeates their education, and the concept of teaching as inquiry helps students avoid the temptation of expecting children to answer questions to which they themselves already know the answers. Rather, students soon learn to ask open-ended and intriguing questions and to develop and display the same sense of wonder that children experience through their own questions and discoveries (Malaguzzi, 1998).

Being an *active learner* means being a careful observer, a respectful listener, and a thoughtful inquirer about teaching and learning in the classroom. Active learning involves making informed decisions, questioning assumptions, and posing problems. We have two sayings that guide this thinking: "Make the problem the project" and "Those with the problems are often the ones with the solutions." Thinking about teaching in this way allows teachers to learn from and with their

Supporting a sense of inquiry and wonder in children is the work of a teacher/researcher.

students by asking and addressing real questions about issues and topics that concern them. We examine two examples of real questions later in this chapter.

BECOMING A REFLECTIVE THINKER

As researchers, teachers fulfill different roles through their inquiries. One important role is that of reflective thinker. *Reflection* is both a process and a product of active learning. Through the process of reflection, students carefully consider their experiences and the experiences of their students in order to improve their teaching and design more responsive curricula. Improvement or change in teaching (a product) happens only when we become aware of who we are, what we bring to teaching, and what our role is in relation to children and parents. Reflection helps us become aware of what is appropriate and possible in the classroom. It keeps us from being mechanical and complacent in our teaching, thus helping us avoid the pitfalls of feeling too good about ourselves when things are going well and feeling lousy about ourselves when nothing seems to work. To be aware of this can be liberating and lead to more thoughtful and caring teaching.

According to John Dewey (1933), reflection requires the development of several dispositions and skills, including introspection; open-mindedness; the willingness and ability to view from multiple perspectives and to synthesize opposing views; the wherewithal to search for alternative explanations of classroom events; and the ability to use new evidence to support, evaluate, and reconsider previous decisions, assumptions, or theoretical positions. Reflection is therefore vital to interpreting and analyzing the experiences, interactions, and events of people holding different perspectives, in particular teachers, students, and parents. In action research that attempts to illuminate the experiences of teachers and students in the classroom, a primary focus of analysis is the identification of understandings that emerge from teaching and learning partners (teachers, students, and parents) about their experiences and relationships in the classroom.

Our students, for an example, are asked to reflect on their experiences in the classroom twice a week. Although it is relatively easy for them to describe these experiences in writing, it is more difficult for them to reflect on the significance and meaning of these experiences for the children and their own teaching. To assist them, we often encourage them to ask themselves the following kinds of questions:

- What was the activity you observed like for the children?
- What was the activity like for you? (e.g., What were you thinking and feeling as you experienced the activity?)
- What decisions did you make? What did you learn?

These questions and others like them help students reflect at a deeper level, evoking an understanding of how both children and teachers can experience the same events and activities differently, and pointing to the need to reconsider and negotiate subsequent curricula for children. Here is one example of a student's reflection on an experience that provoked new thinking.

> On Monday the fire truck came in for a visit with the firefighters and Sparky the Dog. Sparky was a man dressed up in a Dalmatian suit, kind of the mascot for the fire department. The kids went crazy over him. They love seeing people in costumes. First, Sparky came into the class and walked around a little so we would know that it was okay to go outside and see the truck. On the way out, Minoka was walking beside Sparky and asked him if she could ask him a question. She then asked if he knew Clifford, the Big Red Dog. Sparky didn't say anything, and Barbara [another teacher] and I faced each other and smiled. Then I said to her, "That's a good question!" [I learned that] children think on a different level than adults. I would have never compared or rationalized the similarity enough to ask Sparky if he knew another fictional animal character. To Minoka, Sparky belonged to a different

society than us, a type of Mickey Mouse microcosm, and she didn't realize that Sparky was "not Sparky," but someone dressed up to be Sparky. I also learned that there is no way to be able to predict some of the questions of children from this age group.

Joshua Koen, junior in early childhood education

THINK ABOUT IT

How might this reflection foster further inquiry and curriculum implementation?

PROJECTS AS REAL PROBLEMS: USING THE CYCLE OF INQUIRY

Earlier we alluded to the pursuit of a *real question,* in which students explore authentic and meaningful questions of interest to them. It is has been our practice over the last few years to ask our students to work collaboratively with teachers in the lab school on problem-based (action) research projects that promote the development of a deep and elaborate understanding of selected core ideas related to curriculum and assessment. These collaborative projects follow the cycle of inquiry developed by Jeanne Goldhaber and Dee Smith (see Gandini & Goldhaber, 2001), which is further described in Chapter 10.

Consistent with action research processes (e.g., Stringer, 1999), the cycle of inquiry moves from framing and focusing meaningful questions and gathering data (observing, recording, and collecting artifacts) to the analysis, interpretation, and planning or revising of new practices, procedures, or policies. Real or authentic questions are not imposed or assigned, and students do not look for quick-fix solutions; rather, these questions stem from a desire to understand children, teaching, or the classroom environment in profound ways (Gandini & Goldhaber, 2001; Hubbard & Power, 1997). Thus, the questions teachers and students develop should be important and open-ended enough to allow new possibilities to emerge, as questions will no doubt need to be reframed and revised as the result of observation and reflection. Moreover, the inquiry process will likely require original thinking and interpretation, use multiple methods of inquiry, and lead to some meaningful action, such as the resolution of the problem or issue on which the research was focused. Finally, the investigation process or resolution of a problem should help students construct new understanding of the principles and concepts that are fundamental to good practice.

As an illustration of the action research process, we briefly share two projects that were undertaken during the 2000–2001 academic year by teachers and students in our lab school. Each project had as its emphasis practical outcomes relevant to the solution of real problems. The first project addressed a real issue of significance to our lab school program: our desire to improve and strengthen the relationships and activities among the participants and staff of the lab school and our co-located neighbors, the adult day services. The second project, which became the foundation of a teacher's thesis research, demonstrates a primary purpose of action research, that of contributing to and/or improving teaching and learning, in this case teacher practice.

Promoting Intergenerational Activities

We are fortunate to have the Virginia Tech Adult Day Services, a full-day, dependent-care facility for older adults with dementia, located right next door to the lab school. Over the past several years, we have made efforts to increase the opportunities for meaningful and mutually beneficial activities and interactions between the children and older adults, with varying success. Teachers and students from the infant and toddler classrooms worked together to systematically investigate intergenerational relationships between older adults and infants and toddlers, with the hope of developing greater understanding of these relationships and to enhance intergenerational curriculum development and implementation. With the belief that there was considerable value in having the very youngest children and the older adults share experiences with one another, the following questions were posed by the teachers and students in the infant–toddler classroom:

> How can we facilitate positive relationships between older adults and infants and toddlers?
>
> How can we facilitate an experience that is meaningful and beneficial for both age groups?
>
> How will we know when the experience is meaningful and beneficial?

It was reasoned that before positive relationships could develop, trust had to be formed between the children and the older adults. Efforts were made to increase opportunities for interaction between the children and older adults and to find common goals. Three methodologies were employed:

1. A photograph book was made of pictures of the older adult neighbors from adult day services so that the children could become familiar with their faces.
2. A second book was developed containing pictures of the children interacting with special older adults in their families (e.g., grandparents, aunts, uncles, or other older special friends).
3. With the help of adult day services staff, older adult participants visited the infants and toddlers almost every day.

The photo books helped the children develop familiarity with the older adults, construct positive images of older adults and aging in general, and build some connection between their relationships with older relatives and the older adults in adult day services.

The regular visits from the older adults to the infant–toddler room resulted in new ways of thinking about the environmental context and the need to rearrange

Forming a foundation of trust allows positive relationships to grow between children and adults.

this environment to better accommodate the older adults and be more conducive to promoting interaction. For example, the existing couch and chairs were not in a comfortable space for the children and older adults to interact. The teachers realized this problem and adjusted the space to make the "living area" more comfortable and accessible to the children and older adults. This new arrangement soon became an optimal setting for interaction.

Gradually, over the weeks, the children and older adults began to trust one another, and some special relationships began to form between particular children and adults. Children who once would shy away from the older adults began playing closer and closer to them. Interactions between the children and older adults became more intentional as the children sought out their older friends. Moreover, the children and the older adults developed a reciprocal teacher–learner relationship that became very visible in the classroom.

Though it is beyond the scope of this chapter to describe this project in greater detail, the process of inquiry outlined here and its resulting outcomes are important because they fulfill the promise of interpretive action research. This research led to the formation of new and meaningful relationships, benefiting the participants (and staff) of both programs. The infants developed a sense of trust in the older adults who would hold them and nurture them, and this intimate relationship was of tremendous importance to the older adults as well. Interacting with the infants often sparked memories of the older adults' own childhoods or of the children in their lives. Teachers, students, and staff from both programs gained a new understanding of the experiences and possibilities of very young children and older adults together. More joint meetings between teachers and staff of the two programs were implemented to discuss new activities and additional ways to enhance relationships, and there are ongoing attempts to share ideas for developing new curricula and further investigations. This example of collaborative teacher research illustrates the power and promise of inquiry designed to address significant issues and result in practical applications.

Children Teaching and Learning in Collaborative Interaction

The purpose of the teacher research described here was to examine peer teaching in preschool peer group interactions in order to better understand the significance of these experiences (Aschermann, 2001). This student's interest in peer teaching and learning developed from daily observation of and reflection on children observing and interacting with one another as they explored materials and became engaged in activities in her classroom. Specifically, the questions that framed her investigation were:

> What does peer teaching look like among preschool children?
>
> In what ways does peer teaching contribute to children's learning in the classroom?

Because what we wish to emphasize about this project is the motivation for undertaking such an investigation, we do not attempt to describe the study in detail. In the case of this teacher, the motivation to pursue the preceding questions came from her strong desire to figure out what she was observing in the classroom. The peer interactions she had observed over an entire semester, and the discussions she had regularly with her students, revealed something significant about children's interactions and activity choices, and it was her hope to gain a deeper understanding of these interactions.

> I hoped this study would help illuminate what peer teaching looks like during children's collaborative interactions, and also provide insight into how these interactions assist children on a cognitive and social level. Both the process of children's collaborative experiences as well as the product in relation to development were of utmost importance in this research in order for me to begin to understand the value of these interactions. (Aschermann, p. 7)

Through ethnographic (i.e., long-term, naturalistic) observation and documentation of what she termed *ordinary moments*, occasions when children came together in play to interact purely through their own interest and without outside adult influence, this teacher was able to uncover some new insights about specific acts of teaching and ways of learning among peers in her classroom. The documentation method she used when observing and recording the children's interactions was constructed based on her experiences with the children as a teacher in the classroom; her critical review of "traditional" research literature, primarily observational studies of preschool interactions; and her understanding of child development theories. This is critical because, to be useful, teacher research, like any form of research, must be formulated and conducted in ways that connect personal knowledge (i.e., knowledge based in one's own experience and practice) with knowledge based in research and derived from theory (Snow, 2001).

These two research projects, one developed to improve and strengthen relationships and program activities and the other to suggest new teaching strategies and foster personal and professional development, suggest that much can be gained by applying the tools of inquiry to the development and resolution of problems in educational settings (Stringer, 1999). Further, they point to the value of the "insider's perspective," which enables teachers to look more deeply into the issues, problems, and wonders of classroom life. As researchers, teachers integrate formal theory and personal knowledge to formulate questions and generate new understanding concerning the subject of interest through reflection, inquiry, and action.

One Final Example: How Children Learn from a Teaching as Inquiry Approach

The story related at the beginning of this chapter demonstrates the value of teachers and children learning together through inquiry. Before concluding this chapter, we present one other very personal and meaningful example of how this process, internalized by Andy Stremmel's son from his experiences with teachers and peers in the laboratory classroom, can be generalized to other teaching and learning contexts.

THE WONDER OF DISCOVERY

It was an Easter Sunday, as I recall, when my five-year-old son Joel and I went on an "adventure." This was a common undertaking. We would load up his backpack with all kinds of scientific exploration gear, including a magnifying glass, compass, pencil and paper, small containers (for rock or bug specimens), a small rock hammer and other tools, plastic ziplock bags, a container of juice, and some graham crackers (for nourishment on long treks). I, of course, carried a pocketknife (in case we ran into wildlife that needed taming). On this particular day we went looking for bugs, because he received a "bug box" for Easter that I purchased at the Science Museum in Roanoke, Virginia. The bug box was cylindrical, made out of clear plastic, and had a magnifying lens for a top, with small holes so the specimens could breathe. Onward we went "as far as the road takes us," as Joel always says.

We captured for our study a black ant. It was Joel's idea, upon returning home, to observe this ant very closely, using his bug book as a resource. He explained to me that he needed to document his discovery, something commonly done in his classroom at lab school, so he proceeded to draw a picture of the ant and color it in with black and brown crayons (he observed that the ant had a brown spot on its abdomen). As he drew the picture, he remarked that the ant had three body parts, six legs, and two antennae and was remarkably strong (he knew that ants can carry several times their weight). We wrote down these features in his "journal," with me providing the correct letters and Joel printing them on the paper. Joel would carefully look at the ant, in between putting down the words, and frequently referred to his book, noting in particular that this ant was not dangerous, unlike its counterparts the red fire ant or the army ant.

Joel mentioned the importance of having a hypothesis, and when I queried him on his understanding of a hypothesis, he answered with an example that was stunning. "A hypothesis," he said, "would be like, well, black ants are big because they need to be strong to carry food." Right or wrong in his assumption, he seemed to understand the meaning of a hypothesis. It was then that I began to wonder why it took an entire semester, if not longer, for some of my students to understand what a hypothesis is. Perhaps, I reflected, it was because we, as teacher educators, often fail to teach them as we do our children—listening closely to their interests and ideas, building on them, pursuing "their" authentic questions, and engaging them in meaningful inquiry.

We ended our "science lesson" with my son proclaiming that the ant should be let go, free to live out the rest of the day in ant fashion. However, he wanted to make sure that the ant did not get mixed up with the ants that were building a rather large anthill in our front yard. His reasoning: "You see, this black ant might get attacked if he invades the colony of the other [smaller brown] ants." This ability to take perspective and show caring, regardless of its level, was gratifying.

Why relate this story in a chapter on teachers as researchers? Though Andy Stremmel enjoys showing off his son's talents and passion for discovery, there is a more noble purpose intended here. It demonstrates, in our view, how children *appropriate* (i.e., internalize and reconstruct according to their own meaning capacity) the process of inquiry through their participation in an educational program in which teachers value and promote engagement with meaningful questions that emerge from children's interests and theories about the world.

As researchers, teachers play a central role, then, in the generation of new knowledge and understanding about teaching and learning. Whether this knowledge is directly applied to new developments or the solution applied to problems in the classroom or school; used to inform one's own teaching practice and understanding of children; or used to add to an academic body of knowledge, teacher research has an important place in schools and in teacher education programs. Teachers as researchers have the power to make a difference not only in the lives of children but also in their own professional lives, in their educational settings, and in the shaping of their discipline.

GETTING STARTED ACTIVITIES

We believe there are two characteristics of good teacher research to be considered at the outset of any investigation:

1. Teacher research represents an approach in which teachers and students learn from one another.

2. Teacher research addresses real questions you want to learn about, not those that others assign you.

Doing Teacher Research

1. Brainstorm and list several questions you have or problems you face as a teacher in your classroom. Try to narrow your list to three to five possible questions. Your questions should be open-ended enough to allow possibilities to emerge. What interests you? What intrigues you? What are your observations and reflections revealing to you? Consider broader teaching dilemmas that have arisen in your classroom ("making the problem the project").

2. Review the literature related to these questions and talk with other teachers about your questions. Decide which questions would be most significant or informative to the early childhood education community. Select one question for your research.

3. Develop a plan for conducting your research. What data will you collect? How will you collect it? For how long? How will you analyze your data?

4. Collect, organize, and analyze your data.

5. Write a report of your teacher research project, discussing how you developed your research question; the methods you selected and why you chose them; and your findings and what they mean. Then determine appropriate subsequent actions to improve the classroom or your teaching.

6. Develop a presentation on your findings.

RESOURCES

On the Web
http://gse.gmu.edu/research/tr/index.shtml
> Teacher Research, George Mason University Graduate School of Education. Learn more about teacher research and how to conduct it in the classroom by visiting this site.

http://education.ucsc.edu/faculty/gwells/networks
> *Networks: An On-line Journal for Teacher Research* is the first online journal dedicated to teacher research. The journal provides a forum for teachers' voices, a place where teachers working in classrooms, from preschool to university, can share their experiences and learn from one another.

Readings
Eisner, E. (1998). *The enlightened eye: Qualitative inquiry and the enhancement of educational practice.* Upper Saddle River, NJ: Merrill/Prentice-Hall.

Fu, V., Stremmel, A., & Hill, L. (2002). *Teaching and learning: Collaborative exploration of the Reggio Emilia approach.* Upper Saddle River, NJ: Merrill/Prentice-Hall.

Hubbard, R. S., & Power, B. M. (1999). *Living the questions: A guide for teacher researchers.* York, ME: Stenhouse.

Mills, G. (2000). *Action research: A guide for the teacher researcher.* Upper Saddle River, NJ: Merrill/Prentice-Hall.

Stringer, E. T. (1999). *Action research* (2nd ed.). Thousand Oaks, CA: Sage.

Wells, G. (2000). *Action talk and text: Learning and teaching through inquiry.* New York: Teachers College Press.

REFERENCES

Aschermann, J. (2001). *Children teaching and learning in peer collaborative interactions.* Unpublished master's thesis, Virginia Polytechnic Institute and State University, Blacksburg, Virginia.

Ayers, W. (1993). *To teach: The journey of a teacher.* New York: Teachers College Press.

Dewey, J. (1933). *How we think: A restatement of the relation of reflective thinking to the educative process.* Boston: D. C. Heath.

Gandini, L., & Goldhaber, J. (2001). Two reflections about documentation. In L. Gandini & C. Edwards (Eds.), *Bambini: The Italian approach to infant/toddler care* (pp. 124–145). New York: Teachers College Press.

Hansen, J. (1997). Researchers in our own classroom: What propels teacher researchers? In D. Leu, C. Kinzer, & K. Hinchman (Eds.), *Literacies for the 21st century: Research in practice* (pp. 1–14). Chicago: National Reading Conference.

Hubbard, R. S., & Power, B. M. (1997). Finding and framing a research question. In L. Patterson, C. M. Santa, K. G. Short, & K. Smith (Eds.), *Teachers as researchers: Reflection and action* (pp. 19–25). Newark, DE: International Reading Association.

Kerlinger, F. (1973). *Foundations of behavioral research* (2nd ed.). New York: Holt, Rinehart and Winston.

Malaguzzi, L. (1998). History, ideas, and basic philosophy: An interview with Lella Gandini. In C. Edwards, L. Gandini, & G. Forman (Eds.), *The hundred languages of children: The Reggio Emilia approach—advanced reflections* (2nd ed., pp. 49–97). Greenwich, CT: Ablex.

Snow, C. (2001). Knowing what we know: Children, teachers, researchers. *Educational Researcher, 30*(7), 3–9.

Stremmel, A. J., Fu, V. R., Patet, P., & Shah, H. (1995). Images of teaching: Prospective early childhood teachers' constructions of the teaching–learning process of young children. In S. Reifel (Series Ed.), *Advances in early education and day care: Vol. 7* (pp. 253–270). Greenwich, CT: JAI Press.

Stringer, E. T. (1999). *Action research* (2nd ed.). Thousand Oaks, CA: Sage.

CHAPTER 4

THE PREPROFESSIONAL PORTFOLIO
Documenting Self

Our deepest business is to know who we are.

Mary Rose O'Reilley, *Radical Presence*

At the beginning of the semester, Nora, an early childhood education sopho-more, reviews her portfolio from the previous year. Her portfolio begins with a poem she wrote that expresses who she is as a person, such as characteris-tics that describe her, her hopes, passions, cares, and dreams. It also contains a metaphor, or image, of her view of teaching. Nora sees herself as a coach, someone who stands on the sidelines and cheers on, supports, and encour-ages students to do their best work, to think creatively, and to work together in the learning process. After this personal reflection, Nora's portfolio con-tains a self-selection of artifacts (e.g., work samples, reflections, and other items) that she believes provides evidence of her teaching beliefs and values and of her growth and effectiveness over the first year of her teacher educa-tion program. Reviewing this portfolio will prove useful over the course of her development as a teacher, for this process of revisiting, or "looking again," will help Nora clarify and reconstruct her views, compare her past and present performance in the classroom, and rethink her understanding of what it means to be a teacher.

In this chapter, we discuss how a portfolio can be an important doc-umentation tool for helping beginning students of teaching to re-search and learn from their own experiences. We address several questions about portfolios as a means of assessing personal and pro-fessional development.

- What is a portfolio?
- Why do a portfolio?
- What should be included in a portfolio?
- Are there different types of portfolios?
- How can you use your portfolio to show who you are as a developing person and professional?

Because teaching is a complex, human-centered activity, learned by living and doing it, portfolios increasingly have been recognized as an authentic means of documenting teachers' personal and professional development in the real context of their lives (Ayers, 1993; Grant & Huebner, 1998; Wolf, 1994). Portfolios typically are created for the purpose of providing to some external group (e.g., a school board or personnel committee) a comprehensive view of one's performance in context; however, the portfolio also can be an important documentation tool for helping beginning teachers research and learn from their own experiences. Portfolios as a means of making visible the work, the intentions, and the growth of teachers have the power to illuminate teacher practice and foster the development of self-awareness. As a documentation of self, portfolios represent the notion that the past has power to influence the future. This chapter discusses how the preprofessional portfolio can be developed to reveal the student's own learning and in the process enable the exploration and reconstruction of self.

In this chapter, we distinguish between the *preprofessional* and the *professional portfolio* for purposes of clarifying its intended use as a documentation tool for self-growth and learning. That is, what makes the preprofessional portfolio different from the professional portfolio is simply the notion that the development of the former begins well in advance of the actual act of teaching. Just as you as a student continue to change and develop, the preprofessional portfolio is a living documentation of thinking, beliefs, and encounters that change over the course of the entire teacher education experience.

WHAT IS A PORTFOLIO?

Generally speaking, portfolios have been referred to as organized documented histories of one's efforts, accomplishments, and developmental progress in one or more areas, authenticated by work samples and realized through careful and intentional reflection (Paulson, Paulson, & Meyer, 1991; Wolf, 1994). The portfolio is a purposeful collection of artifacts that includes the individual's own participation in selecting and evaluating the contents, determining the criteria for selection, and reflecting on its overall worth (Paulson et al., 1991).

Portfolios represent a movement toward a more public, professional view of teaching. They reflect teaching as a scholarly activity that begins with inquiry into the self. Self-reflection is the most powerful tool available for improving teaching and developing greater self-awareness. Proponents of portfolios as a means of

Students reflectively and selectively choose the contents of their portfolio.

documentation assert that they show evidence of skills, including the ability to reflect, that exams, standardized tests, papers, and even projects cannot demonstrate (Panitz, 1996). Because portfolios are documentation of work, experiences, and growth over time, they represent a more holistic and authentic assessment of the individual.

WHY DO A PORTFOLIO?

Portfolios foster self-directed learning in ways that other performance measures cannot. As a form of authentic assessment, a portfolio represents a self-selected representation of what a person considers valuable. For students in the process of becoming teachers, portfolios provide a concrete way to take control of their learning and develop the ability to value their own work (Paris & Ayres, 1994). When you assume responsibility for deciding what to include in your portfolio, you learn to think carefully about your work and to examine evidence of your progress over time. Through opportunities to critically reflect on your performances, you can develop increased awareness of yourself as a teacher. Thus, in addition to making public your work, portfolios make visible *your standards* for good work and the qualities you value in teaching.

THINK ABOUT IT

Portfolios make visible your standards for good work and the qualities you value in teaching. What are the standards and values that underlie and motivate your teaching?

TYPES OF PORTFOLIOS

Portfolios serve different purposes at different times and in different settings, and they can vary considerably in format. Nevertheless, it is important to recognize that a portfolio is not simply a compilation of everything you have done. More than a collection of course work and artifacts that bear on your teaching performance, a portfolio is a thoughtful selection of information that provides evidence of your development and effectiveness as a teacher.

Students can develop three different types of preprofessional portfolios: the working portfolio, the course portfolio, and the presentation portfolio (Campbell, Cignetti, Melenyzer, Nettles, & Wyman, 1997). A _working portfolio_ is a comprehensive, ongoing collection of work selected from course work (e.g., tests, papers, assignments, notes, handouts, projects, entire journals, teacher-made materials, etc.) and other teaching-related experiences (e.g., community activities and field experiences) that forms a framework for self-documentation and goal setting (Campbell et al., 1997). This work might be stored on a computer disk, in a filing cabinet or file boxes, or in several notebooks organized by course, subject, or topic. For example, Nora, the student in our opening vignette, chooses to keep all of her work in cardboard file boxes. Everything related to teaching, from class notes and handouts to completed assignments, is systematically filed away in these boxes. This documentation can be referred to as needed and later selected in the development of either a presentation portfolio or a course portfolio, which, as you will see in a moment, represents specific artifacts that best reflect achieved competence and personal and professional development over an entire course or curriculum.

Course portfolios are compilations of all class materials, including notes, assignments, handouts, papers, and other performances, from a specific course. An instructor might determine the items to be included based on course goals and objectives, the content to be learned, or particular roles and responsibilities that students should demonstrate in the classroom. For her course on guiding young children's behavior, for example, Nora is given an outline by her instructor that indicates the specific items to be included in her portfolio over the semester. As part of her grade for the course, she will be evaluated on her adherence to guidelines, the organization and appearance of the portfolio, and reflective evidence of growth in understanding course content and classroom effectiveness. In our view, course portfolios should include some prespecified materials, but when they are used primarily for improvement and self-directed learning, most items should be chosen by the student in collaboration with the instructor or others who may serve as consultants. More will be said about this later.

The *presentation portfolio* is assembled by the student for the stated purpose of giving others a clearly discernible portrait of personal and professional growth and competence over time (Campbell et al., 1997). This portfolio is highly selective and consolidated and allows others the opportunity to get an accurate representation of the individual without having to read a lot of material. This type of portfolio is what Nora will bring to an interview when she is ready to look for a teaching position.

THREE TYPES OF PORTFOLIOS

- A working portfolio is a collection of work that is systematically organized and stored over the course of the teacher education curriculum. It may be referred to as needed and drawn from in compiling a presentation portfolio.
- A course portfolio is a systematic compilation of class materials, assignments, and performances from a specific course. It includes both instructor-specified and student-determined items.
- A presentation portfolio provides a portrait of achieved competence and personal and professional development over the entire teacher education curriculum.

Increasingly, *electronic portfolios* are being required for students who are meeting the various professional standards for teaching and learning. Materials from course work and field experiences are stored in computer files (HTML, text, photos, PDF, video, sound), and portfolios are designed for electronic access on the Web. Although a broader discussion of electronic portfolios is beyond the scope of this chapter, there are many excellent web sites on portfolio construction, a few of which are listed at the end of this chapter. It should be noted that electronic portfolios are neither electronic scrapbooks nor fancy multimedia presentations. As authentic assessment tools, web-based electronic portfolios are a convenient and efficient way of demonstrating to prospective employers your knowledge, skills, and views about teaching and your suitability for a specific teaching position.

In sum, the type of portfolio you develop will depend on your audience. Information contained in the course portfolio, for example, will be organized to the specifications and interests of those (e.g., university course instructors or advisors) who look at and evaluate the portfolio. However, each portfolio is unique and reflects both the individuality and creativity of the creator and the expectations of the person who requires or assigns it. So it is important to remember that you, either individually or with the assistance of others, will identify the aspects of learning that you value enough to document (Paris & Ayres, 1994).

WHAT TO INCLUDE IN A PORTFOLIO

Most likely one of your initial questions will be, "What should I include in my portfolio?" Although there is no single answer, most portfolios are organized in some systematic way to represent what is meaningful to the creator and to those who are likely to view and evaluate the portfolio. Portfolios might be organized around a set of standards or goals, and might, therefore, include things that provide tangible evidence of movement toward the achievement of those goals (Campbell et al., 1997).

Ultimately, what you put into your portfolio should reflect what is valued. This often includes accomplishments and performances; evidence of your ability to reflect on and evaluate experiences; personal perceptions of your progress or development; your satisfaction as a teacher; and your educational beliefs. Although usually there are some basic items that represent products of good teaching and statements of beliefs and values, in the end it will be up to you to decide just what to include.

Based on our own work as teacher educators and on the work of colleagues who have used portfolios, the following major areas seem to be common or frequent components of a portfolio:

- A table of contents
- Material on the student, including such things as a résumé, philosophy of education, and personal goals
- Materials on experiences with children, including a child study, journal entries, personal reflections, children's artifacts, and observations
- External evaluations and observations from those who have observed the student in the classroom
- Self-observations
- Videotaped performances (e.g., activity plan implementations)

We believe that you should not limit your portfolios to only your "best work." Instead, including a wide variety of representative "work samples" allows you to see evidence of your progress over time. Further, indicating *why* each work sample has been selected helps a reviewer or evaluator understand the context of your work and what it says about your progress or growth as a teacher.

INQUIRY INTO THE SELF: DEVELOPING
THE PREPROFESSIONAL PORTFOLIO

When you entered your teacher education program, you brought with you a set of experiences and beliefs that form the basis of your understanding of what it means to be a teacher. Research suggests that the perspectives, values, and beliefs that students embrace and that influence their teaching decisions and actions are largely implicit and unexamined (see, for example, Stremmel, Fu, Patet, & Shah, 1995). However, these implicit understandings need to be made explicit in order to make sense of them, rethink inaccurate or naive assumptions, and develop more sophisticated views of teaching. This perspective is consistent with the philosophy of John Dewey, who described education as the process of reconstructing one's experience. To grow, to become better at what we do, requires that we rethink our positions in light of new experiences and, in the process, transform ourselves.

Self-knowledge may be the most important, yet least attended to, kind of knowledge teachers need to possess (Ayers, 1993). If this is true, then a major goal of teacher education should be to help students develop an increased understanding of self (Bullough & Gitlin, 1995). Therefore, there is value in having students begin developing portfolios in their first year that serve the purpose of assisting them in the exploration and understanding of self. In our teaching, we have posed three questions to help guide students' self-exploration during the first year of their journey in becoming a teacher: *Who am I? Where did I come from? Where am I headed?*

Here is one student's self-inquiry:

> *I am a sophomore in early childhood teacher education. I am living on my own for the first time in my life. It is exciting to finally be free and independent, but it is also terrifying. I was born in Iowa City, IA, and grew up in a small town called Hills, which was a great town because everyone knew each other and would do anything for one another. I moved to Roanoke [when I was 9] because my Dad got transferred. That move was one of the most difficult times I went through during my childhood. I had few friends and got teased a lot about being fat until I grew older and my body evened out. I was an outsider, very shy, and felt self-conscious. I had to get used to a new school system that was completely different than what I was used to. For example, at my school in Iowa, grades were mixed together, and for certain subjects, like math and reading, [teaching seemed to be more individualized]. It was hard to make the adjustment. Now as a college student, I have made the adjustment to a large campus, and have finally gotten used to large classes and the 20–30 minute walks across campus to get to my next class. I am excited to be in early childhood education because teaching is what I would love to do in life and this major is very competitive. . . . In ten years, I see myself married, having two children, and teaching elementary education in northern Virginia. . . . In twenty years, I will still be teaching or be doing some kind of administrative work as a principal or assistant principal.*
>
> Tawnya Jarrard, sophomore in early childhood education

THINK ABOUT IT

How do you think this student's experiences, understanding of her past, and hopes about her future will influence her as a teacher?

Self as Person: "Who Am I?" "What Do I Believe?" "What Helped Shape Who I Am?"

The great philosophers of the world tell us that one of the most important questions we can ask is "Who am I?" or "What is this thing called self?" (de Mello, 1990). Self-awareness and understanding are critically important in teaching because we teach who we are. Our conceptions of ourselves as learners and teachers are grounded biographically. Teachers need to know what theories, values, and beliefs are driving their teaching, and they need to be able to defend them or reconstruct them when conditions change. Understanding who we are and what we bring to our teaching enables us to understand that children also bring something to us.

Although there are numerous artifacts you might choose to include in a portfolio to represent who you are, some of the possibilities include:

- An autobiographical sketch, which is a brief statement or paragraph about who you are that may include information such as words you would use to describe yourself, something you love, something you fear, something you hope for, and something you feel passionate about, and so forth. We have found that this activity is often a fun and easy way to begin thinking about self.
- The story of your name. This is another fun and relatively easy activity, and it gives you an opportunity to research how you got your name and to tell the story behind it.
- A story of a time in your life when you learned something important about yourself: This is sometimes more difficult, but it can help you reflect on significant events and people in your life that have helped you construct your understanding of self.
- Teaching images or metaphors that represent implicit theories or views of "self as teacher." Developing a personal metaphor is a great way to help you articulate and consider who you think you are and who you want to be as a teacher, and it helps generate simultaneously emerging images of the child, parents, and other aspects of what it means to teach. Following is an example of a third-year student's image of teaching as it evolved over time:

I feel that the image of a teacher and her students at a crossroads represents my ideas about teaching. I see myself moving with my students, helping and guiding them, but as a partner in the learning process rather than a dictator of it. There are many different paths to take that may or may not end up in the same place. I want to work with my students to help them discover more about the world that they live in, allowing them to choose the direction that we take, and never being afraid to try something new and different. In this image, I see my own personal philosophy that the process, or the path chosen, is just as important and rewarding, if not more so, than the end product or destination.
Erin Burke, junior in early childhood education

Self as Learner: "Who Am I as a Student?"

The preceding artifacts are examples of how you might begin documenting your understanding of self and your image(s) of teaching. But, before you can effectively teach, you must understand who you are as a learner. Thus, an important question for the first-year student is "Who am I as a student?" Again, you might begin to address this question in many different ways. We ask beginning students to include in their portfolios images of self as a learner based on inquiry into their major *intelligences,* or the special and individualistic abilities they have to solve problems and create products using various means of representation (e.g., see Armstrong, 1993), as well as their interests, passions, hopes, talents, and preferred modes of learning. In addition, we ask students to include assignments they have been most pleased with and those that have posed the greatest challenge and effort over the first year. This includes a "best piece" and a "most difficult piece" analysis in which the student reflects: "I think this is my best work because . . ." and "I think this has been the most difficult thing I have done because . . ."

The process of selecting which assignments to include is necessarily an evaluative process. Students must think carefully about their work, a practice that is likely to lead to improvement and self-awareness, both as a student and as a teacher. It also forces the students to think about the standards or expectations they have set for themselves.

"I THINK THIS IS MY BEST WORK BECAUSE . . . *AND* **THE MOST DIFFICULT THING THAT I HAVE DONE BECAUSE. . . ." A FIRST-YEAR STUDENT'S VIEW**
The project of creating a portfolio has proved to be some of my best work, because I had to put a lot of effort and thought into the expression of who I am and my goals as a teacher. But I also felt that this was the most difficult thing I have had to do because it has made me step back and establish where I am and where I want to be. It made me better understand myself as a learner and why I want to become a teacher.
                              Kylie Felps, first year student in early
                              childhood education

THINK ABOUT IT

How do you see yourself as a student and what might this tell you about the kind of teacher you will become?

Continuing the Journey: "Who Am I as a Teacher?"

Teaching is a developmental phenomenon, and as a student you must stay alive to its dynamic nature. As you continue the exploration of self, somewhere along your journey you must confront the questions: "What is teaching?"; "What does it mean to be a teacher?"; "What image or images do I hold of the teacher?"; "How do these relate to popular cultural images of the teacher?"; and "Why do I want to be a teacher?" Over the course of your teacher preparation program, no doubt you will have numerous and varied opportunities to experience teaching both directly and indirectly and to discuss what it means to teach. As mentioned earlier, one of the ways to explore "self as teacher" is to make visible and reflect on unarticulated and unexamined views of teaching. We have found the following avenues helpful to students at all levels of teacher preparation:

- Get together on a regular basis with students who are in their student teaching year to discuss teaching experiences and issues related to teaching in general.
- Shadow a teacher or student teacher for a couple of hours in his or her classroom to get a feel for what teaching is like.
- Serve as or seek out a student teacher mentor who will provide social support and a forum for sharing experienced information.
- View videos, read teacher autobiographies or books on teaching, and make use of various media to examine teaching-related diversity issues.
- Demonstrate, using multiple languages (e.g., visual representations and performances), popular images and cultural stereotypes of teaching, along with previously unexamined personal metaphors of teaching.
- Write a formal autobiography (see Bullough & Gitlin, 1995, for a cogent look at educational biography) that documents how you came to the decision to become a teacher, the people or critical incidents that influenced this decision, and your thinking about the aims of education and the role of teachers.

Any one of these activities might become part of the preprofessional portfolio included under the category of self. As stated earlier, because the preprofessional portfolio is a living document that changes over time with the addition of new experiences and one's reflection on these, new artifacts are continually being added and old ones are removed and placed in the working portfolio. This is an ongoing process that reflects a continuing cycle of critical analysis of one's work, beliefs, and practices, in which the opportunity exists to reinvent and reconstruct personal experience.

Teacher as Researcher

As you can see, teaching is more than action and activity; it is also reflection and speculation. Our knowledge of teaching is embedded in everyday practice, reflection, and questions about what we do. As noted in Chapter 3, teachers are researchers of their own experiences. The concept of teacher as researcher suggests a way of questioning assumptions and posing problems that extends across the professional life span. Therefore, it is essential that students begin to embrace the processes of inquiry and personal and professional renewal as a lifelong endeavor prior to the student teaching year. Questions such as "How can the study of self contribute to who I am as a teacher?"; "Who do I want to be in the lives of children?"; "What role do relationships play in the educational process?"; and "What is curriculum?" become critical in the development of self-understanding.

Portfolios have been described in this chapter as a major tool for documenting reflected experiences, views, and beliefs. Over the course of your teacher education program, you should be developing a keen ability to observe and document children's interactions and encounters, and to plan activities and experiences that derive from the questions, interests, passions, and abilities of children. The preprofessional portfolio can assist you in developing an equally acute ability to reflect on and learn from these experiences, opening up the possibility for you to confront and reconstruct your thinking about teaching. In addition to any of the previously mentioned items, we list below a few other important artifacts that should be included in your portfolio by the time you finish your teacher education program:

- A philosophy of teaching that includes core values. Distinct from, yet related to, an autobiography, a philosophy of education is a narrative that reflects your view of how children learn and how, therefore, you should teach, which will have been reconstructed over the course of your program. Also, a listing of your core values or "commitments" to teaching helps to identify part of who you are and what you bring to teaching children. For example, one of our core values is the belief that all children have capacity.
- Your image of the child, including a carefully constructed image of a particular child who is the subject of a systematic child study. Who is the child? What does it mean to be a child? These philosophical questions are at the heart of effective teaching and relate to one's understanding of self (see Chapter 5).
- Participant observations conducted in other classrooms. You can learn a lot about your own teaching style and views when you have opportunities to observe and reflect on a variety of classrooms and schools, comparing observed elements to your personal experiences in the classroom.
- Engagements in practical inquiry (e.g., pursuing "real questions"; problem-based activities; projects; and action research). Projects that involve the pursuit of a real question, in which students pursue authentic and meaningful questions of interest to them, require original thinking and interpretation and multiple methods of inquiry, and promote the development of a deep and elaborate understanding of selected core ideas related to curriculum and assessment. As articulated in Chapter 3, this form of inquiry is part of the routine and expected function of teachers' daily lives in the classroom that can be documented in a portfolio.

Self-Observation

In the process of putting together a portfolio, you can't help but learn one of the most important skills of becoming a teacher: the ability to observe and evaluate yourself. No one can teach you this skill, but when you take the time to watch, listen to, and study your experiences carefully, you begin to develop a greater self-awareness. Without self-awareness, you cannot test your deepest values and beliefs, and you lose the capacity for renewal and growth (Ayers, 1993). We believe that students should observe themselves frequently and write down what they discover. Doing this makes it easier to write a self-assessment of your overall growth and development for inclusion in a course portfolio at the end of a semester or a presentation portfolio at the end of each year. This self-reflective statement makes public the knowledge, skills, and dispositions you feel you have developed as well as the increasing ability to evaluate yourself as a learner and teacher in the process of becoming. Self-observation also enables you to revisit and revise your goals and to develop new goals for the immediate future.

SELF-OBSERVATION
Lori Orndorff, junior in early childhood education

In the past, it has always been our goal to observe others: teachers, parents, and students. For the first time in my teaching experience, I was able to observe myself as a teacher and reflect on my own feelings, understandings, and practices. In order to observe myself while in the classroom, I sporadically wrote down what I was doing and feeling at certain points throughout the day. Revisiting these moments after their occurrence has allowed me to develop concerns, questions, and ideas about my own teaching techniques/ practices. Completion of my self-observation involved designing a self-portrait of how I see myself in the classroom. Creating my artifact has also permitted me to reflect on the feelings I experience throughout the course of a school day. I have realized that reviewing personal teaching strategies/ practices [is] just as important as observing others.

Finally, observing my own teaching techniques and interactions has really benefited me because it has allowed me to truly reflect on what I do in

A student teacher's artifact, created to represent her personal theory of teaching.

the classroom and whether or not it is appropriate and effective, as well as
beneficial for the children. Now I understand how observation is not only
critical for the children and parents, but it is very constructive when it comes
to personal reflection and thought on teaching techniques and philosophies.
Reflecting on previous experiences will only benefit what is done, practiced,
and explored in future experiences.

The Importance of Collaboration

Following the notion that teaching practice is learned in a social context, portfolios are best prepared with the guided assistance of others, notably those who serve in a mentoring capacity, as well as those who share in the learning community. Portfolio development should involve interaction and assistance in the same way that all learning reflects the efforts and contributions of the self and others in the construction of knowledge and meaning. Therefore, opportunities to discuss your work with peers and instructors are essential.

Peers can review one another's portfolios, exchange ideas, confer on artifacts, and even assist one another in the documentation of teaching and the preparation of their respective portfolios. Instructors and supervising teachers serve as consultants or mentors who provide support, encouragement, suggestions, and resources during the preparation of the portfolio. Collaboration in the design and preparation of the portfolio promotes collegial exchange focused on the art and scholarship of teaching.

Representation and Reflection

Many of the artifacts described in this chapter can be representations (e.g., physical models, poems, artistic portrayals) using your own "language." Promoting multiple representation of experience enables you to get in touch with your talents, abilities, and different nuanced ways of learning in ways that written work alone cannot provide.

Reflection on the significance of each artifact encourages you to think more deeply and carefully about what you are learning, and to gain insights into your motives, methods, and images of teaching. Hopefully, the result is a more critical self-examination of teaching that will lead to greater understanding and mindfulness. Therefore, one of the most important pieces of information you can include in a portfolio designed to document self-learning and development is a reflective summary about the things contained in the portfolio. This might take the form of a one-page narrative that precedes each major topic area or category. This narrative provides a careful explanation of why you chose particular artifacts and what you learned about yourself, children, or teaching from these artifacts. The following is an example from one student's portfolio:

> *In this section [on Philosophy of Education,] I include several artifacts that*
> *represent my philosophy of teaching and learning. The first, entitled*
> *"Influences on My Career," is about some of the people, events, and*
> *experiences that have had a deep influence on who I am and how I envision*
> *myself as a teacher. Also included is a paper entitled "Students Don't Work,*

They Learn" which is a critical analysis of an article I read that helped me think more carefully about teaching and learning. Finally, you will also see my most recent philosophy of teaching that I wrote this semester. Together, these artifacts demonstrate my ever-changing philosophy of teaching, which has moved from a rather simplistic view to one that is complex, student-centered, and constructivist.

Kim Martin, junior in early childhood education

Revisiting the Self: "Who Am I Now?" "Where Am I Headed?"

In this chapter, we have discussed how students might begin their formal teacher preparation programs by exploring and discussing who they are as persons, as learners, and as students, moving toward an increasing focus on self as teacher. The preprofessional portfolio can be an important tool for documenting views, beliefs, and performance. Moreover, it allows students to revisit their thinking, compare where they were with where they are now, and see visible evidence of learning and development.

Just as students need to think about the what, why, and how in planning activities for children, they also need to think carefully about the planning and organization of their portfolios. For example, they need to decide what goes into the portfolio, why these items are significant or meaningful, and how can they be organized to best document their development as teachers. Questions pertaining to this decision include "What knowledge, skills, and dispositions do I want to demonstrate?"; "Which artifacts represent my best work?"; and "How can I best organize my information to demonstrate teaching improvement?"

The end product must contain information that demonstrates that the student has engaged in self-reflection that leads to heightened self-awareness and understanding. In the end, the effectiveness of the preprofessional portfolio as a documentation tool may be based on the degree to which the selected artifacts:

- Encourage and represent critical reflection on practice and how to improve it
- Demonstrate the rethinking and reconstruction of teaching strategies, beliefs, and images
- Document personal and professional development over an extended period

In conclusion, the preprofessional portfolio reflects you; your unique experience, talents, and perspectives; and your journey into the wonders and mysteries of becoming a teacher and a lifelong learner.

GETTING STARTED ACTIVITIES

In this chapter, we emphasize that, ultimately, what you put into your portfolio should reflect what *you* value. In addition to instructor-determined or other prespecified items such as those presented earlier, here are just a few of the items or artifacts that we personally value as teachers and include in our teaching portfolios. They are included here, with some ideas or questions to get you thinking about your own portfolio.

1. *A personal narrative or autobiography that reflects a sociohistorical look at the experiences, events, and people who have helped me construct my image of teaching and learning.*

   Who are the persons who have been significant in shaping your interest in and views of teaching?

2. *A description of my core teaching values (e.g., one is that I believe in the capacity of all children to learn).*

   What is it that you value? Develop a list of your core teaching values, write them down, and revisit them often.

3. *Reflections on both satisfying and successful teaching experiences and frustrating or unsuccessful teaching attempts.*

   Teaching is an intellectual challenge, and it doesn't always go as you envisioned. By collecting and including lesson plans or reflections on teaching that show both challenges and frustrations and joys and successes, you can demonstrate development in various aspects of your teaching.

4. *Stories on teaching that powerfully and vividly demonstrate my learning.*

   Stories record and communicate who we are and the significance of daily teaching experiences. Reflect on and write down some stories you recall about interactions with children, parents, or curriculum planning that convey evidence of your learning and development as a teacher.

5. *Examples of original projects or curriculum development.*

   This speaks for itself. Creative and innovative plans, assessments, and teaching methods that you developed and implemented should be a must for inclusion in your portfolio.

6. *Preceding each artifact, some statement of its significance or meaning, to put the work in context.*

   Perhaps most important, always write a clear and concise statement of why a particular piece of work is significant so that those reading your portfolio can understand the reason behind its inclusion, how it demonstrates something about who you are, who you have become, and who you hope to be as a teacher.

RESOURCES

On the Web

www.teachnet.com/how-to/employment/portfolios/index.html
   Teachnet.com: Good information on how to create and organize a teacher interview portfolio.

www.electronicportfolios.com
   ElectronicPortfolios.com: A comprehensive site about developing electronic portfolios, with a lot of helpful links.

www.chre.vt.edu/TeacherEd/electroportfolio.htm
   Center for Teacher Education at Virginia Tech electronic portfolio guidelines.

Readings

Bullock, A., & Hawk, P. (2001). *Developing a teaching portfolio: A guide for preservice and inservice teachers.* Upper Saddle River, NJ: Merrill/Prentice-Hall.

Campbell, D., Cignetti, P., Melenyzer, B., Nettles, D., & Wyman, R. (1997). *How to develop a professional portfolio: A manual for teachers.* Boston: Allyn and Bacon.

Stone, B. (1998). Problems, pitfalls, and benefits of portfolios. *Teacher Education Quarterly, 25*(1), 105–114.

REFERENCES

Armstrong, T. (1993). *Seven kinds of smart: Identifying and developing your many intelligences.* New York: Plume.

Ayers, W. (1993). *To teach: The journey of a teacher.* New York: Teachers College Press.

Bullough, R. V., & Gitlin, A. (1995). *Becoming a student of teaching: Methodologies for exploring self and school context.* New York: Garland.

Campbell, D., Cignetti, P., Melenyzer, B., Nettles, D., & Wyman, R. (1997). *How to develop a professional portfolio: A manual for teachers.* Boston: Allyn and Bacon.

de Mello, A. (1990). *Awareness: The perils and opportunities of reality.* New York: Image Books, Doubleday.

Grant, G. E., & Huebner, T. A. (1998). The portfolio question: The power of self-directed inquiry. In N. Lyons (Ed.), *With portfolio in hand: Validating the new teacher professionalism* (pp. 156–171). New York: Teachers College Press.

Panitz, B. (1996). The student portfolio: A powerful assessment tool. *ASEE Prism, 6,* 24–29.

Paris, S., & Ayres, L. (1994). *Becoming reflective students and teachers with portfolios and authentic assessment.* Washington, DC: American Psychological Association.

Paulson, F. L., Paulson, P. R., & Meyer, C. A. (1991). What makes a portfolio a portfolio? *Educational Leadership, 48,* 60–63.

Stremmel, A. J., Fu, V. R., Patet, P., & Shah, H. (1995). Images of teaching: Prospective early childhood teachers' constructions of the teaching–learning process of young children. In S. Reifel (Series Ed.), *Advances in early education and day care* (Vol. 7, pp. 253–270). Norwood, NJ: Ablex.

Wolf, K. (1994). Teaching portfolios: Capturing the complexity of teaching. In L. Ingvarson & R. Chadbourne (Eds.), *Teacher appraisal: New directions* (pp. 108–132). Victoria: Australian Council for Educational Research.

PART II

The Child as Provocateur

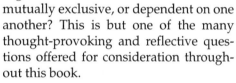

art Two is a brief but highly influential section designed to examine the child. Chapter 5 offers a historic retrospective in which the reader is treated to a review of the child as a cultural invention. Here you will begin to formulate your own image of the child and consider how this image coincides with your earlier attempt to write a definition of "the image of the teacher." Are these definitions mutually exclusive, or dependent on one another? This is but one of the many thought-provoking and reflective questions offered for consideration throughout this book.

Waterfall
It molds its world with every drop just as we are molded by life. Whether it is a trickle or a torrent, a stream, or a river. We are molded by our experiences as if they were the waterfall of life.
Julie Bryan, Early Childhood
Student Teacher

CHAPTER 5

THE CHILD AS CULTURAL INVENTION
Reconstructing Images of the Child

If anyone gives you the impression that he has the answers now to the great timeless questions about childhood, you can smile and listen politely or you can turn your back and walk away, but in any case don't believe him.

Melvin Konner, *Childhood:*
A Multicultural View

I am a ship
That voyages the sea
I am the wind
That blows through the trees
I am the sun
That shines brightly for all
I am the strength
Proudly standing tall
I am a lost kitten
To be taken in
I am lonely
And in need of a friend
I am the rain
That nourishes the grass
I am a clown
So that you can laugh
I am a garden
For tiny seeds to grow
I am a kite
Who knows where I'll go?
I am a tear

In a puddle of sadness
I am a sparkle
In a smile of gladness
I am a candle
With an eternal flame
I am a stranger
With everyone's name
I am the hope
Of the world for tomorrow
I am the light
And the dark and the sorrow
I am all of these things
And it all lies within you
For I am a child
Teach me what to do.

The beautiful poem that opens this chapter was written by Brooke Elliott, a junior in early childhood education. It represents her image of the child. In this chapter, we offer a brief overview of images of the child through the ages, as perpetuated by developmental theory and historical and cultural influences. We pose the following questions for continued and deliberate reflection throughout your teaching journey.

QUESTIONS TO BE CONSIDERED

- Who is the child?
- What does it mean to be a child?
- How do our images of childhood in general and of the children we teach in particular limit possibilities for understanding children more fully and prevent the inquiry necessary for theory building and the conduct of future research?

WHO IS THE CHILD?

Who is the child? What does it mean to be a child? Have you ever asked yourself these questions? We have all been children, and we have all experienced the joys, the triumphs, the challenges, and the woes of childhood, to a greater or lesser extent. But when we stop to reflect on what childhood is, or what it means, we are likely to draw on many sources. We may think about the views of childhood held by our society, or the many theories of the child that have emerged in developmental psychology. Very likely we have constructed our conceptualizations of the child from the many and varied personal experiences we have had caring for and working directly with children. Brooke's poem is one early childhood education student's "image of the child" constructed from the *personal practical knowledge* (i.e., understanding constructed from reflection on experience) and *formal* (i.e., theoretical) *knowledge* she has gained over many years as an observer and student of childhood. In this chapter, we explore images of childhood constructed by society and culture and by early childhood education students who are in the process of becoming teachers. We discuss how certain images limit possibilities for understanding children more fully and foreclose the reflective inquiry needed for developing responsive curriculum and teaching methods that grow out of children's interests and strengths. Espousing the image of the child as competent, strong, and a protagonist in the pursuit of meaning, understanding, and culture, we provide some examples of how to encourage reflection and renewed thinking about long-held conceptualizations of childhood.

THINK ABOUT IT

How do you view children?

Where do these views come from, and what might these views reveal about the ways you interact with children in the classroom?

The premise of this chapter is that childhood is a social and cultural construction. This suggests that conceptions of childhood, views of what it is and means to be a child, cannot be separated from culture (Kessen, 1979). How we view children and their lives has been constructed differently in different places and times (socially and historically) (Aries, 1962). Further, how we view children is related to important questions such as:

1. What does our society hope and expect for children?
2. How should children behave?
3. What do children think? What are they like at a particular age or stage of development?
4. What does it mean to educate children—how should we teach them and how do they learn?

How students of teaching answer these questions relates to the kind of teacher they want to be and how they will conduct themselves in the classroom.

When we, as teacher educators, ask our students why they want to be teachers, most of them will say, "Because I love children." This is not the only reason, of course, but there is little question that love of and concern for children are primary reasons that people are drawn to teaching. And yet the observed actions and decisions of prospective teachers and experienced teachers alike often seem inconsistent with a loving, caring view of the child. More specifically, we may say we love children, but to what extent do we view them as multidimensional and capable

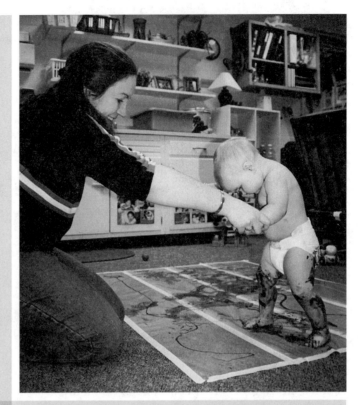

How should we teach children and how do they learn? It all depends on your image of the child.

human beings? To what lengths do we go to really understand and get to know them? To what degree do we base our teaching practices on a deep respect for and understanding of children and their personhood?

IMAGES OF THE CHILD

One of the most transforming questions we have pondered in recent years is from William Ayers, who asks, "When we teachers look out over our classrooms, what do we see?" (2001, p. 28). The response cuts to the heart of our views of the child. Do we see a collection of deficits, or do we see human beings with both limitations and remarkable gifts? Do we know them? What are their hopes and dreams, their passions and fears, their cares and concerns? The point is, Ayers so convincingly states, that "in the human-centered act of teaching, all attempts to create definitive categories lower our sights, misdirect our vision, and mislead our intentions" (p. 29).

Clearly, then, how we view the child can limit and narrow the possibilities we have for good teaching, or they can open up new avenues for understanding and knowing the children we teach and engaging them in an adventurous journey of learning. Consider the following examples, which in our experience are typical of how students often think about children:

In many ways the child is much like an adult and needs only to be given numerous experiences and lots of love. Children need to be taught right from wrong and how to do the things that will make them competitive in our society. This includes knowledge and skills related to math and reading and writing. Children's work must meet the expectations of the teacher and the school and [be] evaluated according to these expectations. I think that when children do not have expectations they just get by and never really learn anything important. Children also must learn respect. Sometimes the children I have observed seem to lack respect and are disobedient. I know that as a teacher I will have my work cut out for me.

I think children are curious, questioning, and interested in the world around them, and this should always be encouraged. Children are always learning, growing, and experiencing, and they benefit from energetic, involved adults. Children trust and respect when they feel trusted and respected. With the proper guidance and the necessary skills from adults, children are able to solve their own problems. Children should always be given chances to succeed, and to make choices about their own lives and education.

These examples represent two different constructions of what a child and an adult–child relationship ought to be. The former view is typical of a first-year student, the latter of a third-year student. Both examples reflect images of the child as perpetuated by developmental theory and social and cultural influences. These different assumptions and attitudes about children will likely affect the way students interact with children in the classroom.

THINK ABOUT IT

How do our images of children (as reflected in our labels, categorizations, definitions, and evaluations of children) affect our expectations of them?

Let us now take a further look at some common images of the child that have guided thinking, inquiry, practice, and even policy in this country:

- Children as little adults
- Children as incomplete
- Children as needy
- Children as deficient
- Children as depraved
- Children as property

Children are always learning, growing, and experiencing.

Although these are not the only images promulgated by our culture, they are those often implicitly or explicitly found to underlie our thoughts about and behaviors toward children, especially in our classrooms and schools (cf. Anderson & Johnson, 1994; Corsaro, 1997; Kessen, 1979; Stremmel, 2002).

It was the historian Philippe Aries (1962) who made the assertion that childhood does not exist in a finite and identifiable form—there is no universal image of the child. In earlier periods, children were regarded as "little adults," who were at once different from adults in terms of particular defining characteristics such as size, strength, or how much work they could do, but who were not thought to differ in terms of how they think or behave. Most teach-

THINK ABOUT IT

What other images of the child can you think of?

How have children been portrayed in the media, past and present?

ers today, it is assumed, would agree that children are not little adults but little people, beings in the present. Nonetheless, as suggested by the first-year student in the preceding example, the image of the child as an immature or incomplete adult having unequal value persists in the many ways we think about and act toward children in our society. For example, James and Prout (1997) point out that in Western conceptions of childhood, age is often a dividing line to legally exclude children from adult spaces. Ages set boundaries and limits to children's activities. Children are assigned to age groups in all manner of activities; age is a determinant (often a primary one) of when children go to school and when they can vote. Adults ask children incessant questions about their age (e.g., "What do you want to be when you grow up?").

Another example that often goes unnoticed by those who work with children is the implied similarity between adult work (paid employment) and schoolwork, which is often conducted like work in factories. Calling children's play or learning "work" denies or downplays the present of childhood and subordinates it to adulthood. Students are viewed as under the authority of the teacher, who imposes tasks, monitors and regulates behavior, and evaluates performance, all in the service of preparing children for a position of good standing in the competitive market (James & Prout, 1997). Children's play and learning are significant activities in their own right; to call them work reduces their value as real and meaningful activity in the here and now.

THINK ABOUT IT

Calling children's play or learning "work" denies or downplays the present of childhood and subordinates it to adulthood.

Implicit constructions of the position (or status) of children in the life course deny time present in the life of a child and focus on the interrelationship between time past and time future, the movement toward adulthood. Childhood is not something to be passed through or to be remembered; it is something to be lived.

THINK ABOUT IT

Childhood is not a prelude to adulthood. Can you think of other ways in which we treat childhood as provisional and preparatory?

Robert Fried (2001) has stated, "The early years are so full of learning that its velocity and abundance cannot be captured by even the most ardent of parent chroniclers" (p. 127). In spite of this insightful reasoning, we live in a society that disregards the problems of children, squelches their ideas, denies their feelings, and ignores or diminishes the significance of their daily experiences (Stremmel, 2002). In schools we talk about meeting children's needs, planning according to children's needs, and waiting until children are "ready" to learn, all of which assumes children are lacking and in need of something that adults have and children do not.

Woodhead (1997) suggests that the idea of children's needs has been constructed as part of a universal or standardized model in which childhood is viewed as a period of dependency, defined by relationships in which adults are dominant providers and children are passive consumers (p. 78). Child development theory, particularly maturational (age and stage) theories that have promoted normative and universal images of how children develop, have contributed to our image of the child as dependent and needy. Although there is now more widespread recognition of development as socially and culturally determined, as children actively seek out and learn through enduring and reciprocal relationships with others, we must be cautious of what theories offer (Stremmel, 2002). Theories, at best, help us understand that childhood is a unique time of life, not a phase or a precursor to adulthood. Children actively contribute to their development, and although they are in need of and dependent on others, they also need love, encouragement, and support in their attempts to make sense of the world.

Unfortunately, schools are a good place to look for examples of how we view the child as needy and deficient in our society. The truth is that students often are defined in school by what they don't know and can't do, as opposed to what they know and value. Curriculum and teaching practices are built on a deficit model, which assumes teachers (and tests) determine and control what is taught, what is learned, and the outcomes (who fails and who is promoted). The heavy focus on child outcomes, our national obsession with standards and accountability, and our intrepid efforts to remedy children's problems and deficiencies by teaching them isolated skills and facts that will eventually be forgotten because children have little interest in them—all without considering children's passions, curiosities, and potentials—constrain teachers' efforts to address children's unique attributes and see children "at promise," as opposed to "at risk" (Ayers, 2001; Fried, 2001; Meisels, 2000). Contrast this with the following image held by an early childhood education student, which acknowledges children's potential and capability and sees children with hopefulness:

> *Children are curious by nature. They enjoy seeking out knowledge and construct it actively. Through different mediums, children learn how to represent and organize the world around them. Through many and diverse experiences, they grow and develop, sometimes gradually other times by leaps and bounds. I believe that through experiencing a child's world, adults learn more about the world themselves, for children are often the best teachers.*
> Sarah Guschke, junior in early childhood education

If children were asked about themselves, who they are and what they like, most would willingly tell you something positive about themselves, things that make them feel strong, competent, secure, and worthwhile. Then there are those children who would tell you the opposite, that they feel dependent and insecure, stupid and worthless, because this is what they have heard others tell them, perhaps not di-

Children are often the best teachers.

rectly in words, but through their actions and attitudes and through teaching that focuses on deficiencies and shortcomings. As Ayers (2001) states, "We must see beyond the unstated assumption driving most schools, the wacky idea that children are puny, inadequate adults and that the job of education is to transport them as quickly as possible from that sorry state" (p. 33).

Schools are not the only place children are treated as deficient. In many places in our society, children are abandoned, mistreated, neglected, abused, and criticized because they are viewed as small, needy, incompetent, annoying, and degenerate. This is evident in the alarming increase in cases of child abductions and in the many acts of sexual and physical abuse reported in this country. It is also apparent in regulations that permit private foster and adoption agencies to allow foster and adoptive parents to use certain forms of physical punishment as long as they are not "abusive," and in homes and classrooms where children are ridiculed, isolated by means of "time out," or otherwise punished because they fail to meet adult expectations that may be arbitrary and inappropriate. All children, and especially marginalized children,

THINK ABOUT IT

You cannot teach someone whom you don't expect to learn. How can we create environments in which we can see children as capable and passionate learners?

are vulnerable and in need of compassionate, nurturing environments in which they can develop trust in others, a sense of self-worth, and the ability to care.

> **THINK ABOUT IT**
>
> Some adults feel that children are to be seen and not heard. But children are not subordinate to adults. They must be respected for who they are and what they can do. What are some ways you try to foster mutual respect?

Finally, though we do not want to admit it, children are often viewed as the property of adults. Think about the following illustrations:

> From a parent to a young child: "You brat, you never listen to me when I tell you what to do. I work hard to give you a home and food on the table. I expect that you will mind me and be grateful."

> From a parent to her college-age daughter: "When you are in my house, you obey my rules. I don't care what you do in college; here you abide by my restrictions, you keep my curfew, and you remember that I am your mother."

All of parenting is a struggle with the reality of giving up control, which often begins when parents watch their child walk away from them for the first time. It may continue well into the child's adult years, as parents continually remind their children of the "correct way" to discipline their own children, or fret when a daughter refuses to be "given away" in marriage because she wants to be her own person. Children are a gift, not a possession; parenthood is a trust, not a right. Teachers need to be mindful not only of this truth but also of the fact that they, along with schools as a cultural-political institution, are in loco parentis. Children are entrusted to those who care for and teach them. Children do not belong to us, but in a sense we belong to them. Teachers exercise a responsibility in loco parentis toward every child who is entrusted to their care (see van Manen, 1991). This means that teachers and schools are not only responsible for preparing children for the larger society, but they are also responsible for protecting children from possible risks and for providing caring environments in which children can flourish and be successful (van Manen, 1991). Although it may sound strange to speak of the relationship between parents and children, or teacher and children, in terms of hospitality, this understanding is at the core of the teaching–learning relationship. Children are not properties to own and rule over; they are human beings to cherish and care for.

A CHILD
Alison Fox, junior in early childhood education
A child is not bad, he's just a good kid who sometimes does bad things.
A child is not a loser, he's just a winner who sometimes doesn't win.
A child is not dumb, he's just a smart kid who sometimes gets stumped.
A child is not a mistake, he's a blessing in disguise.

Children are a gift, not a possession.

THINK ABOUT IT

To see children more fully as human beings, teachers need to create a wide range of ways for children to tell us about themselves. Think about how you can foster the child's personhood and help the child become more whole and more fully alive in the classroom.

A MORE POSITIVE VIEW OF THE CHILD

As discussed earlier, the construction of childhood in Western societies has built on the idea of children as small, dependent, and needy. In contrast, a growing number of writings about childhood (see, for example, Edwards, Gandini, & Forman, 1998; Fried, 2001; James & Prout, 1997) view children as capable agents in their own socialization and development. Accordingly, every child comes into the world with a desire to learn that is as natural as the desire to be loved and cared for. Fried (2001) states, "The desire to learn, to discover, to figure something out, and to be able to do something well enough to proclaim it as one's own must surely be as strong as any impulse in the human soul" (p. 127). This image of the child is championed in

Reggio Emilia, where a profound respect for children and deep belief in their potential contrasts with the American view of the child as needy and dependent. Among other things, this view of children as competent, intellectual, and strong enables teachers to take seriously both the process and the products of children's learning, lending dignity to children's work that is often lacking in our schools. For teachers to envision all children as capable, gifted, and passionate, it becomes their responsibility to discover those abilities, gifts, and passions. Ayers (personal communication, March 12, 1999) suggests that teaching begins with faith, a faith in children as capable. But children don't always show us their gifts. Children have more dimensions than we can see, measure, or quantify.

THINK ABOUT IT

The Reggio Emilia approach to early childhood education and constructivist thinking in general require us to see children as strong, competent, and intellectual—at capacity and fully human. To what extent do you feel schools are set up to see this truth?

This alternative construction of childhood holds greater promise for understanding and respecting childhood as a legitimate part of the human experience. When children are seen as having potential, they are seen not as having needs, but as having rights. That is, children are entitled to quality care and education because of "who they are," not because of what they need (Hendrick, 1997, p. 43). According to Woodhead (1997), "Children's rights breaks through the web of paternalist, protectionist constructions that emphasize children as powerless dependents, separated-off from adult society and effectively excluded from participation in shaping their own destiny" (p. 80). The following image of the child, contributed by a third-year (junior) early childhood education student, thoughtfully portrays the child as a unique human being who is worthy of respect, capable of initiative and intelligence, and active in his or her own development:

A child is a unique being—no child, even twins, [is] exactly identical. Because all children are individuals, unique and special, they are hard to describe in terms of characteristics, demeanor, intelligence, and attitude. I consider children to be the greatest creation of all; children are sharp, caring, learning, teaching, and interactive with each other. It is astonishing and somewhat difficult to entirely conceptualize a child and his/her representative qualities, or characteristics. A child is intelligent, loving, and authentically wants to learn about the environment around him or her—a child can learn so much so fast (children can learn a second language and fluently speak it in far less time than an adult). Some people say that children need to be taught all about their environment from adults. This philosophy almost communicates that children are unintelligent—but more often than not, children are smarter, more creative, and [more] unconventional than adults. If an adult gives a child credit and values his or her opinion, children can teach adults some truly amazing things. In fact, children have not had to learn the "conventions" and rules that govern most everyday relations—thus they are similar to Einstein and constantly break the rules; but in reality they are not doing anything bad. Maybe children are truly smarter and more creative than adults. The only thing I feel is certain is that the children of today are going to be the citizens and leaders of tomorrow. *One of the ways that I can help children, as a teacher, is to help them understand their environment, and help them learn new things, by providing the means and experiences for the development and intellectual expansion of the whole individual. A child can, and will, take care of the rest.*

John Lincoln

IDENTIFYING CHILDREN'S STRENGTHS

How can we help students of teaching begin to see children's capacities? One excellent activity we have had our students participate in is a "descriptive review of the child" (see Himley & Carini, 2000). This activity, similar to a case study, focuses the student's attention on the child's strengths and on the multidimensional aspects of children as learners. Students write separate narratives on:

1. The physical presence and gesture of the child (e.g., size and build; how the child moves, enters the classroom, and positions himself or herself in relation to the other children; and characteristic ways of expressing thoughts, feelings, and ideas)
2. The disposition and temperament of the child (e.g., the child's attitudes toward school and life; the child's sense of rightness or justice, loyalties and personal commitments; the child's passions and how deep feelings tend to be expressed)
3. The child's connections with others (e.g., relationships with peers and adults, especially friendships, attachment relationships, and learning relationships)
4. The child's modes of thinking and learning (e.g., how the child thinks, learns, and uses multiple "languages" to explore and make sense of the world)

What is important about this exercise is not the specific categories or ways of describing the child, but rather the notion that the child can and should be seen, described, and encountered along many dimensions, in particular his or her strengths and primary ways of living and learning in the world. In this way, we come to see and know the child from many perspectives as capable, unique, and worthy of our deepest respect.

A DESCRIPTIVE REVIEW OF JONAH'S MODES
OF THINKING AND LEARNING
I perceive Jonah as a bodily-kinesthetic thinker and learner. He has a need for movement and action. He usually has a structure made of Legos in hand as he creates an adventure for his dramatic play. It seems that he always has a

different object to carry around with him that he incorporates into his play. He has to be able to touch and manipulate things to understand them.

Jonah uses his body to communicate with others. He holds Emily's hand or puts his arm around Stephen to let them know that he cares about them. He expresses his feelings of affection and camaraderie by being in physical contact with his friends.

Jonah is in his element when he is outdoors. I can tell that he needs to move about and stretch out in the space he occupies. When he comes out to the playground, he comes alive.

In summary, Jonah is a very lively and energetic person. It is his nature to express himself physically and to have that need in order to experience things. I hope to use this knowledge to bring out the best in Jonah. I would like to plan activities that allow him to move and to touch. Opportunities for group work and interaction with others would also be meaningful to Jonah in the classroom.

Donna Ritchie, junior in early childhood education

SUMMARY

Images of the child throughout the ages, as perpetuated by culture, history, and theory, have often cast childhood in an unfavorable light. Concepts of childhood and their attendant practices, beliefs, and expectations about children should be neither timeless nor universal but must take into account the temporal and cultural specificity of ideas and social constructions (James & Prout, 1997). A more hopeful and promising way to conceptualize the child, then, is to see the child from many perspectives in order to understand them more fully. Moreover, we should see children for who they are and for what they can offer. Amelia Gambetti, executive consultant for Reggio Children, has stated that just as children have potential for learning, in their ideas lies the potential for teaching (personal communication, January 1998).

Research shows that teachers are more likely to be guided by their commitments to and images of the child than by instructional theories (Stremmel, 2002). Childhood has its own validity; it is not simply a functional stage or a preparation for life. Teachers must avoid obstacles that prevent them from accurately seeing the child in his or her fullness. Children arrive in this world with their own gifts. If teachers recognize this, they listen and observe carefully to what children like, what they are drawn toward, and what they do and say.

When teachers listen to children and their stories, they learn what is real to them, and they learn what questions to ask and how to teach; for in children's ideas and stories, their questions and their theories are revealed, which is the information needed to enhance their learning. Furthermore, when teachers begin (or are able) to see their own stories in those of the children they teach, their expectations of children may rise, as may their ability to change their teaching for the benefit of children. As Ayers (1995) indicates, "Assuming an intelligence in children—perhaps obscure, perhaps hard to access, but nevertheless there—is the only hopeful way to approach teaching" (p. 7).

GETTING STARTED ACTIVITIES

1. What is your image of the child? Think about your conceptualizations of the child. Now represent your image or images using a different "language" or means of representation to construct this artifact. For example, instead of writing about your image of the child, draw, sculpt, create a three-dimensional object, or perform your views of the child. Provide a caption (written reflection) that explains your representation, offering insights into your personal understanding of children and theories of child development.

   As you have more and more experiences with children, revisit your image of the child. How has it changed? What have you learned? You may wish to review data you have collected through your observations of a single child or group of children and from other sources of gathered information (portfolio entries, recorded conversations with children, meetings with parents, discussions with teachers, etc.).

2. If you could choose only three, which attributes would you wish to bestow on all children? (These should not be physical or material.) Now go find evidence of these in your neighborhood, community, schools, and elsewhere. What did you find out?

3. Think back to your own childhood. What are some of the things you enjoyed about this time? How did these experiences contribute to some of the characteristics that best describe who you are? Now think about where you are most genuine, most yourself. Are these qualities ever apparent in the classroom? When? Where?

4. When you plan curriculum, what tends to be your focus? Is it the child who guides your thinking about what, why, and how to plan? What can you say about the complexity and meaning of the activities you provide?

RESOURCES

Readings
Cleverley, J., & Phillips, D. C. (1986). *Visions of childhood: Influential models from Locke to Spock* (Rev. ed.). New York: Teachers College Press.

Corsaro, W. (1997). *The sociology of childhood.* Thousand Oaks, CA: Pine Forge Press.

Fried, R. (2001). *The passionate learner: How teachers and parents can help children reclaim the joy of discovery.* Boston: Beacon Press.

Matthews, G. B. (1994). *The philosophy of childhood.* Cambridge, MA: Harvard University Press.

REFERENCES

Anderson, H., & Johnson, S. B. (1994). *Regarding children: A new respect for childhood and families.* Louisville, KY: Westminster John Knox Press.

Aries, P. (1962). *Centuries of childhood: A social history of family life* (R. Baldick, Trans.). New York: Knopf.

Ayers, W. (1995). *To become a teacher: Making a difference in children's lives.* New York: Teachers College Press.

Ayers, W. (Ed.). (2001). *To teach: The journey of a teacher.* (2nd ed.). New York: Teachers College Press.

Corsaro, W. (1997). *The sociology of childhood.* Thousand Oaks, CA: Pine Forge Press.

Edwards, C., Gandini, L., & Forman, G. (Eds). (1998). *The hundred languages of children: The Reggio Emilia approach—advanced reflections.* (2nd ed.). Greenwich, CT: Ablex.

Fried, R. (2001). Passionate learners and the challenge of schooling. *Phi Delta Kappan, 83*(2), 124–136.

Hendrick, J. (1997). Reggio Emilia and American schools: Telling them apart and putting them together—can we do it? In J. Hendrick (Ed.), *First steps toward teaching the Reggio way* (pp. 41–53). Upper Saddle River, NJ: Merrill/Prentice-Hall.

Himley, M., & Carini, P. (Eds.). (2000). *From another angle: Children's strengths and school standards.* New York: Teachers College Press.

James, A., & Prout, A. (1997). Re-presenting childhood: Time and transition in the study of childhood. In A. James & A. Prout (Eds.), *Constructing and reconstructing childhood: Contemporary issues in the sociological study of childhood* (pp. 230–250). Washington, DC: Falmer Press.

Kessen, W. (1979). The American child and other cultural inventions. *American Psychologist, 34*(10), 815–820.

Meisels, S. J. (2000). On the side of the child: Personal reflections on testing, teaching, and early childhood education. *Young Children, 55,* 16–19.

Stremmel, A. J. (2002). The cultural construction of childhood: U.S. and Reggio perspectives. In V. R. Fu, A. J. Stremmel, & L. T. Hill (Eds.), *Teaching and learning: Collaborative exploration of the Reggio Emilia approach* (pp. 37–49). Upper Saddle River, NJ: Merrill/Prentice-Hall.

van Manen, M. (1991). *The tact of teaching: The meaning of pedagogical thoughtfulness.* Albany: State University of New York Press.

Woodhead, M. (1997). Psychology and the cultural construction of children's needs. In A. James and A. Prout (Eds.), *Constructing and reconstructing childhood: Contemporary issues in the sociological study of childhood* (pp. 63–84). Washington, DC: Falmer Press.

CHAPTER 6

CREATING AN ENVIRONMENT FOR CHILDREN TO BE KNOWN AND VALUED
Educational and Caring Spaces

When we talk about relational space, we mean an integrated space in which the qualities are not strictly aesthetic but are more closely related to "performance" features. This means the space is not composed of functional zones but of the fluidization of functional zones. In the relational space, the predominant feature is that of the relationships it enables, the many specialized activities that can be carried out there, and the information and cultural filters that can be activated within the space.

> Giulio Ceppi and Michele Zini, *Children, Spaces, Relations: Metaproject for an Environment for Young Children*

I described the physical layout of the classroom for infants by drawing a floor plan accompanied by a written narrative. I observed that the message conveyed by this room is that it is child-focused with an attempt to make the space, as much as possible, a continuation of the infants' homes. This child-focused message is further made visible, on the walls, with documentation of the infants' activities and life in their classroom.

The classroom projects a safe and secure environment where the infants are free to explore and interact. For example, in the soft area, the rocking chairs, a couch and a "nest" on the floor are arranged in a way that provides optimal interactions and relationships among the infants and teachers, combining care-giving and learning. The message is that caring relationships [are] important in a community for teaching, learning, and care giving.

> Olivia Schoch, junior

At the beginning of every school year, the early childhood educa-tion students participate in an environment walk around the school, led by their respective supervising teachers. This exercise fa-miliarizes them with the physical environment and gives them an opportunity to study how the environment supports teaching and learning from a social constructivist, inquiry-based curriculum. They pay special attention to the classroom they are assigned for their stu-dent teaching. After the environment walk, the students illustrate the floor plan and write an accompanying paper that describes what they have seen and learned. The preceding paragraph is a synopsis of Olivia Schoch's observation of the classroom for infants.

In Chapter 2, "How You Teach Is Who You Are," we make clear that schools and classrooms are places where the search for the mean-ing of self and life takes place, where education is based on relation-ships. Paola Strozzi (2001) reflects that Malaguzzi considered school one of the places for the search for the meaning of life and the future—it is active, creative, "livable, documentable and communicable, a place of investigation, learning, recognition, and reflection." The goal is to create an *amiable classroom* where children, teachers, and families feel that "care and attention [are] given to the environment, which creates a sense of harmony and 'communicativeness'" (p. 58). Chap-ter 8 in this book provides ideas for the building of an amiable school.

QUESTIONS TO BE CONSIDERED

- How does the classroom environment foster children's development?
- How do you create an amiable and safe environment for learning and teaching?
- How does environment promote teaching and learning as inquiry among children and teachers?

Studies on learning, cognitive development, and teaching have highlighted the im-portance of learning based on the relationship between individuals and the learn-ing environment (context). Knowledge emerges as a result of activities engaged and shared in an environment that connects individuals, materials, cultural tools, and symbol systems (Strozzi, 2001; National Research Council, 2000a, b, c). Part Four, The Tools of Teaching and Learning: Life in the Classroom, documents how these activities are part of life in the classroom.

Spaces that are fluid and ever changing develop from a teacher's research into the life in the classroom. No space is static or ideal but rather one "that is capable of generating its own change, because an ideal space, and ideal pedagogy, an ideal child or human being do not exist, but only a child, a human being, in relation with their own experiences, times, and culture" (Rinaldi, 1998, p. 115). You are invited to take a tour of a school that focuses on how individual spaces are created as a part of the whole environment—"creating a space of life and of the future" (p. 114).

In creating an environment that reflects these ideas, Lynn Hill (1998) suggests that we need to continually find ways to be truly collaborative, keeping in mind that such an environment has the following characteristics:

- *An atmosphere that teaches,* one that is aesthetically beautiful and respectful of its inhabitants, one that allows for greater connections to be made among the protagonists, and one that constantly engages and challenges
- *Attention and appreciation for the time the protagonists spend together,* emphasizing the opportunities to collaborate and celebrating a community of learners
- *A negotiated program,* one that reflects the members of the community, allows for the contributions of all the protagonists, and respectfully documents, displays, and reflects on the life in the classroom (school)
- *Many opportunities for continued research,* expanding the community to include others with similar interests, developing projects that might inform, and continually questioning, searching, and learning (see Chapter 3, "The Teacher as Researcher")

Let us take a photographic tour of a school. On this tour, pay attention to how different spaces in an environment promote and provoke the development of "joy, curiosity, interest, affection, autonomy, possibility, responsibility, desire, expectation, tranquility, satisfaction, intimacy, individuality, belonging" (Strozzi, 2001, p. 58).

LIFE IN THE CLASSROOM: THE CLASSROOM ENVIRONMENT
How a classroom is physically arranged says a great deal about the spirit of that classroom. From the moment you walk into the classroom for 4-year-olds at the Virginia Tech Child Development Center, the environment sets a soothing tone of camaraderie and mental stimulation. When entering the room, you want to explore and discover, yet feel welcomed and calmed at the same time. A closer look at the dynamics of the classroom helps us to understand why this tone is set and how the environment plays such a major role in education and child development.

The first thing one sees when entering this classroom is that it is kid-friendly. The table and chairs are appropriately proportional to the average size of a pre-kindergartner. Most of the materials are at the children's level and can be easily accessed by the children. By having appropriate furniture and accessible materials the classroom sends the message that the children are respected, welcomed and that they belong in this room. This room reflects the belief that children are capable, have control of their environment, and can actively take part in their own learning and development.

The classroom is also aesthetically pleasing. Most of the artifacts on the walls are created by the children. The alternative lighting, such as lamps and spotlights, plants, and sofa add a "homey" touch and takes away the institutional feeling found in many classrooms. The display of children's artifacts, their photos, documentation of their work all enhance the children's sense of belonging.

How do the children conduct themselves in this classroom? The best example I can give is [that] the first thing in the morning . . . all the children arrive at the classroom and dive right into the materials set out by the teacher and begin exploring and constructing their own learning. Seldom does a child approach me and ask what he or she should be doing or ask for help to find something to work on. This is just what every teacher should strive for: a classroom where the children take an active part in their own learning because they feel comfortable enough to engage themselves in using materials to explore and learn, in their own ways.

The room provides tables and large floor areas for groups to learn and play together as well as smaller individual spaces for one-on-one interaction with a partner, or simply [to] work individually. By giving children the responsibility to decide who they want to play with or how to play, the teacher sends a message of trust and valuing the children's choices.

However, we believe the most wonderful aspect of the environment [is] the materials found in this classroom. Very few toys and materials are store-bought. What can be found are items found in nature and art materials that offer the children many ways to use these materials in their play and in making their own toys and props. We are still amazed at how a stick can begin the children's thought process of creating a house, deciding on roles of the people who live in the house, and then to move on to wanting to write a play involving their house. All this came from looking at a stick and thinking "what can I do with this?" This creative process helps the children learn to develop their own sense of autonomy while learning among their peers. Most likely this feeling will stick with them for the rest of their lives as they continue exploring and learning because at a young age they developed a love of learning.

Nicole Butler, early childhood education junior

THINK ABOUT IT

In reading the rest of this chapter, reflect on:

How is Nicole's descriptions of the environment represented in the classroom?

What other insights have you discovered about an environment that values children?

A SCHOOL THAT VALUES THE CONTRIBUTIONS
OF A COMMUNITY OF LEARNERS

The walls in the entryway of the school are covered with artifacts and documentation of the life in the classrooms. Materials that encourage creative ways of learning and multiple ways of knowing are placed on shelves to invite exploration and experimentation, connecting the school to the outside environment. The artifacts send a welcoming message to all who enter the school to be a part of its experience. This is a living school that is always changing. The documentation panels are narratives that connect what is happening right now with "a memory of the past and 'memory'

A school that is active and alive is projected through documentation and materials—inviting children, parents, and visitors to revisit the past and look forward to the future.

of the future" (Rinaldi, 1998, p. 118). Documentation (see Part Four) panels provide a feeling that you are welcome to become a part of the stories of life in the classrooms.

THINK ABOUT IT

In what ways does the entry into the school project the philosophy of the school?

How does the ritual of arrival and departure to and from the school promote home–school communication?

LIFE IN THE CLASSROOM

Just as the day begins with greetings, my day ends with greetings also. I greet the parents into the classroom, inform them of the day's events for their children and then say goodbye to the children individually. It is very important to have these positive social interactions when the children leave as [well as] when they arrive. By having these interactions the parents have a sense of what happened that day and the children feel a sense of closure in their day and look forward to com[ing] back the next day.

Martha Drinkard, junior

Children Arriving and Departing

The children arrive at the school saying goodbye to their parents, and parents exchange information with the teachers. As they enter their classroom, the children survey the room for familiar objects and friends while looking for different "surprises" that both foster continuity of experience and provoke different ways of knowledge building. On arrival the children get together with their friends, talking, playing, and engaging in investigations that provoke and challenge them to expand their ways of knowing.

During departure time, the children say goodbye to their teachers and friends and reunite with their parents, and teachers share the happenings in the classroom with the parents. These sometimes fleeting moments are precious time taken to build relationships and emotional well-being among all the protagonists.

Classroom Environment and Organization

The spaces in the classroom are aesthetically organized yet flexible—an environment of possibilities. Movable shelf units display children's work and materials.

The classroom is aesthetically organized yet flexible—an environment of possibilities.

Personal spaces convey respect for and the value of individual children.

Respect for each child's sense of self and being valued is reflected in personal spaces and places, such as a cubby marked with the child's name for his or her belongings. Children are encouraged to bring things from home to share and to promote continuity between home and school as a means of fostering relationships between the children, teachers, and families. Each child has a mail "box" to receive mail from friends and others in the school and a backpack to collect materials on field trips and to bring things from home to school and vice versa.

Creative Materials and Tools with Multiple Possibilities

Materials displayed in transparent and easily accessible containers invite children to explore, experiment, investigate, and represent their learnings in a variety of ways. These materials are "open" to many possibilities and do not impose particular ways of using them. Instead they invite the desire to investigate: to explore, ask questions, and pose hypotheses.

Many tools and materials of learning and knowing are readily available—markers, pens, pencils, chalk, paper, clay, books, and so much more. Light tables, light boxes, projectors, computers, cameras, and other forms of technology extend learning possibilities, ways of exploration, and documentation.

A variety of "open" materials invite children to experiment and represent their varied ways of learning and knowing.

THINK ABOUT IT

How does the organization of space and material encourage inquiry and multiple ways of learning?

How do materials that are open to many possibilities promote the use of different "languages" for learning and representing one's learning?

Individual and Group Identity

In an educational and caring environment, children solidify their individual identities in the company of others. They learn about themselves as members of a group engaging in routine tasks, collaborative projects, and individual activities. Daily assembly provides an opportunity for children and teachers to share their life in the classroom—to tell their stories, share the artifacts they have created, reflect, revisit experiences, and plan for the next steps. Small groups of children meet with the teacher to share ideas, reflect, and plan.

Children meet with the teacher to share ideas, reflect, and plan.

Identity is enhanced through seeing oneself in different dimensions and perspectives.

Individual identity is made visible through photographs, drawings, action figures, and artifacts children have constructed and documented. Children enhance their identities by representing themselves through different mediums such as clay, paint, and wire, and these artifacts are displayed in the classroom. For example, action figures are transformed into three-dimensional statues using a variety of mediums and are displayed in a group, providing yet another way of seeing and understanding self and others.

Possibilities of Light, Shadow, and Reflection

Light, shadow, and reflection are integral parts of the world we live in, which includes the classroom. Vea Vecchi (qtd. in Hill, 1998) states that

> to live is to observe light. A human being is a chrysalis for light. Light transforms the environment with a touch of one finger . . . [and] common materials become more precious in the presence of light. One child [in the presence of light] becomes

Light and shadow connect the real world and the world of possibilities.

more dramatic, others will enjoy the optical [appeal], and others are more willing to construct. Light offers variety and individuality.

Space for Collaboration

The children move around the classroom observing, watching, and exploring their different interests. Often they join one another to form collaborative groups to play and to work on projects that are either child or teacher initiated. Flexible spaces in the classroom foster these moments of collaboration and negotiation.

Space for Individual Exploration and Ways of Knowing

A child-centered environment offers flexible spaces for individual exploration and to ponder and reflect. Just as multiple materials and mediums promote individual children's different ways of knowing, such space allows children to explore and learn in ways that are most meaningful to them, because they attend to and accommodate multiple intelligences and ways of learning and knowing.

Space for collaboration and negotiation.

Experimenting, investigating, and exploring possibilities.

Constructing, reflecting, and making sense "my way."

THINK ABOUT IT

How does space encourage both collaborative and individual learning and knowing?

What are the benefits of collaborative learning?

What are the benefits of individual learning?

In what ways do these ways of learning interact and enrich learning experiences for the group and the individual?

Space to Be Alone and for Special Relationships

Sometimes the children wish to be alone. Spaces apart from the busy life in the classroom allow children to be alone, to play alone and reflect, or to be with a few children to converse, share a secret, or tell a story. Children value these moments, which are important times for social and emotional development.

A moment to be alone—to explore and understand oneself.

Special time with special friends, to share and to relate.

Caring for Others, Animals, and the Environment

Caring is an important part of an education based on relationships. Caring goes beyond caring for one another in daily authentic encounters in a classroom. Caring happens in relationships with children in other classrooms. Children often navigate to other classrooms to share special time with younger or older children.

Caring is also expressed through cleaning and tidying up the classroom, doing different routine tasks, and tending to plants and animals.

THINK ABOUT IT

How do relationships with other children and adults, animals, and nature enable the development of a curriculum of caring for self and others?

Caring for plants and all living things.

Cultural Reproduction and Reconstruction

In the classrooms in this school, there is always a dress-up area for children to engage in play. In play, children reconstruct their understanding of the culture, its people, relationships, custom, values, and so on. This area can be extended into other areas of the classroom as children create real and imaginary places, playing both real and fictional characters (family members, firefighters, police officers, sports figures, superheroes, dinosaurs, animals, and a variety of other imaginative characters). In the process of play, they reproduce the culture(s), reflect, revisit, revise, and in creative ways reconstruct the culture(s). Through play they make sense of relationships in different ways, exploring and finding meaning in relationships among themselves, making connections with adults, and creating a world that could be.

Relationships between Adults

The teachers are the builders and creators of a caring learning environment by taking into account the image of the child, how children learn, and how space fosters

Parents, teacher, and child review portfolio and documentations and gain deeper understanding of the child's growth and development.

the children's development in all domains. The teachers listen, observe, and interpret children's activities in order to extend the children's explorations and projects.

The teachers collaborate with one another to reflect on, interpret, and design provocations to extend learning activities and to document children's projects and happenings in the classroom. In reviewing the documentation and the children's portfolios, parents and teachers reflect and gain deeper understanding of the children's learning, growth, and development. The parents are welcome to share their experiences and to participate in and experience the life in the classroom.

Connecting the Outdoor and Indoor Spaces for Learning

The learning environment extends outdoors to the playground and places children visit on field trips. There is a seamless continuity between the indoor and outdoor learning environments. Natural materials collected outdoors are brought indoors to enhance learning and experimentation. Learning through play, exploration in relationships continues outdoors, with others, and by oneself, . . . and one's identity is tested and redefined in different ways.

Relationships are extended and enhanced in outdoor play.

The learning environment is dynamic, challenging, aesthetic, and ever-changing with the interests, projects, and needs of the children in a community for learning. In this community one is safe to imagine, to value difference in a space "already made for me; both snug and wide open, with a doorway never needing to be closed. Home" (Morrison, 1998, p. 12).

THINK ABOUT IT

How would you construct and organize spaces that enable children:

To express their potential, abilities, and curiosity?

To explore and research alone and with others, both peers and adults?

To perceive themselves as constructors of projects?

To reinforce their identities, autonomy, and security?

To work and communicate with others?

To know that their identities and privacy are respected?

(adapted from Rinaldi, 1998, p. 120)

One's identity is tested and redefined
on the playground.

GETTING STARTED ACTIVITIES

Classroom Observation and Reflection

Plan to visit in a public or private classroom (P–6) and spend at least two hours observing and (if possible) participating in the life of the school. Be sure to call in advance and secure approval for your visit. In writing up your observations, include:

1. The demographics of your visit (teacher's name, school, grade, etc.)

2. A drawing of the environment and your reflection on its value with regard to the notion of "an environment that taught"

3. Your impression of the image of the child that was evident in the space

4. A critical review of the curriculum implemented in the classroom

5. How this observation fits with your philosophy of teaching or how was it different

6. What you will take with you from this experience

RESOURCES

Readings

Ceppi, G., & Zini, M. (Eds.) (1998). *Children, spaces, relations: Metaproject for an environment for young children.* Reggio Emilia, Italy: Reggio Children.

Gandini, L. (1998). Educational and caring spaces. In C. Edwards, L. Gandini, & G. Forman (Eds.), *The hundred languages of children: The Reggio Emilia approach—advanced reflections* (2nd ed., pp. 161–178). Greenwich, CT: Ablex.

Greenberg, P. (2000). Display children's art attractively. *Young Children, 55*(2), 89.

Hubbard, R. S. (1998). Creating a classroom where children can think. *Young Children, 53*(5), 26–31.

Malaguzzi, L., & Gandini, L. (1993). For an education based on relationships. *Young Children, 49*(1), 9–12.

Ratcliff, N. (2001). Use the environment to prevent discipline problems and support learning. *Young Children, 56*(5) 84–88.

Sutterby, J. A., & Frost, J. L. (2002). Making playgrounds fit for children and children fit on playgrounds. *Young Children, 57*(3), 36–41.

REFERENCES

Hill, L. T. (1998). *Chronicling change at the Virginia Tech Child Development Laboratory School.* Unpublished manuscript, Virginia Tech, Blacksburg.

Morrison, T. (1998). Home. In W. Lubiano (Ed.), *The house that race built* (pp. 3–12). New York: Vintage Books.

National Research Council. (2000a). *Eager to learn: Educating our preschoolers.* Washington, DC: National Academy Press.

National Research Council. (2000b). *From neurons to neighborhoods: The science of early childhood development.* Washington, DC: National Academy Press.

National Research Council. (2000c). *How people learn: Brain, mind, experience and school* (Exp. ed.). Washington, DC: National Academy Press.

Rinaldi, C. (1998). The space in childhood. In G. Ceppi & M. Zini (Eds.), *Children, spaces, relations: Metaproject for an environment for young children* (pp. 114–120). Reggio Emilia, Italy: Reggio Children.

Strozzi, P. (2001). Daily at school: Seeing the extraordinary in the ordinary. In Project Zero & Reggio Children (Eds.), *Making learning visible: Children as individual and group learners* (pp. 58–77). Reggio Emilia, Italy: Reggio Children.

PART III

Families, Schools, and Communities
Learning from One Another

In this section there is a strong emphasis on the willingness of the school to share and partner with families on behalf of the education of the children. Examples are offered of strategies for bringing communities together for a common cause. Also included is a detailed story of one school's attempt to define and build an amiable system of schooling in which all members are respected for what they bring to the whole.

Caterpillar
Relationships go through many stages
and emerge from them ready to fly.
Julie Bryan, early childhood education student teacher

CHAPTER 7

A FAMILY-CENTERED MODEL
Parent–Teacher Partnerships

We cannot really be child-centered if we are not also family-centered.

William Ayers

Freddy's teacher recently has noticed an increase in his aggressive behavior toward the younger children in his classroom. In particular, Freddy has been hitting and pushing other children, creating some fear among his classmates. The teacher decides to talk to Freddy's mother and asks, "Can you think of anything happening at home lately that may be contributing to Freddy's behavior in the classroom?" Somewhat taken aback by this question, Freddy's mother replies, "No, nothing I can think of, but I am certain it has to do with the way you are running your classroom. Before Freddy came here, he never had any problems in school."

This conversation, familiar to many teachers, often characterizes parent–teacher communication about issues and incidents that occur in school. Reflected in this scenario are mutual blame, lack of trust, and a relationship that is distanced by difficulties in communication. How could this encounter be altered to reflect a more family-centered approach, one in which partnership, collaboration, and mutual respect and trust are evident? In this chapter, we ask this and other questions with the aim of encouraging you to reflect on important issues related to your work with families and helping you to establish supportive family–teacher partnerships.

- What are some assumptions underlying traditional views of parent education?
- How do traditional ways of working with and involving parents fail to support partnerships?
- What does it mean to be family centered?
- What are some of the barriers to creating a family-centered approach?
- How can we move toward family-centered partnerships and collaboration?

Parents are a child's first and primary teacher. How many times have we heard that statement? In our experience, however, this is one of those known essentials of early childhood education that often becomes forgotten in practice. For example, parent involvement, an important component of what we have come to expect in high-quality early childhood care and education, has often included a variety of activities such as accompanying children on field trips, volunteering in the classroom, participating in parent conferences and home visits, assisting with fundraising events, and communicating regularly with teachers and administrators

Parents traditionally have not been recognized as experts in life experiences with skills not available in the everyday curriculum.

(McBride, 1999). Although parents have been welcomed to be involved in these and other activities that are part of the established structure of the program, parents traditionally have not been involved in decisions related to curriculum or program goals. Indeed, parents are seldom recognized as authoritative sources of knowledge about their children and as experts in life experiences and skills that may not be available in the conventional curriculum.

In this chapter, we advocate a family-centered approach, which views parents as meaningful partners in the classroom, in the school, and in the educational lives of children. We acknowledge the importance of the family in contributing to school environments that encourage and support family strengths, relationships, and experiences.

THEMES UNDERLYING PARENT EDUCATION AND INVOLVEMENT

A brief look at parent education and involvement in children's education in the United States reveals three central themes of child psychology that have influenced thinking and practice:

- The home is important and basic for human development.
- Parents need help in creating the most effective home environment for children's development.
- The early years are important for lifelong development.

The assumptions that children need home and parents, particularly the mother, for optimal growth will not be disputed here, other than to suggest that this mid-nineteenth-century ideology has been an underlying premise of the need for parent education (Kessen, 1979). Unfortunately, it has led to another assumption—that when something goes awry in the course of a child' development, parents are to blame. Our main point is that each of these themes has for most of the last century dominated our approach to parent–teacher relationships and the view of parent education as a means of compensating for deficiencies in parenting and home life (see Powell & Diamond, 1995).

THINK ABOUT IT

What are some of the ways our society continues to promote the idea that parents or families are somehow deficient or lacking in their abilities to socialize and educate their children?

Powell (1989) has noted that the significant influence of parents on their children's development has been long acknowledged by educators. This recognition has been accompanied by recommendations for providing parents with child-rearing information and guidance. Moreover, as Kessen (1979) has noted, all theories of child development claim that lay persons, especially parents, need expert guidance in the raising of young children. Finally, early intervention programs such as Head Start have been based on the assumption of the importance of family and community influences on child development (Zigler & Styfco, 1993). Acknowledgment of the family's role as a primary socialization agent also has contributed to the notion that early educational experiences must be reinforced at home for preschool to have a significant impact on the child's development (Powell, 1989). This notion underlies a major purpose of traditional parent involvement programs.

TRADITIONAL APPROACHES TO PARENT INVOLVEMENT

Traditional parent involvement approaches can be subsumed under two major ideas:

- The importance of bringing parents into the life of the program
- Instructing parents about child development and informing them about how the curriculum "teaches" their children

Historically, parent involvement in early education programs has been viewed from a program perspective. From this point of view, parents are encouraged to participate in the program in a variety of ways that support program goals, but certain boundaries limit the parental influence on program operations and decisions. Teachers are considered to be the experts who determine and implement interventions and strategies without any family input or participation. When parents do provide information to teachers about their children, it usually is solicited by teachers in order to enhance their interactions with children (see Powell & Stremmel, 1987). Although soliciting information from parents is desirable, when parent-provided information is used to generate inferences about the causes of behavior in school, as our opening scenario suggests, it often assumes parental blame for things that happen at school without considering ways parents and teachers can work together to help and support children.

USES TEACHERS MAKE OF PARENT-PROVIDED INFORMATION
- To enhance their interactions with children
- To develop inferences about the causes of children's behavior
- To monitor parents' perceptions of the program
- To develop a better understanding of parents (Powell & Stremmel, 1987)

Disseminating information to parents that will encourage them to adopt and extend the ideologies and practices of the program is another common purpose of parent education and involvement. The goal here is to inform and educate parents about what happens and why, with the often hidden agenda that parents need to conform to the ideology and practices of the program; little or no attempt is made to acknowledge and respect the diverse perspectives and practices of parents. In the study referred to by Powell and Stremmel (1987), teachers expected parents to use teacher-provided information to develop positive feelings about the program and to reinforce at home what children were learning in the classroom. Moreover, teachers felt that some parents who held inappropriate expectations regarding their child's development would refine their perceptions and interactions to be more closely aligned with program views and practices. In many ways, this is more comfortable and less risky than inviting input from parents that may create the possibility for negative feedback and illuminate inconsistencies in beliefs and practices. Yet any culture built on the idea of collaboration and empowerment must be free to discuss parents' perceptions, concerns, interests, and responsibilities for participation without feeling threatened.

TEACHERS' EXPECTATIONS FOR HOW PARENTS USE INFORMATION
- To develop positive feelings about the program and their child's experiences
- To reinforce what children are learning in the classroom
- To alter existing perceptions of and interactions with children (Powell & Stremmel, 1987)

THE FAMILY-CENTERED MODEL

The theoretical position we advocate in this book suggests the need to consider the entire ecosystem of the child and move toward a more *family-centered* view of the home–school relationship. The family-centered model views parents as true partners in the child's care and education and values parent interaction and participation as a means of "strengthening the enduring relationship between parent and child" (Bronfenbrenner & Morris, 1998). It means carefully considering parents' input and addressing their individual needs and interests to a much greater degree.

Authentic partnerships with parents look very different from the traditional patterns of parent participation and involvement. First, developing such partnerships involves a shift in thinking about parent involvement from a program perspective to a family perspective. It means adopting the premise that families are the center of children's lives. According to McBride (1999), the first value of family-centered practice recognizes that all family members, not just the child, should benefit from intervention and educational services. Second, family-centered practice calls for programs to recognize and respect families as decision makers in the practices that affect their children's education and care, and as collaborators in the development of program goals. This includes, among other things, working with teachers and children as collaborators in inquiry; serving on parent advisory committees that have input into curriculum decisions; and participating on parent–teacher committees that focus on a specific problem or issue. Third, family-centered practices respect family culture and diversity and are responsive to the diverse needs of families. Services and practices are designed to foster and strengthen family relationships and

> **THINK ABOUT IT**
>
> What is the image of the family promoted by the family-centered model?
>
> In what ways does a family-centered program support the connections between children and families?

Family-centered programs respect families as decision makers for children and themselves.

family functioning, and teachers learn about each child as they both develop through relationships with the child's family (Bredekamp & Copple, 1997; McBride, 1999).

FAMILY-CENTERED PROGRAMS
- Acknowledge the importance of parents as true partners in child development and early education
- Respect families as decision makers
- Value and support parent interaction and participation as a means of strengthening the enduring relationship between parent and child

Barriers to Creating a Family-Centered Approach

Creating a family-centered approach requires action on the part of both families and teachers or program providers. Often a family-centered community is difficult to achieve because it requires a mutual commitment to common goals, something that does not happen easily. Time is needed to get to know families and to understand the values and goals they hold for their children. There also must be a perceived equality in the teacher–parent relationship. Unlike partnerships in traditional models, in which parents are passive consumers of knowledge and information, in the family-centered partnership parents are empowered in ways that enable them to contribute to the environment and the curriculum so that they reflect the desires, strengths, and culture of families; parents have a real opportunity to effect change. However, parents know as well as teachers that school has been historically the territory of teachers and that teachers potentially have the power to make children's lives miserable if parents are too intrusive. Further, perceiving the teacher as expert, parents are often uncertain about their own expertise in parenting.

Two-way communication is an important aspect of successful parent–teacher partnerships. Families have something to offer and teachers must be willing to listen. Teachers must use everyday or common language that is descriptively specific and free of value judgments, and they must take responsibility for creating *intersubjectivity,* or shared understanding or purpose, to prevent ambiguity, confusion, and defensiveness from becoming barriers to communication. Honesty, openness, and respect for values, beliefs, and perspectives are also essential to forging authentic partnerships. When parents feel lied to or manipulated, not trusted or respected, communication breaks down.

A Story for Reflection

Years ago, Andy Stremmel was teaching in a Head Start program when the following incident occurred:

> After a child had been engaging in inappropriate behavior (hitting and biting), I firmly rebuked him for what he had done. The child reported to his mother that I had hit him, even though this was not true. (Though, I admit, on reflection, I would have handled the situation much differently and more tactfully.) The mother, unabashed, told me that it was in my power and authority as the teacher to hit her child if I so desired. She added: "It is the only way we can get him to listen at home."
>
> I was upset by this incident, thinking that these parents must be strict and uncaring, not understanding the effects of hitting on a child's learning and development. As time went by, and as I got to know the family better, I became rather attached to this child and his family. Watching the daily interactions between the parents and their son, I saw how both parents cared deeply for him. I also came to realize that this family held certain assumptions about power and authority and had learned the social realities of the neighborhood where they lived. I learned that these parents had developed the notion that children had better learn to defend themselves physically if they were going to survive. Although I disagreed strongly with hitting as a means of guidance, and I could not agree with these parents' view of physical violence as a way of solving problems, I realized the need to listen, to try to understand a perspective different than my own, and to learn that there are different realities. This growth in my own understanding was necessary for establishing a space for dialogue and shared understanding. (Stremmel, 1996)

Becoming Family Centered: Family as Protagonist

In Chapter 5, we discussed the positive image of the child held by Reggio educators. This extends to the family as well, for children develop in relationship with the family, other children, teachers, and the community. In general, social relationships are considered to be basic to the learning process and to the construction of meaning.

In Reggio Emilia, education is a system of relations, with the quality of the program inextricably linked to the quality of relationships among and between adults. Parents' participation in the school is expected and supported, and they are an active part of their children's learning experiences. Just as children have rights to high-quality care and education, so too parents have rights to be involved in all aspects of their children's school lives (Gandini, 1997).

Parent–teacher partnerships are based on the nurturing of collaborative and reciprocal *pedagogical relationships.* A pedagogical relationship is two-dimensional in nature, in that both players (parent and teacher) contribute to the construction and maintenance of the relationship in a spirit of collaboration, intersubjectivity, and mutuality. The realization of such a relationship is dependent on the teacher being thoughtful and caring in attempting to understand and feel for the other person's reality (Noddings, 1984).

THINK ABOUT IT

Collaborative parent–professional partnerships are manifest in the ongoing dialogue and negotiation of these and other culturally and socially relevant questions:

What do we want for our children?

What do we know about them that will help us all to better teach them?

How can parents and professionals support each other's roles in the child's development?

Parents are powerful protagonists in their children's development. Yet they remain an often underutilized source of information about their children (Ayers, 2001). It is easy to view parents as overly involved, having nothing better to do with their time, especially when we feel they are overstepping their bounds in offering views and advice that we see as too subjective or intrusive. However, the insights of parents and their invested knowledge of their children are precisely what we need to become family centered (Ayers, 2001).

Assessing How Family Centered You Are

By now, we hope we have firmly established the idea of family centeredness, calling for collaborative parent–teacher (home–school) relations from the perspective of parental rights, parent empowerment, and responsiveness to family values, perspectives, and cultural diversity. The following questions are presented as a means of assessing how family centered a program is:

- Are most parent meetings and interactions with parents problem focused?
- How easy is it for a parent to find out what is going on in the classroom?

- Are parents a regular source of information? Is parental input valuable, and does it ever influence change in what the program does?
- Do parents typically come to school to discuss positive activities?
- Are parents informed when their children are doing exciting and interesting things in the classroom? When children are doing well?

It is important to address these questions before moving toward a more inclusive model of parent–teacher partnerships. As you will read in Chapter 8, inquiry into these and other questions leads to critical analysis of what authentic parent–teacher partnership means.

SOME ESSENTIAL ELEMENTS OF PARENT–TEACHER PARTNERSHIPS

Before concluding this chapter, we want to provide some essential elements or principles of authentic parent–teacher partnerships. All policies and practices associated with a family-centered approach should be based on these principles.

Families don't need fixing. When families and professionals are true partners, there is an attempt to get to know families and understand and build on family strengths.

It takes a village to raise children. This saying may seem trite given its use in recent years, but the truth is it does take a collaborative effort. Families and schools working together can make a significant impact on the care and education children receive.

Communication among administrators, teachers, and parents is essential. For best results, a policy on parent involvement needs to be clearly defined and articulated. What is expected and what is valued? If partnerships are valued, how can programs welcome all families as partners in the program? Further, good communication requires a commitment to building trust between parents and teachers. Because teachers tend to control the flow of information between school and home, they are uniquely positioned to initiate and foster good communication.

Parents and teachers engage as collaborators in the education process. Whereas teachers possess information about child development and about children's experiences in group settings, families have information about their children as individuals across time and in a variety of settings beyond school. Therefore, parents and teachers must collaborate in the process of education; they must create opportunities to learn together and to share in decision making. This might involve including parents in staff development and training, developing committees to focus on common issues of teaching and parenting; or engaging in action research designed to address problems, issues, and concerns in the classroom or school.

THINK ABOUT IT

People are the experts of their own lives, the only authentic chroniclers of their own experiences. Therefore, we must develop the perspective that parents have expertise as well.

How can we go about nurturing this perspective?

Understand that parents develop too. It is easy to forget that parents develop along with their children (and teachers too). We have often seen this truism manifested in the following assumptions:

- All new parents want perfection for their children. It can sometimes seem that they expect teachers to treat their children as if they were the only ones who mattered.
- All of parenting is a struggle with the reality of giving up control. It is difficult for parents to give their children over to the care of someone else.
- All parents need support and encouragement in their child-rearing practices. Opportunities to talk with other parents and teachers can be a tremendous source of support, as parents discover that others experience, desire, and need the same things.

Expect differences and, at times, conflicts in values, attitudes, goals, and parenting styles, and be sensitive to these differences. Two-way communication includes creating avenues for families to share their culture and to participate fully in the discussion of what is in their child's best interest.

Understand that the development of "authentic" home-school partnerships requires a shift in thinking about what parent partnership really means. Most of what we have presented in this chapter makes the assumption, largely from the point of view of teachers and care providers, that authentic partnerships with parents are not only desired but also that they look a certain way. We need to keep in mind that partnership may mean different things to different people. For example, it may mean for one family that they want to be well informed of what goes on in school and want teachers to know about things happening at home that will make them better teachers of their children, yet they may not wish to participate in parent meetings or committees or as volunteers in the classroom. This does not make them less caring or concerned parents. As stated before, teachers must get to know family members individually if they are to respect and support them in their goals for their children.

Moral contracts and Declarations of Intent. A Declaration of Intent is a pledge of mutual trust and respect, an agreement on goals and strategies, and a sharing of rights and responsibilities. Although not a required element of effective parent–teacher relationships, we feel quite strongly that a formal statement of intent conveys a powerful message of commitment to the development of a community of collaboration, mutual respect, and responsiveness. Our own school's Declaration of Intent is the subject of the next chapter.

SUMMARY

Increasingly, in early childhood education there is a movement toward family-centered approaches that view parents as true partners in the child's care and education and that value parent interaction and participation as a means of "strengthening the enduring relationship between parent and child" (Bronfenbrenner & Morris, 1998). Based on the growing recognition that the family is the primary influence in all aspects of a child's development and education, family-centered approaches reflect an ecological view of the child as a member of a family system, which itself is part of a larger system of community, society, and culture. Overcoming the potential barriers to parent–teacher partnerships will require both new skills in communication and changing perspectives on family strengths, values, and beliefs, including an understanding that early childhood educational programs serve families, not children alone.

GETTING STARTED ACTIVITIES

Throughout this chapter, we have posed many questions, all of which we believe are worth your serious reflection and discussion. In addition, the following questions and activities are offered for your consideration:

1. What are some of the perceptions of families you hold that may prevent the formation of authentic partnerships in your classroom?

2. What are some potential "turf" issues that may threaten the development of equal partnerships with parents? What are some of the things teachers do to undermine or prevent parents from being part of a mutual decision-making process?

3. How might you alter or design parent–teacher conferences to better reflect the ideals of collaboration and partnership inherent in the family-centered approach?

4. Based on your understanding of the principles of a family-centered approach, how might you deal with an overly aggressive or hostile parent whose ideas and beliefs run counter to yours or the philosophy of the school in which you work?

RESOURCES

On the Web

http://npin.org/library/1999/n00091/n00091.html
> National Parent Information Network, NAEYC, Building Parent–Teacher Partnerships: This article offers some good suggestions for how to build positive parent–teacher relationships.

http://ecap.crc.uiuc.edu/pubs/katzsympro.html
> Parent–Teacher Partnerships: A Theoretical Approach for Teachers, ERIC/EECE Publication: This paper discusses the research on parent–teacher partnerships, including factors that affect the development of effective relationships.

Readings

Berger, E. (1987). *Parents as partners in education: The school and home working together* (2nd ed.). Columbus, OH: Merrill.

File, N. (2001). Family–professional partnerships: Practice that matches philosophy. *Young Children, 56*(4), 70–74.

Powell, D. (1989). *Families and early childhood programs*. Washington, DC: NAEYC.

Powell, D. (1998). Reweaving parents into the fabric of early childhood programs. *Young Children, 53*(5), 60–67.

Workman, S., & Gage, J. (1997). Family–school partnerships: A family strengths approach. *Young Children, 52*(4), 10–14.

REFERENCES

Ayers, W. (2001). *To teach: The journey of a teacher.* (2nd ed.). New York: Teachers College Press.

Bredekamp, S., & Copple, C. (Eds.). (1997). *Developmentally appropriate practices in early childhood programs.* (Rev. ed.). Washington, DC: NAEYC.

Bronfenbrenner, U., & Morris, P. A. (1998). The ecology of developmental processes. In W. Damon (Series Ed.), R. M. Lerner (Vol. Ed.), *Handbook of child psychology (Vol. 1): Theoretical models of human development* (pp. 993–1028). New York: Wiley.

Gandini, L. (1997). Foundations of the Reggio Emilia approach. In J. Hendrick (Ed.), *First steps toward the Reggio way* (pp. 14–25). Upper Saddle River, NJ: Merrill/Prentice-Hall.

Kessen, W. (1979). The American child and other cultural inventions. *American Psychologist, 34,* 815–820.

McBride, S. L. (1999). Family-centered practices. *Young Children, 54,* 62–68.

Noddings, N. (1984). *Caring: A feminine approach to ethics and moral education.* Berkeley: University of California Press.

Powell, D. R. (1989). *Families and early childhood programs.* Washington, DC: NAEYC.

Powell, D. R., & Diamond, K. E. (1995). Approaches to parent–teacher relationships in U.S. early childhood programs during the twentieth century. *Journal of Education, 177,* 71–94.

Powell, D. R., & Stremmel, A. J. (1987). Managing relations with parents: Research notes on the teacher's role. In D. Peters and S. Kontos (Eds.), *Advances in applied developmental psychology, Vol. 2: Continuity and discontinuity of experience in child care* (pp. 115–127). Norwood, NJ: Ablex.

Stremmel, A. J. (1996). *Diversity: Training guide for the U.S. Marine Corps Child Development Program.* Blacksburg, VA: Department of Family & Child Development, VPI & SU.

Zigler, E., & Styfco, S. J. (Eds.) (1993). *Head Start and beyond: A national plan for extended childhood intervention.* New Haven, CT: Yale University Press.

CHAPTER 8

THE AMIABLE SCHOOL
Incorporating Everyone into the Equation

To feel a sense of belonging, to be a part of a larger endeavor, to share meanings—these are the rights of everyone involved in the educational process, whether teachers, children, or parents. In our schools, the active participation of the families and collegiality among staff and children working in groups is essential.

Carlina Rinaldi, *The Hundred Languages of Children*

Our school was concerned about family participation. It seemed that no matter how hard we tried to encourage parents to be involved in the life of our school, they continued to seem removed from the real experience of true participation. Parents rarely showed up at school meetings that were scheduled to inform them of child development issues, and school functions were also poorly attended. When we surveyed the families for our National Association for the Education of Young Children (NAEYC) accreditation, the issue that stood out for parents as the greatest concern was "the lack of communication between home and school." We were disappointed that despite all our efforts families still wanted more, more, more. We were beginning to feel a sense of hopelessness and exhaustion and even a little resentful because we felt that our efforts were not reciprocated by the families. We felt they needed to make a greater effort to at least meet us halfway. This chapter is the story of our school's attempt to find amiability in the midst of discord, mistrust, a breakdown in communication, and an enormous desire to change our way of participating together.

This chapter offers a reflection of the concept of an amiable school. The idea of a strong home–school partnership is sometimes difficult to grasp and even more difficult to practice. A story of one school's painful but rewarding transformation is shared.

127

QUESTIONS TO BE CONSIDERED

- How do we overcome personal feelings and perspectives but continue to have a dialogue and to reinvent ourselves by taking into account others' thoughts, values, concerns, and needs?
- How do we have a dialogue across differences?
- How do we trust each other's intentions?
- How do we overcome external controls and interferences in the shape of attempts to intimidate, dislodge participants, and incite conflict?
- In order to build an amiable school, we have to begin with building a trusting, working relationship among participants. How do we get along together and intensify relationships? It is not an easy journey. Various ups and downs continue to interfere and challenge us even with our best intentions.
- How do we negotiate conflicting feelings of divided loyalty?
- How do we build a new culture of care and possibilities?

The journey began while visiting the schools of Reggio Emilia, Italy. Several of us from our school had traveled to Reggio Emilia with the main focus of learning from the schools in Italy how to think about and enhance our home–school relationships. It was immediately evident that we needed to pay a new kind of attention to parent participation back home. In the schools in Reggio, we noted an amazing sense of loyalty, affection, and dedication coming from the parents of children in their schools. They attended most of our meetings in the schools and were often the main spokespersons for the school, sharing information about philosophy, systems, projects, and the reciprocity that existed between the families and their school.

When we returned home, we redoubled our efforts to talk with our own families to explore their impressions of their place in our school, as well as their understanding of parent participation. We also began to analyze the ways in which parents had been made visible in our school in the past. It didn't take long for us to acknowledge that we barely had parent involvement, and that we were a long way from partnership.

We needed to find a variety of ways to communicate with families and to convey our desire for their partnership in the education and care of their children. In short, we needed to create a more welcoming, amiable atmosphere in our school, one in which we could all feel a sense of ownership, responsibility, and commitment to the lives of the children, the teachers, and the families.

With a desire and a passion to provide an environment in which children, families, and teachers might be challenged to flourish, we embarked on our first Declaration of Intent, a collaborative effort to study an issue of shared interest. At the first formal gathering of our entire school body at the beginning of the school year, we unveiled our Declaration of Intent. It read: *How can we create an Amiable School which recognizes families as true partners and collaborators in the program?*

Family engagement and participation is the mission of most schools. In the past, this relationship was structured in alignment with historical philosophies of child development and school movements, teacher preparation, child study, and parent education. In more recent years, due to changing societal and institutional contexts, there has been an ongoing need to reconstruct programs to make them more responsive to the lived experiences of parents, children, and teachers. Among the changes has been a call for more parent involvement. This demand was a challenge of the 1990s among all early childhood programs, with varied success in its implementation. Educators seem to need to share stories of struggle and success in order to make family participation an integral part of school systems.

THINK ABOUT IT

How would you begin to bridge the gaps between parents and teachers, between home and school?

From an ecological perspective, a school is situated in a multilayered system. It is embedded within the contexts of knowledge, power, and politics and serves many unique perspectives. These unique perspectives are often at odds. It is essential for schools to face and negotiate these external pressures that challenge and at times test our relationships of trust and divide our loyalties. We really had our work cut out for us to begin facing the challenges and making the enormous changes that we felt were necessary to establish a system in our school that would be more welcoming of parents, more reciprocal, and more amiable.

We began our struggle by acknowledging to ourselves that we had not done a good job in the past of listening to the voices of all the protagonists. We admitted that we tended to *inform* parents about their own children, about school functions, and about their responsibilities as parents in the school. We recognized that we rarely involved them in dialogue or asked their opinion about issues that were directly related to their role as parents. This was obviously going to have to change in order for the lines of communication to open up between home and school. *How* was the big question we faced.

THINK ABOUT IT

How can you build a community from a large group of individuals who are used to thinking about *self* before *group*?

About that same time, we took stock of how the rest of the protagonists in our school were feeling about their ability to make contributions to the school. Did the teachers and children really have a voice? As we found with the families, it appeared that the loudest voice was the administration's and that the rest of the members of our "community" were practically mute.

TRY TO REMEMBER THAT YOU ARE A COMMUNITY IN THE MAKING

No community is a perfect community. If any community is "perfect," it falls into the way of doing things "small." It will not grow, develop, or change. It stagnates. A community in the making is one that is constantly revisiting its past and reinventing its future—what it could and should be. It is looking at things "large" with faith and determination while struggling to build and rebuild a culture and context based on relationships and possibilities. Each protagonist must have the courage to change, to unlearn and yet learn as he or she reflects and digs into the deepest sense of self, so that together we can search for ourselves as a community. We could no longer be satisfied with the ordinary and the comfortable, as that seemed to us to be doing things small. We needed to be doing things large, and in building an amiable school we had to fight against having others determine exactly who we were. We were all drawn to the words of Loris Malaguzzi (1998) as he described the importance of amiability within a school community:

> Our goal is to build an amiable school. . . . It must embody ways of getting along together, of intensifying relationships . . . of assuring complete attention to the problems of education and of activating participation and research. (p. 65)

Above all, we decided that issues, concerns, opportunities, and challenges should be brought to the community by its members in the spirit of collaborative problem solving, in the hope of creating shared understandings, and with the aim of establishing a safe place for learning and growing. Our primary goal became to establish a community that was a safe space for members to:

- Show themselves fully to one another and be welcomed
- Enter into dialogue with one another
- Be listened to and affirmed
- Solve real problems and think creatively
- Learn from one another and make mistakes with minimal cost
- Perform roles and responsibilities in a way that says, "I trust your abilities to perform and succeed"
- Foster and share multiple perspectives
- Be at the center of authentic and intimate learning experiences
- Reflect on experiences and see this as a valuable source of growth and development

THINK ABOUT IT

How can we create a community that allows all participants to share in the effort to create and sustain a vibrant community of learners?

What are some of the ways of thinking and acting on this goal?

LISTENING TO THE VOICES OF OUR FAMILIES

The Journey toward Amiability

Our next step was to elicit input from the families. We wanted an open forum for dialogue. With great enthusiasm, we created an interactive documentation panel for our school's hallway. This, we hoped, would be the place where we would all be empowered to offer our ideas, thoughts, and suggestions for improving our school. We sent out flyers to all the families and asked for their input in our process of becoming more "amiable."

Next, we hosted a home–school dialogue on the Reggio Emilia approach. This meeting included a description of our philosophy and a slide presentation about the elements of the Reggio Emilia approach. Families then worked in small groups with teachers to brainstorm suggestions for the improvement of the school. We shared the following quotation with our families as they considered their goal of creating a more welcoming and amiable setting:

> Our objective, which we always will pursue, is to create an amiable environment, where children, families, and teachers feel at ease. . . . Thus, we have put together a mechanism combining places, roles, and functions that have their own timing, but that can be interchanged with one another in order to generate ideas and actions. All this works within a network of cooperation and interactions that produces for the adults, but above all for the children, a feeling of belonging in a world that is alive, welcoming, and authentic. (Malaguzzi, 1998, pp. 63–64)

That night the families came up with some definitions of their own amiable school:

> An amiable school is reciprocal.
> An amiable school is mutually rewarding.
> An amiable school is collaborative.
> An amiable school is welcoming.

These definitions blended beautifully with Carlina Rinaldi's (1998) thoughts related to belonging to a community:

> To feel a sense of belonging, to be part of a larger endeavor, to share meanings— these are the rights of everyone involved in the educational process, whether teachers, children, or parents. In our schools, the active participation of the families and collegiality among staff and children working in groups is essential. (p. 114)

During the meeting, our parents also came up with some suggestions about how to move closer to a true amiable school:

- "We need to move beyond the 'child care mentality' where we merely drop off our children and pick them up again and call that our contribution."
- "Let's have an information session where we can find out who we are and what we can do to contribute."
- "Let's try journaling between home and school as another form of dialogue."
- "Maybe we could document conversations from home and bring them in as a contribution to the child's portfolio."
- "It sounds like in order for us to practice the Reggio Emilia approach that we've got to learn how to become *great listeners*."

After a great start to our new year and after a strong group commitment to the mission of amiability, we got down to work. Work and play in the classrooms began to consume our attention. Some challenging behaviors were evident in a couple of the classrooms, and we were busy attending to these concerns. Other classrooms were easily developing a rich sense of community, and the staff was happily engaged in ongoing professional development.

Perhaps because we were so immersed in the day-to-day experiences in the school, we did not notice at first that all was not amiable as far as the parents were concerned. One day as we were reviewing the comments that had been posted on our interactive documentation panel in the hallway, we were stunned to realize that many of the anonymous comments were quite negative. Some of the comments included:

- "We need to bring back a teacher-directed circle time with some structure!"
- "The snacks are not appropriate."

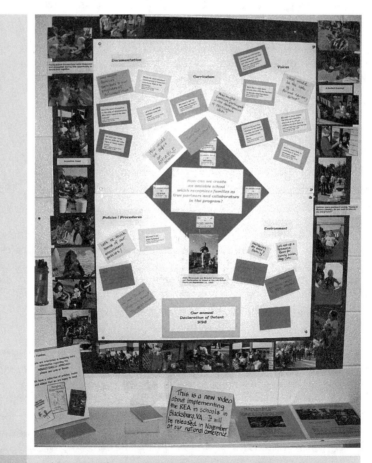

An interactive documentation board can offer the community an outlet for making suggestions, offering ideas, and venting emotions.

- "How about discipline? Teachers do not seem empowered to handle the problems in the classrooms."
- "Make the classrooms more comfortable for parents. They are too crowded."
- "You need to provide some drop-off transitions for younger siblings."
- "Why is the curriculum so 'art-based'? How will they ever learn to read and write?"

In some cases, we noted, parents had begun to use the documentation board to debate among themselves. One parent wrote: "Some parents stay too long in the classrooms. This is disruptive to the teachers and the program and to the other children in the room." Another parent responded: "I thought that we were all welcome in the classroom throughout the day!"

Our initial response to this turn of events was to feel hurt and even a sense of mistrust toward the parents. Some members of our staff insisted that because the interactive documentation panel was not being used as intended, we should dismantle it. Many of us were embarrassed to have such negative comments displayed in such a public way, but we felt that removing them would be a form of censorship that would conflict with our commitment to amiability. It was certainly a time of great confusion and distress.

Finally, after some time for reflection and discussion among the staff, we realized that for some parents the panel had become a substitute for face-to-face discussion and conversation. The anonymity of the comments made it difficult for us to know how to approach the concerns being voiced on the board in the hallway. So we developed a new plan: We proposed to our families that we might begin to hold open dialogues designed around the themes emerging on the board. These new "round table discussions" would be opportunities for us to examine and re-examine the issues from all perspectives.

About that time, Lella Gandini, a liaison to North American schools from Reggio Emilia, arrived in town to consult with us and to assist in our quest to understand the Reggio Emilia philosophy. As she toured our school, she asked for more details about the interactive documentation that was extremely visible on the walls in our hallway. With hesitancy, we described the events that were unfolding in our school. Her response was liberating. She said, "Don't be afraid of your process. Document it and display it with pride so that the entire community can feel a sense of movement and process!"

THINK ABOUT IT

What are some ways to engage families in the life of the school?

And with those wise words always in our minds, we vowed to turn our problems into a project. As is often the case, these feelings of disappointment, disequilibrium, and tension forced us to think beyond the problem.

Parent Advisory Groups were set up as one means by which issues, problems, projects, and community events could be discussed. Monthly meetings were held, and slowly but surely the families began to take on more and more of the decision-making role in our school.

When parents take on a role of shared responsibility in the school, all members of the community benefit.

Special committees were formed to assist with schoolwide projects. Parents eagerly volunteered to help with gardening projects, fund-raisers, computer maintenance, and support for projects that coincided with their own interests and expertise.

Parents became an integral part of the curriculum as their own expertise began to be considered a part of the negotiated days we spent together.

Parent–teacher–child conferences with detailed portfolios were held twice a year. Older children were invited to attend these meetings and to contribute their ideas and memories regarding their own development. Parents contributed additional artifacts and documentation from home to make the portfolio more complete.

New parent orientation to the school was held at the beginning of each year to help families feel a sense of belonging from the outset and to introduce our mission of amiability. It was during these early meetings that families could sign up to work on Parent Committees.

A *Buddy system* was developed to help new families feel welcomed to the school. Each new family was assigned a mentor family to help ease the transition into the school.

LISTENING TO THE VOICES OF OUR TEACHERS

Once we felt that our families were becoming more solidified in the school culture, we turned our attention to our teachers. In our school, we have head teachers who

THINK ABOUT IT

How can these goals for teachers in high-quality early childhood programs be attained?

remain in the school for two years as part of their assistantship for graduate school. This means that our turnover in staff is quite significant and cause for some lack of stability, consistency, and understanding. We desperately wanted to be a strong, viable community, but our teachers complained that sometimes they felt there was little room in the system for their novel ideas for change.

Following are the goals for teachers in our amiable community:

- Teachers should strive to become thoughtful, caring, passionate, creative risk takers and mistake makers who are critical, forgiving, and deliberate about their teaching.
- Teachers should consider themselves teacher researchers and demonstrate an understanding of the importance of observation, self-awareness, reflection, and change as the foundation of the work in the classroom.
- Teachers should come to value the gift of an education based on relationships and find satisfaction in creating intimate, nurturing, and sustaining relationships with children, families, and colleagues.

In order to give the teachers a strong and meaningful voice in the school and to recognize them as researchers in their classrooms, we created the opportunity for supported Declarations of Intent, or action research projects, in each classroom. When a teacher is curious about an aspect of her or his classroom, that teacher can begin to study and analyze the details of the query, often creating an atmosphere of inquiry that can be contagious. (See Chapter 3 for more details on the teacher as researcher concept.)

SOME HELPFUL GUIDELINES IN DEVELOPING A SUCCESSFUL ACTION RESEARCH PROJECT

1. Soon after the beginning of the school year, the teacher should make a formal declaration of her or his intent to study a specific aspect of the classroom.
2. The declaration should include a methodology and a discussion of the data that will be collected in the classroom.
3. Using a mentor or coresearcher is always a positive way to work. Such a partnership offers the opportunity for the exchange of ideas and a deepening development of the topic. A strong research question should be formed at this early stage in the research.
4. Make regular opportunities for forums of discussion of the ongoing projects in the company of a supportive community so that the data can be discussed and analyzed with others.
5. Final reports should be documented for the entire school community and made visible in multiple formats. Presentations at local, regional, and national

conferences will contribute to the professional development of the teaching staff, as would publishing the results in professional journals.

6. Most important, all projects should have strong implications for changing school policy, procedures, and mind-set and give the teachers a sense of having a strong and meaningful place in the amiable community.

One Teacher's Action Research: Angi Primavera's Communication Project

This is how one teacher's action research project got started:

- *Identifying a need:* Noting from the parents' comments on the interactive documentation board and from other sources that families were hungry for more communication between school and home, Angi Primavera (2002) easily identified a problem area that might benefit from the attention of an action research project.
- *Visualizing a project:* Because Angi had skill, expertise, and interest in the use of technology, she proposed that technology might be an answer to part of the breakdown in communication within the school.
- *Receiving validation:* Angi pitched her idea of an interactive web site that would connect with families from her classroom and received an enthusiastic response from everyone.
- *Generating new questions:* Her central research question became: Can the use of technology in the classroom cause increased communication between home and school and a wider community of common relationships?

The purpose of this study was to document and examine the use of technology to facilitate communication between the three protagonists of learning—parents, teachers, and children—in an early childhood education classroom. Specifically, the process of the coconstruction of a web site by parents and teachers and subsequent use of the web site for information exchange and parent involvement, were documented and examined by the researcher using ethnographic methodologies.

QUESTIONS TO GUIDE THE STUDY
- How can the documentation made visible through the use of technology—i.e., a web site—facilitate communication between the three protagonists of learning—parents, teachers, and children?
- How do the protagonists contribute to the development and use of the web site?
- What factors influence parents' participation in the development of the web site?
- How do I, the researcher, provide information for and make revisions to the web site that are responsive to the parents' expressed interests?

The web site was able to share curricular details and also served as a calendar reminder for upcoming events. Parents and children reviewed the web site together from home, thus giving children the opportunity to share details of their day with their parent, which in turn enhanced the learning process and strengthened the home–school relationship.

Lessons Learned from This Action Research Project

Suggestions for policy changes surrounding home–school communications in our school include using a closed, password-protected web site to ensure limited access; using an encrypted address; getting the consensus of the group pertaining to access of the web site and the use of images; and obtaining informed consent from all families before beginning.

During the course of this action research project, and others that had occurred in the school that year, we noted that the project promoted the voices of teachers in the school and contributed to a stronger sense of place for all of them. In addition, the project led to an enhancement of the teacher researcher role, which in turn contributed to the abilities of the teachers, children, and families to understand the exhilaration of representing in multiple languages. These multiple strategies led to outlets for publication, enhancement of our program, continuity and stability within our program, and, most important, a sense of solidarity among the community.

LISTENING TO THE VOICES OF OUR CHILDREN

And then we turned to the voices of the youngest members of our community. Where and when do they have a chance to express their needs, desires, wishes, hopes, and ideas regarding our school? We decided to focus our attention on a couple of children who seemed to be telling us through their actions that they were unhappy with their place in the school.

THINK ABOUT IT

How could you use a system of observation and assessment to determine what the children are passionate about, what they are experiencing, thinking, and wondering?

The teacher spent lots of time with the children in the group helping them understand the appropriate ways to interact with others. Still, some of the younger children were expressing fear, anxiety, and worry about being close to the older, larger, more robust children in the group. During a parent advisory meeting, the parents suggested that the "problem child" be removed from the school because he was causing a domino effect of troubling behavior in the system. The conversations were passionate, and empathy was absent. Each family was concerned for their own child only. All was not well in our school!

THINK ABOUT IT

How can a community respond to and support a child whose behavior is more aggressive than is typical?

How can you assure the other families that their children are safe in the classroom with this more volatile child in their midst?

Learning from previous experiences, we decided to make our problem the project. There seemed to be little sense of community within our school. Each family was concerned only for their own child, not for the group or for the school as an organization. We decided to embark on a group project with the hope that thinking, creating, laughing, and sweating side by side would be the key to building more amiable relationships. We also hoped that this time spent together would give our families an opportunity to get to know one another more deeply and intimately. We were thrilled when a couple of parents stepped forward to supervise the project, thus making the project more family-friendly. We hoped that in the end the relationships might deepen to a place where *expertise* was recognized as easily as *problems.*

When teachers carefully and thoughtfully observe the children's interests, it becomes more apparent where problems can be the sources of great opportunities for learning.

When parents step forward to work in a collaborative way with school personnel, perspective taking and intersubjectivity can thrive.

When children work together in groups, they begin to understand and appreciate one another's expertise, skills, needs, and personalities, thus moving toward the development of a true community.

Finding ways for children to work in tandem on projects promoted friendship and gave them a sense of group accomplishment. Celebrating the uniqueness of each child in the classroom and *listening* carefully to them helped all of us move from a sense of "I" to a sense of "we." We relished this comment from Carlina Rinaldi (1998):

> Listening means giving value to others, being open to them and what they have to say. Listening legitimizes the other person's point of view, thereby enriching both listener and speaker. What teachers are asked to do is to create contexts where such listening can take place. (p. 120)

Finding "classroom experts" gives the children the opportunity to find their own niche and figure out how to work together to solve problems. In this way, we found ways to reevaluate our image of the child and ensured that we helped children in their journey to becoming strong, capable, competent children by giving them the opportunities to practice these arts. We also worked harder to establish a warm generosity of attitude in the classroom that encouraged a spirit of caring and appreciation for one another and all the different styles and ways of being that are always found in an inclusive classroom. Most important, we found ways to engender family support and friendships outside of school walls. We set up a weekly newsletter to share details of upcoming events and found parents who were willing to help with this task. Sometimes it's much easier for a parent to approach another parent about volunteering time or energy than it is for the teacher to take on this role. Organized bowling nights, pizza outings, and cleaning up the local creek were all opportunities that brought families together in ways not typically possible

A strong image of the child is contagious within a community.

Working and playing together outside of the regular school hours contributes to the building of an affectionate and powerful group.

in a traditional classroom—and they went a long, long way toward building amiable communities.

SUMMARY

Listening carefully to the main protagonists in the school can make a strong impact on the organization, system, and educational process. To be successful, community must be established first. It is also important to remember that adult attitudes influence those of the children, so a careful analysis of the adults' image of the child should be considered. Interdependence within the community is also a valuable commodity, along with a profound ability to take the perspective of another. Nurturing the concept of "I am who we are" is equally crucial. The process of building community takes *time.* Don't shortchange it or try to rush it. Savor it.

Our own ever-transforming definition of an amiable school has become: "an intentional, interdependent community where all protagonists are respected and give respect, are valued and give value, are challenged and who challenge others to listen carefully in a shared attempt to continue a passionate transformation of self and school" (Hill, Wells, & Fu, 1999, p. 43).

GETTING STARTED ACTIVITIES

1. In order to establish crucial relationships between and among children, families, and schools, we recommend a looping process whereby teachers and children and

their families remain together over the course of two or more years. How might you organize this complex system within a preschool setting or in a public school? Write a proposal to your supervisor in favor of this concept. Use the important highlights from this chapter to assist with your proposal.

2. Consider ways and means of getting new members of the community acclimated as soon as possible. What would those means be?

3. If relationship building *is the curriculum,* what ways could you find to bring this important element into your classroom each day?

4. Write a personal definition for an amiable school and share it with your peers.

RESOURCES

On the Web

www.ericece.org/reggio.html

This site offers an opportunity to chat with others across the world who are interested in the Reggio Emilia approach. A detailed and helpful archives from past conversations is also available.

www.ecrp.uiuc.edu/v4n2/index.html

This site is a helpful organization of articles regarding early childhood issues.

Readings

Bateson, M. C. (2000). *Full circles, overlapping lives: Culture and generation in transition.* New York: Ballantine Books.

Bersani, C., & Jarjoura, D. (2002). Developing a sense of WE in parent–teacher relationships. In V. Fu, A. Stremmel, & L. Hill, (Eds.), *Teaching and learning: A collaborative exploration of the Reggio Emilia approach* (pp. 69–81). Upper Saddle River, NJ: Merrill/Prentice-Hall.

Galardini, A., & Giovannini, D. (2001). Pistoia: Creating a dynamic, open system to serve children, families, and community. In L. Gandini, & C. P. Edwards (Eds.), *Bambini: The Italian approach to infant/toddler care* (pp. 89–105). New York: Teachers College Press.

Kaminsky, J. (2001). A conversation about family and community participation at Chicago Commons with Dorothy Kelsie Miller, Jennie Seacat, & Miguel Archundia. *Innovations, 8*(3), pp. 7–21.

Power, B. (1999). *Parent power: Energizing home–school communications. A guide for teachers and schools.* Portsmouth, NH: Heinemann.

Rinaldi, C. (1998). Projected curriculum constructed through documentation—Progettazione. In C. Edwards, L. Gandini, G. Forman (Eds.), *The hundred languages of children: The Reggio Emilia approach* (pp. 113–125). Norwood, NJ: Ablex.

Starting small: Teaching tolerance in preschool and the early grades. (1997). The Teaching Tolerance Project: Southern Poverty Law Center, New York.

REFERENCES

Hill, L., Wells, K., & Fu, V. (1999). *The amiable school project.* Unpublished manuscript, Virginia Tech, Blacksburg, Virginia.

Malaguzzi L. (1998). History, ideas, and basic philosophy. In C. Edwards, L. Gandini, & G. Forman (Eds.), *The hundred languages of children: The Reggio Emilia approach—advanced reflections* (pp. 63–65). Greenwich, CT: Ablex.

Primavera, A. (2002). *The life of a website: An inquiry into parent–teacher communication.* Unpublished master's thesis, Virginia Tech, Blacksburg, Virginia.

Rinaldi, C. (1998). Projected curriculum construction through documentation—Progettazione. In C. Edwards, L. Gandini, & G. Forman, (Eds.), *The hundred languages of children: The Reggio Emilia approach—advanced reflections* (p. 114). Greenwich, CT: Ablex.

The Tools of Teaching and Learning
Life in the Classroom

In this final section, we bring the reader directly into our classrooms by describing in detail the means by which curriculum can be negotiated between teacher and child. Joyful, challenging, and inspiring learning is the goal of this brand of teaching, as is the emphasis on children growing and developing as inquiring thinkers. We share several stories to express our belief that community projects can be the impetus for multiple styles of teaching and learning. Finally, four teachers who work in a public school system with a variety of age groups respond to interview questions that challenge them to elaborate on how this brand of teaching and learning can be successful in settings beyond those devoted to the youngest of learners.

Reflection
Illuminating the uniqueness of each day.
Bringing out the many colors of life.
Reminding us how much there is to miss.
Julie Bryan, early childhood student teacher

9

NEGOTIATING THE CURRICULUM
"The Long Story"*

They became aware of the connectedness of all the parts of the system: space, materials, organization, collaboration among colleagues, and participation by parents. They realized how everything contributes to making it possible to really listen to children and to start to work in a truly different way.

Gandini, 1997, p. x

Life in the Classroom: An Example of One Long Story

The Revolving Door project occurred at the Virginia Tech Child Development Lab School during the 1997–98 school year in our Maroon Room, which is the learning community comprising sixteen four- to five-year-old children, one professional early childhood teacher, one graduate student teacher, and several undergraduate teaching assistants. In addition, the curriculum coordinator (studio teacher) participated in the project, as did many parents, grandparents, and community resource folks.

Although the main emphasis of the project occurred during this school year, it is important to set the context of the experience because the project did not occur in isolation, but rather was influenced greatly by personalities, interests, parallel experiences, time of year, the talents and skills within the group, and our own level of understanding regarding the process of a project.

---

*Author's note: "The Long Story," Malaguzzi, L. (1992). A message from Loris Malaguzzi [video]. (L. Gandini, Trans.). Amherst, MA: Performanetics. This chapter includes a "long story" that occurred in the Virginia Tech Child Development Lab School. The author of the chapter, Lynn Hill, served as the curriculum coordinator and studio teacher during the course of the project. Kelly Wells was the master teacher for the classroom in which the project originated. Both of these protagonists' voices will be heard throughout the chapter, as well as the voices of a parent and of the children who were involved. Chapter subheadings are used to delineate each voice.

Any time the story of a project is told, it is important to understand that there are multiple perspectives from which the story might be told. We were keenly aware of this when we went to document the project for the hallway in our school. How do you put on a few panel boards all that transpires during the course of a project like this one? Or, in knowing and realizing that there is no way to tell everything, how do you choose which pieces to tell and which to hold back? For this retelling of the story, we hope to be successful in sharing the multiple voices of the protagonists. You will hear from the teacher, the mother, the studio teacher, and the children.

This chapter takes you on your very own "long story." We review the impetus of long-term relationships and then explore the process as it unfolds in a preschool classroom over time.

QUESTIONS TO BE CONSIDERED

- How does a teacher make a decision about the course of the curriculum in his or her classroom?
- How does the teacher ensure that all children are engaged and challenged during project work?
- What role can families play in this brand of curriculum?
- Define *project dissonance* and discuss its benefits.
- Why are group meetings important aspects of the development of a classroom community?
- How do you feel about sharing (negotiating) the curriculum with other teachers and with the children?
- How might this style of thinking and learning be successful in older grades as well?

Sometimes during the course of time spent together in school, an amazing phenomenon may occur. When all the pieces of the system of respectful education have been carefully attended to, as we have seen in the first three sections of this book (child, teacher, family), and when there is a "connectedness" (Cadwell, 1997, p. x) among the protagonists, the space, the materials, and the organization, the magic of a shared and sustained interest can blossom. The impetus for this shared interest may grow from the careful observation of the children at work, or it may occur because of a serendipitous moment; but suddenly it becomes obvious that a "big idea" (Oken-Wright & Gravett, 2002) seems to have taken on a life of its own in the school. Loris Malaguzzi referred to projects in the Reggio Emilia preschools as *long stories* (qtd. in Cadwell, 1997, p. 35). He believed that these stories should offer both familiarity and possibility in order to engage the children over time. Since then, other professionals have offered additional considerations.

Flexibility, spontaneity, fluidness, and trust are essential ingredients in a school as a project unfolds. Certainly there is a strong component of adult consideration and planning, but these plans must be seen as possibilities and "reconnaissance" (Edwards, Gandini, & Forman, 1998, p. 461) as opposed to strict time schedules and lessons. Respect for and allegiance to the child's suggestion and refinement of ideas are essential and add to the overall feeling of excitement and anticipation as the project takes on its own rhythms.

HOW DO PROJECTS BEGIN?

The fascinating long-term projects from the schools in Reggio Emilia have been documented in multiple ways and captured the attention of educators all over the world. It is instructive to review a few of the projects to determine the impetus and rationale for their development. In the *Amusement Park for Birds* (Forman & Gandini, 1994) the project began as the children in LaVilletta school studied photographs of playgrounds of U.S. schools and began to make comparisons to their own outdoor play spaces. When one child declared, "If our playground is boring for us, think about how the birds must feel," the project was launched. In other cases, a project might be the result of a shared dilemma when teachers and children join together to investigate solutions to a problem over time. In the delightful *Shoe and Meter* (Malaguzzi, Castagnetti, & Vecchi, 1997), a broken table must be replaced for the school. The children commit to assisting in the building of an exact replica of the injured table but first must invent a system for measurement. Together they contrive an innovative technique for calculation based on the fixed scale of one child's shoe. Another meaningful project is related in *To Make a Portrait of a Lion* (Commune di Reggio Emilia, 1987), in which the children revisit the stone lions in the town's piazza. A renewed interest in and deeper understanding of these almost taken-for-granted fixtures in the children's lives were the result when a wise teacher saw the possibility for joyful learning. Projects, therefore, can spring from several sources, including the observation of a child's interest, the desire to solve a problem, and a teacher's prediction of possibility based on an intimate knowledge of the children. The remainder of this chapter invites you to follow along as we carefully examine one long story that celebrates attention to a child's interest, a concern in the school, and the benefits of shared learning over time.

THE REVOLVING DOOR PROJECT

Lynn Sets the Stage

As an instructor for the Department of Family and Child Development, I had the responsibility and privilege of teaching the Curriculum and Program Planning course. This is a five-credit-hour class that requires students to work in the lab school for six hours each week. My job was to observe their work and provide feedback, support, and reflection on their development as teachers.

It was during my observation of my student teachers in the Toddler Room that I first noticed Christina. She was not quite two years old, and she was the child who played alone, always on the periphery of the group, rarely joining in with other children or with any group activities. She did not like to talk with strangers and at the beginning of the year was quiet and distant with the student teachers. Instead, she would sit for long periods with a stuffed animal in her lap, occasionally thumbing through a book. She seemed to prefer this.

Because the student teachers were learning about negotiating the curriculum and about allowing the child's interest to fuel their planning, they were stumped about how to plan for Christina. We decided that if we were having trouble finding an interest area for Christina, we probably weren't paying close enough attention to her. So we redoubled our efforts. What we noticed was that Christina had a favorite stuffed animal that she attached herself to as soon as she arrived at school. Some of the student teachers started to try to talk with her about her choice of "friends" and discovered that Christina had another favorite friend at home and that she was quite distressed that she was not allowed to bring him to school. Beethoven, her stuffed St. Bernard, was allowed to ride to school with her each morning, but she had to leave him in the car when she came inside. Because I was new to the lab school system and only working as an adjunct teacher, I was unaware that this rule was school imposed. The policy stated that there should be "no toys from home." The thinking behind the policy was that toys from home could be distractions for the children, preventing them from fully engaging in the activities prepared for them at school. In Christina's case, it seemed that perhaps she was not fully engaging with the activities at school because she did not have her important transitional object with her. After great debate, the school decided to relax its policy for Christina and allowed her to bring her precious Beethoven to school.

Having Beethoven with her each day seemed to give Christina a new sense of ease and comfort. She began to play with some of the other materials in the classroom, always incorporating Beethoven into the play. But still her relationships with the other children were distant. During this period, we began to form a more intimate relationship with Christina's mother.

The Parent's Perspective: Christina's Mom Shares Her Part of the Long Story

When Christina was two months old, her father was diagnosed with cancer and we were told that he had three to four months to live. Her father and I were immediately thrust into a medical environment in another state, and Christina and her brother were left at home. Christina lived with different relatives during that time, and I didn't see her sometimes for two to three weeks at a time. So that was very difficult, especially since she was a newborn. She was well taken care of, but she didn't have one person or reference point in her life. Her relatives loved her and took care of her physical needs, but she didn't have her mother with her all the time.

At the end of that four-month period and after my husband's death, I came home to be confronted with my father's illness. Once again, I was needed to assist.

It wasn't until Christina was almost two years old that we began to have some sense of a regular and consistent home life.

Christina started full time in the lab school when she was eight or nine months of age. She was a withdrawn and fearful baby—something more than separation anxiety. After I dropped her off, I would watch through the observation windows, and she would separate herself from everyone else. She had her little stuffed animals. She had two special dogs at different times in her life, and anyone who knew Christina also knew Beethoven and Patch—they were part of the family. But at that time, it was policy that kids weren't supposed to bring toys from home. I don't know if it was an exception or if the policy got changed, but about the time that she was two she was able to bring her dog to school. This was a good thing because in retrospect, had that been taken away from her too, it would have been even more traumatic than everything she was already experiencing at home. This would have been one more loss.

So Beethoven and Patch were her best little friends, and when she'd come to lab school she would usually detach herself from the rest of the group and she'd sit with her animal friends and she'd watch. She just wasn't comfortable with a large group, and I don't think she knew how to join in.

Lynn Continues: Christina Finds Her Own Language

We watched carefully that year as Christina's expertise at block building grew and flourished. She would work for long periods on a structure. And then we noticed something interesting about most of her structures. They were usually enclosures of some kind. We knew that the building of block enclosures is a typical stage in block development, but what Christina seemed to be doing was inserting herself and Beethoven into the enclosure and from that vantage point safely observing the rest of the activities going on in the classroom.

> **THINK ABOUT IT**
>
> What could you as a teacher do to strengthen this child's social and emotional perspective?
>
> How would you handle school policies that conflict with your own sense of what is best for the children?

Toward the end of that year, the children in the older classroom became highly involved in the project of building an outdoor playground structure for their pet rabbit. When the time came to put their planned playground structure together, many of the younger children participated in the painting and nailing and preparation. Christina was drawn to this activity and showed a decided interest in the construction and maybe especially the design of the structure—which, as it turned out, was an enclosure similar to the ones she had been building in the classroom for over a year.

School ended for that year, and during the summer Kelly Wells was hired as our first professional early childhood teacher at the lab school. Her expertise was in classroom community building, and she began immediately to incorporate Christina and Patch into the classroom.

Careful observation of Christina's play style indicated her preference for solitary play.

More detailed analysis of her play revealed her repetitive interest in "enclosures."

Kelly's Perspective

I already knew a little about Christina from talking to both her previous teacher and Lynn. I first met Christina during the the home visit. Home visits are important for several reasons. It is the first opportunity to meet the child and to learn more about him or her in the context of the family. There is a strong belief in early childhood education that families are the experts on their children, and the family is an important source of information that enables us to be better teachers for their children. The visits are the beginning of collaborative partnerships with families. (See Chapters 7 and 8 for more details on the importance of family partnerships.) At that time, Christina introduced me to her stuffed animals. It was immediately clear to me that these animals were very important to Christina, in particular Beethoven's friend Patch, who you see pictured here. It was Patch who began coming to school with Christina on a regular basis.

I remember when I took this picture of Christina and Patch. Christina often refused to pose for the camera, but on this particular day she was willing as long as Patch could be in the picture too. I offered the photo to Christina, who at my suggestion painted a self-portrait. Christina identified herself on the right and Patch on the left. Notice that there are more details such as eyes, a nose, and a mouth for Patch than there are for Christina herself. At this point, I seemed to know more about Patch than I did about Christina.

Not long into the year it was obvious that Patch was becoming a valuable part of the classroom community. A variety of mediums were always available for the children to explore and as a means for representing their ideas if they chose. One day several of the children used materials available to them to create a birthday cake and presents for Patch's birthday. It seemed at this point as though Christina and Patch were achieving a strong position in the classroom community.

Christina still often played by herself and still often built enclosed structures. But as we observed Christina

This picture indicates a typical facial expression from Christina while she was at school.

Think about It: What does Christina's painting of herself and her stuffed animal tell you?

closely, we noticed that she was slowly beginning to open up. And one day she opened up her enclosed block structure and invited Alanah to join her inside. This was a wonderful moment and one that we definitely wanted to make the most of.

As Christina's teacher, I wanted this to be an opportunity for her to begin strengthening her relationships with others by working collaboratively with them. So, recognizing the power of working with small groups, I brought Christina and Alanah into a discussion with me. Together we developed a plan for a building that naturally evolved into a house especially for Patch. This house would feature a number of things, including a swirly slide, an experiment room (to do experiments that would gross out other dogs but not Patch's friends), and trees inside so that Patch could go the bathroom (see the list below developed by the children).

A secret passage way
A front door
A back door
A swirly slide for the secret door
An experiment room (to do experiments that will gross
other dogs, but not Patch's friends.)

> *Lights*
> *11 Windows*
> *A car*
> *A wheel chair ramp*
> *An elevator*
> *A small door for the incoming mice*
> *A computer room*
> *A second floor for a bedroom*
> *Trees inside so that Patch can go to the bathroom*
> *Stairs*
> *and it will be white*

THINK ABOUT IT

When should a teacher offer a provocation for the next steps in a project?
When should the teacher hold back and let the children lead the way?

Commentary

When a teacher can see herself or himself as a coresearcher with the children, this shift in attitude can open the door to multiple possibilities. Careful consideration of next steps and the gentle pitch of an idea are part of the craft of teaching during project work. After listening well, observing, scribing, archiving, and analyzing the previous work, the teacher might suggest a possible next step. This teacher direction might then be negotiated and adjusted in collaboration with the children until each feels a sense of shared interest, challenge, and reason to continue with the investigation. This "dance" between members of the investigating group will be successful if they have previously achieved a strong relationship that is characterized by intersubjectivity. (See Chapter 3 for more details on this experience.)

In this case, Kelly recognized that Christina was moving into new territory in her friendship with Alanah. Seeking to support this exciting but fragile new stage in Christina's social development, Kelly proposed a means by which the girls might deepen their commitment to each other. Kelly suggested that they work together to plan a house for Patch, and thus they were charged with a task that was both challenging and cementing. At this point, the project began to develop, and multiple purposes and tasks began to become evident.

Kelly Continues

At this point in the year, the children were getting used to the idea of drawing their ideas and developing a plan before actually implementing them. This is a picture of the outside of the house that Christina and Alanah had decided would be all white. Early Childhood educators place a strong importance on *temporary documentation* in the classroom; it reflects and continues to inspire the children's work and keeps parents informed about the work in the classroom, to name just a few benefits.

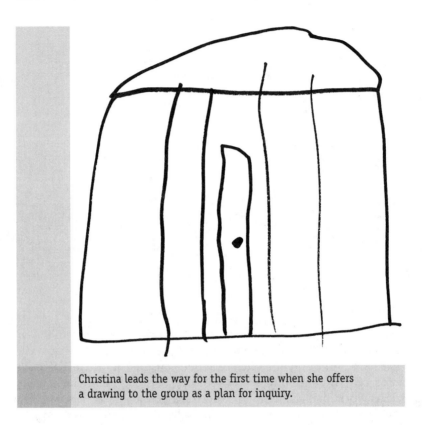

Christina leads the way for the first time when she offers a drawing to the group as a plan for inquiry.

THINK ABOUT IT

What is the purpose of temporary documentation in the classroom for the teachers, the children, the families, and the school?

Commentary

As the work in the classroom ebbs and flows, it is important to keep track of the sounds and rhythms in order to document the processes for all members of the community. Meaningful photographs that depict the important moments in the course of a project can be coupled with transcriptions of the children's conversations and debates. When work samples are added, the result begins to represent the essence of the actual experiences. Further, when these documents can be gathered and displayed almost immediately, this temporary documentation can be extremely beneficial to the community. Recent technological advances now make it possible to digitally photograph or videograph a classroom episode for almost immediate use by the community. Katz and Chard (1996) and Goldhaber, Smith, and Sortino

(1997) have written extensively on the benefits of this interesting process. (See Chapter 10 for a lengthy discussion on this topic.)

Kelly Continues

Christina and Alanah had brainstormed ideas and drawn plans, but I could tell that they were beginning to feel frustrated with the materials they had been using. They needed some new spark to keep them going. I saw a lot of potential, and I just didn't want it to drop. At this point, we also realized that it was time for the teachers to take part in the dance and initiate a new direction for the curriculum.

So I offered them a new medium and a new venue. I presented them with the idea of using LEGOS on the porch (the porch is an extension of our classroom that we share with the adult day services next door). This was just what they needed, and Christina and Alanah immediately got started.

And now I was starting to notice that a few of the other children were beginning to show some interest in Christina and Alanah's work. The children worked for several days on Patch's house. Patch was always close by so that they could refer to his size and build everything to scale.

Commentary

Another way in which the children were drawn into the project was through group meetings. Group meetings are an important aspect of our curriculum. They allow the children to reflect on their thinking and to inform the group about ongoing projects and daily happenings. Group meetings are held each day and offer the children an opportunity to gather together, participate in a shared ritual, carefully review the work in the classroom, and make plans for the next steps. We have found these meetings to be quite meaningful for the entire classroom community for several reasons.

> **THINK ABOUT IT**
>
> What is the purpose of group meetings? For the children, the teachers, the project?

Communication.   As Christina began to share the story of building a house for Patch with the rest of the class, it was obvious that several developmental leaps were occurring. First, her descriptive language skills were greatly enhanced as she sought to find just the right words and just the right emphasis that would communicate the project. In addition, Christina's self-confidence got a boost as she took note of the obvious interest on the faces of her friends. Other children in the classroom asked many serious questions about the work and in the process of questioning allowed the communication between the main protagonists and the rest of the community to deepen.

A Critical Review of the Documentation.   As the drawings, models, and description of the plans are shared with the peer group, it is not unusual for some of the children to offer critical comments. Finding gentle and considerate ways to critique one another's work, then, can become one of the goals for these meetings. Careful coaching about making productive comments is easily modeled on the adult level, as is the fine art of accepting input from others. These basic skills of collaborative learning and democratic participation are crucial to the life of a true community of learners.

Peripheral Interests Are Engendered.   You will remember that as this project began to take shape, Kelly purposefully and thoughtfully invited two children whom she perceived as having complementary styles to participate. This invitation is never meant to be exclusionary, but rather is offered in the spirit of respect for the natural interests of the main protagonists and in an effort to begin the work at some starting point. What often subsequently happens is that additional children in the classroom find a component of the project that holds a special interest for them. Spin-off projects that may or may not directly relate to the original idea are not uncommon. The process of reporting on the progress of a project at the group meeting is often the impetus for the peripheral interests. In addition, it must be added that there are also great educational and developmental benefits for the child who chooses to *observe* the project as opposed to participating at a more intimate level.

Community Ownership Is Established.   We have found the experience of the group meeting to be one that all members of the classroom look forward to with great anticipation. I have often overheard a child excitedly announce to a friend her intention of sharing a recent accomplishment or idea at the group meeting. The children very obviously feel validated by the opportunity to have a forum for sharing their work, their ideas, and their questions. As time passes and as the experience of the group meeting becomes a classroom ritual, the children come to feel a deep sense of community with the other members of their group. Individual expertise is celebrated in a way that allows children to see themselves as making a meaningful contribution to the fabric of the group. Personalities are revealed during these intimate meetings, and children begin to understand what it means to participate in a respectful way in a group setting.

Even if all of the children in the group are not actively involved in the life of the project being discussed at the group meeting, because there is an established sense of community there is a shared ownership of and pride in the experience.

An Inspiration for Continued and Sustained Work.   Finally, the group meeting seems to breathe a constant life into project work. Keeping the work continually visible to the group and allowing for input from various sources fuels the experience and keeps it moving forward.

Kelly Describes a Setback

So now these children have worked for many days. If you remember, the porch is a space we share with others. One day a graduate student from another department was conducting an activity during a time the children were not present. The next day we returned to the lab school to find that the house had been destroyed. I was furious! The graduate student had wanted to move the house to another location so she would have the space to conduct her own project, but in doing so she had completely demolished it. The house was not in a few pieces that could be easily put back together; it was in a million pieces and completely destroyed. I just kept thinking, What is this person's image of the child?

Well, this was not okay! What do I do as these children's teacher? I knew that I had to take some initiative. I could tell that the children were upset and disappointed, but I could also sense that this problem seemed so insurmountable that they would probably drop the entire project and end up feeling disempowered. I wanted them to feel empowered to express their feelings of anger to this grown-up. So Christina, Alanah, and a few others went to the office and typed a letter to the graduate student. This was empowering, but where did we go from here? Thank goodness we had documented the process up until that point. We got out all the original lists of ideas and the children's drawings and photos and moved the building process back into the classroom. Then we got started again.

> ### THINK ABOUT IT
>
> How would you as a teacher have handled this setback in the project?
>
> What are the positive ramifications of project dissonance?

Piaget's Theory of Cognitive Dissonance

Jean Piaget (1973) has contributed the concept of *cognitive dissonance,* which seems quite evident at this stage in the project. The destruction of the house and the children's disappointment certainly could have spelled the end of the effort. However, with the support of their teacher, the children found a way to use the disequilibrium they were feeling to launch themselves into the next phase of their work. Our friends and colleagues in Reggio Emilia have often talked about the importance of conflict in the transformation of relationships: "The process of negotiating through the maze of opposition and of reformulating an initial premise are part of the processes of assimilation and accommodation" (Rinaldi, 1998, p. 115). Certainly, the fact that this small group of children experienced this setback together contributed to their sense of themselves as a group. Rallying around the problem together and working out new ways of negotiating the roadblock caused, in the end, a stronger and more committed effort to be born. We learned that problems and setbacks need not be aspects to fear, but rather may be the impetus for new learning.

Kelly Assists the Children with the Process of Rebuilding

As the children embarked on the rebuilding of Patch's house, they seemed more open to modification of the original plans. The process of rebuilding allowed additional ideas to spring forth and a new direction for the project. One day they found

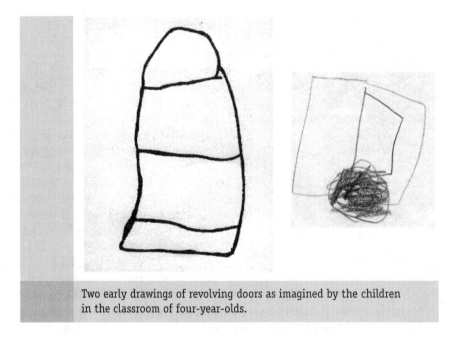

Two early drawings of revolving doors as imagined by the children in the classroom of four-year-olds.

a little revolving door piece, and we just began talking about it. What questions could we teachers ask the children to provoke their thinking? Some children had had experiences with revolving doors and others were less knowledgeable. Then a student teacher said, "Hey! There is a revolving door in the new building across the street!" Now I was getting excited, and soon a small group of children planned a trip to see this revolving door. Before we left, we had a discussion about revolving doors. I wanted to encourage the children to think of themselves as researchers. I asked them to consider what the door looked like and how it might work. They began to develop their own theories and to draw pictures to represent their ideas.

We then began our research. Viewing teachers and children as collaborators in research and remembering above all else to trust the process, we headed off to visit the door. When we arrived at the door, the children instantly inserted themselves into the panels and began their research by thoroughly experiencing the sensation of revolving. They went around, and around, and around. . . .

We visited the door several times. This took a great amount of trust on the teacher's part. We kept asking ourselves if this was the best direction to take things. Each time, the children took their clipboards with them so that they could draw again and refine their original drawings, but they were visibly happiest when they were simply revolving in the door. I kept asking myself, Is this really research, or frivolous play? I was soon to find out.

When I came back from our outing to the revolving door, I was overwhelmed with enthusiasm. I knew that the energy and enthusiasm for the experience that I had just witnessed in the children needed to be capitalized on. It was at this point that I brought Christina's story to Lynn. We regularly collaborated on the processes

Research!

within the classroom and we immediately knew that the children's interest and enthusiasm for the revolving door had that special potential and possibility for providing a meaningful learning opportunity for the group. We weren't sure where the project was going to go from here. We just had to trust and to believe that if you listen very carefully and have a great amount of trust in yourself as a teacher and in children to take control of their own learning, the project will move forward.

Commentary: Moving Forward

Planning, envisioning, and negotiating a meaningful curriculum requires a great deal of time and commitment to the process. On careful review of the ongoing documentation and based on an intimate knowledge of the individual children and their interests, rights, theories, and relationships with one another, the adults in the setting then begin to hypothesize the next steps. Carlina Rinaldi (1998) describes this experience as *progettazione* and suggests:

> Discuss fully all the possible ways that the project could be anticipated to evolve, considering the likely ideas, hypotheses, and choices of children and the direction they may take. By so doing, [the teachers] prepare themselves for all the subsequent stages of the project, while leaving ample space for changes, for the unexpected, and for moments of stasis and digression. (p. 118)

I remember hearing Carlina expound on this concept during a study tour to Reggio Emilia (in the winter of 1994). She told our small group that we must always be open to the ideas and elaborations coming from the children. For every one-hundred ideas an adult might have, the children would have two-hundred. And then, providing a metaphor I will never forget, she suggested that as teachers, we "should hold in our hands a compass rather than a fixed train schedule." This beautiful image of flexibility and guidance as opposed to control and directiveness was what we were aiming for as our project began to gain momentum.

Life in the Classroom: The Studio Teacher Joins the Project: Lynn's Role

We weren't really certain about what to do and where to go with this interest in the door. A small pedagogical team made up of the teacher (Kelly), our pedagogical co-ordinator (Vickie Fu), and the studio teacher/curriculum coordinator (Lynn) met. We asked ourselves:

- What are these children interested in?
- What aspects might have longevity and possibility for sustained interest?
- What does Christina need from us now?

We brainstormed possibilities that included more house planning and model building. We thought about a possible investigation of doors on campus. We considered the concept of revolution and how it related to Christina's development. And finally we felt ready to ask the children for their ideas. The next day a small committee of children came to the studio to discuss their interests.

THINK ABOUT IT

What are the benefits of offering the children the opportunity for small-group meetings?

Are you as a teacher ready to give up some of the control of the daily curriculum in order to give the children the opportunity to thrive and learn in this way?

Commentary

Before the children come into the studio for a conversation, I usually try to prepare some appropriate questions in the hope that I'll be able to tap into their current theories, concerns, questions, and enthusiasm. However, I don't want the children to feel as though I am questioning from a superior position, so having a relaxed and easygoing attitude about the experience is crucial.

Considering how to capture the conversation is also worth some advance planning. Audiotaping has worked well for us, especially if the transcriber is also a member of the conversation. The children in our school have taken great interest in rewinding and replaying and "remembering what we said" during the course of the conversation. One drawback with audiotape is that you miss out on all the subtle, nonverbal forms of communication. A video camera can capture the facial expressions and body language that an audiotape would miss. Transcribing a videotape can be a cumbersome process, however, with lots of time spent at the TV and VCR. Some people are really good at simply jotting down notes as they take part in the banter with the children. Each technique has its advantages and its drawbacks, so when possible, it is best to use multiple forms of data collection in order to capture the essence of the experience.

Inviting children who have a shared interest in the next phase of the investigation is also important. Small groups of four or five children seem to allow for a positive dynamic to occur within the group. Practicing respectful questioning and listening skills is an important aspect for both the children and the adults who participate in the small group.

These intimate conversations can be delightful opportunities to hear the children's musings and to participate together in imagining what might come next. Sometimes during the course of these moments together, a very special essence of shared affection, shared wonder, and shared humor can be almost palpable. This is the point at which intersubjectivity has been achieved. From this status of relationship can come great things.

Lynn's Story Continues

And so five children made their way to the studio that day. They brought with them their previous drawings of Patch's house, the letter they had written to the graduate student after the problem on the porch, and their most recent sketches of the revolving door from across the street. I began by asking them to fill me in on all they had been working on lately. The children launched into a wonderful description of their work in and out of the classroom, from feeding the pet fish, to some early reading, to trips to the duck pond. I soon realized that my initial question was a bit broad, so during an ebb in the conversation, I asked if they could focus for a moment on their work on Patch's house. Christina took the lead here, although she had been one of the quieter members of the group up to this point. She pulled out the documents and began to use them to tell the story of their efforts to build a house for Patch. When she came to the part in the story about how the house was ruined, the other children jumped in with their own feelings about that particular experience. Still smarting for this injustice, they angrily expressed themselves. "So," I said, "are you here today because you want me to help you rebuild the house?"

"Well, maybe," said Christina, "but actually we've gotten interested in building a revolving door."

"Wow! Help me understand what you want to do."

"Well, we just want to build, you know, we've been making all these plans on paper and now we just want to build," said Christina.

"OK, where do we start?" I responded.

At this point, the children all talked in a hurry with their many, many ideas. Carlina's version of children's two-hundred ideas was coming true right in front of me. I could tell that it would take quite some time to sift through all the possibilities, and I wondered if the children would remain engaged for the time it might take to fully explore all their ideas. So I suggested that we make a list of all their great ideas. I could tell that this suggestion was irritating to Christina because she wanted to "just build it" and didn't want to get sidetracked with any more talking. The other children, however, seemed excited about the opportunity to share their ideas and to see them written on the large paper in the studio.

After we generated an extensive list with many diverse suggestions for our next steps, the children then reviewed the list and narrowed down their choices. Finally, they decided on Christina's original suggestion, which was to build a revolving door. Later, as I reviewed this audiotaped conversation, it occurred to me that the children had adopted an unspoken allegiance to Christina and to her ownership of this project. Although they were anxious to share some individual ideas, they were also quite obviously respectful of Christina's feelings about the project. Although we had never had a group conversation about Christina's emotional turmoil, the children seemed to sense it and in their own gentle ways were willing to adjust their personal needs to assist with her healing process. I was in awe of their generosity.

Next, we decided we needed to choose a drawing that would serve as our plan for building the door. We spread all the drawings out on the floor and talked about each one. Some offered more detail, some offered more three-dimensionality, and some offered more creative emphasis. The final drawing in this series is the one the children chose to work from. (It was also interesting that at this point some children began to refer to this drawing as "our directions.")

We were finally ready to begin the physical work, and Christina was thrilled. We talked about materials and affordances and began to look through the studio for parts that might work.

THINK ABOUT IT

What are nontraditional materials and their affordances?
How can these valuable materials be introduced to the classroom?

Three more detailed and knowledgeable drawings of a revolving door. These drawings occurred after prolonged thought, research, and inquiry.

Commentary

Classrooms and studio spaces can be fascinating places in which to create and represent when they are filled with nontraditional materials. These unusual specimens are eclectic. Bins and tubs filled with materials made of plastic, metal, wood, mylar, fabric, wire, and paper can be organized for the children's use. We collect these materials from businesses and industries in our local community. The families in our school also supply us with interesting "beautiful stuff" (Topal & Gandini, 1999) from their own homes and offices. Overruns, punchouts, rejects, and cast-off pieces are captured before being sent to landfills and are channeled into our schools. These materials then become nontraditional learning materials for schools, studios, and homes. We have found that when children are confronted with these "materials without a past," they are naturally drawn to their open-ended quality and enhanced creativity is the result. In addition, the use of these materials fosters problem solving, cooperation, team building, and even a greater sense of self. One additional benefit of using these unusual materials cannot be overstated: When children have the opportunity to experience and appreciate nontraditional ways of thinking at a young age, they are less likely to be biased and prejudiced as adults (Mayesky, 1995). We believe that the use of diverse materials and the resulting comfort level with "the unusual" promotes an appreciation for that which is different.

George Forman (1994) has offered another consideration when using materials to represent ideas and concepts. He suggests that the physical and emotional properties of certain materials make them more or less likely to represent in a satisfying way. "An affordance is the relationship between the transformable properties of a medium and the child's desire to use that property to make symbols" (p. 42). So, for instance, when a group of children in the studio wanted to represent "ice cream land," we talked first of all the physical and emotional qualities of this image and then began to put our hands on some of the materials. A process of suggesting and rejecting materials ensued until the group hit on a satisfying "representer" of their concept. In this case, they chose tiny, clear plastic beakers, which they filled with rolled-up pieces of colored tissue paper. Later, as their understanding of *media literacy* grew and as their plans became more elaborate, they branched out and employed additional materials to represent their growing knowledge.

The Home–School Connection

I remember Christina coming home and talking about a project she was working on at school. She didn't necessarily mention that it was a revolving door project, but she was most excited about the studio. She said that it was a wonderful room with shelves and lots of things, and you could pick out whatever you wanted to do. I remember that she told me that you had to have a plan and that you could get help from Lynn on working through your plan and starting on your project.

I think that she was most excited about being able to plan and create. She loved gathering everything together and getting all the plans on paper. I think that the studio and the gathering of materials was the most exciting part for Christina.

Back to Creating in the Studio

The children chose a red cardboard pole for the center pole, three large pieces of foam core for the door, and colored cellophane for the see-through quality of the door. They also knew that each door needed a handle, so they opted to duct-tape smaller pieces of the red cardboard pole to each door as a handle.

The building process took about a week; the children came to the studio each day for some part of the day. Christina and Alanah were always in attendance, and sometimes other children came along as well. It was during this stage of the work that Christina began to volunteer to share some of the details of the building project with the group during group meeting. This was indeed a milestone for our young friend.

After the week of building was over, the kids showed off their replica, first to their friends at group time and then to the other classrooms. Finally, they propped up the door in the hallway, and together we fashioned some documentation that would describe to the families just what it was and how the children had made it. At this stage in the work, I noticed a change in the children's attitude. They did not seem as anxious to come to the studio to work with me and they seemed less enamored with their final product. I felt that in some way the product was lacking for them or that perhaps this project had just run its course. I decided to meet with them one last time to debrief and to review the project together. Once again the group joined me in the studio. This time Kelly came along; she had gathered together all of the documentation from the project. We spread all of this on the floor and began to talk about our process as we organized the data in a chronological way. When we came to the end of the long story, Christina appeared sullen.

> **THINK ABOUT IT**
>
> What are the benefits of teacher collaboration?

"What's up?" I asked her. "Why are you so quiet?"

"We thought it was gonna really go around by itself," she said.

"We forgot to put a floor on it; that's why it won't go by itself," offered Alanah.

"And its not big enough, that's why," added Christina.

Kelly and I looked at each other at this moment of reckoning. Finally, it dawned on us that they had been expecting their own revolving door to be more similar to the one across the street—in both size and function. We didn't want to disappoint them, but we were both stumped as to how to help them accomplish their dreams.

Commentary

It seems important at this stage in the long story to comment on the special relationship in this case between the studio teacher and the classroom teacher. These two professionals have been able to achieve a true sense of community and shared trust without which this project could not have evolved as it did.

Thomas Sergiovanni (1992) has written extensively on the topic of school community. His three-part definition is worth mentioning here because it seems well represented in the relationship between Kelly and Lynn. His definition of community is "relationships of people who work in the same place (community of place), feel a sense of belonging and obligation to one another (community of friendship) and are committed to a common faith or values (community of mind)" (p. 63). Establishing such a strong foundation is essential in collaborative relationships. Next, a sense of trust must exist between and among the teachers. When each person makes the child the focus of her or his work, then individual expertise can be devoted to a mutual goal. This status requires a deep intersubjectivity in which the adults know and understand one another well enough to both challenge and complement one another. In this kind of relationship there is a willingness to be spontaneous together and a willingness to learn from one another. (See Chapter 11 for a more detailed account of the concept of community building.)

> **THINK ABOUT IT**
>
> What are the opportunities associated with scaffolding as a teaching–learning tool?
>
> How does the teacher achieve this important status with his or her students?

Vygotsky's concept of the *zone of proximal development* (1978) is embraced by social constructivists like our friends and colleagues from Reggio Emilia. They have helped us understand the dance that transpires between teacher and student as they negotiate the experience of learning together. Finding the "pitch" level is the work of the teacher. With the goal of neither frustrating nor boring the child, the teacher must find the individual challenge level that will allow the child to take the next steps in the learning process.

At this point in the project, the children were telling us that they wanted to build a more elaborate representation of the revolving door. Certainly, they had learned quite a bit about media literacy, about drawing to learn, about the size and function of doors, and about measurement and calculation during the course of this experience—*and the possibility for an even deeper understanding seemed palpable.* However, for us the greatest achievement had been Christina's enormous social and emotional gains. With this "big idea" in mind, then, our pedagogical team met once more. Using our respectful knowledge of the child as a guide, we planned to continue to support Christina's emotional development by endorsing this group project.

Where Do We Go from Here?

Kelly and I met with Vickie to talk about this turn of events. We considered many aspects of the project to date in trying to decide where to go from here. First and foremost, we were thrilled with the way Christina had blossomed during the course of this work. She had attained a new status in the classroom, and her expertise in and talents for planning, drawing, and constructing were widely known and valued by her peer group. She had also surprised and delighted us with her new leadership skills and her abilities to plot a course for the project and delegate responsibilities to her new friends. And then we needed to consider the issue of time. Unfortunately, it was already mid-April, and our school would end for the year during the first week of May. If we were going to do something elaborate, which was what the kids were proposing, we were going to have to do it quickly and we were going to have to get some help. Although we had loads of other responsibilities that came with the end of the year, we knew we would kick ourselves later if we failed to take advantage of this great opportunity that had fallen into our laps, so we took the leap.

We told the kids that we would help them create their dream of a "real revolving door" but that they were going to have to work really hard to accomplish it by the end of the year. There was no problem with the level of their commitment or enthusiasm.

For this segment of the project, we led the children a bit more than we typically like to do. But because our immediate emphasis was on creating an opportunity for Christina and her friends to have this group experience, we felt that in this case we could justify a shift from our more typical style of a slower, more negotiated curriculum.

First the children chose a location for the door—right outside their classroom, of course. Then they began to think about how to build it in order to make plans for materials and dimensions. One of the most heated debates of the project occurred at this point. Christina could not understand what actually made the door move. She was really trying to think about the engineering of the door, and in her mind she was certain that the three-paneled door must be attached somehow to the floor and that when you stepped onto the floor you were automatically propelled around. Articulating this theory to her friends proved to be quite frustrating for her. But Alanah hung in there with her and gave her the support (peer scaffolding) she needed to get her over this next bump in the road.

Here is a brief segment of the transcribed conversation about "how the door works":

Christina: If the *floor* doesn't move, what makes the *door* move?

Alanah: You just push it and it moves.

Christina: If you push it . . . it wouldn't move if you didn't push it . . . but what *makes* it move?

Alanah: Nothing moves really . . . only when the people push it it goes around.

Christina: But what *makes* it move when the people push it?

Alanah: Well, the door *can* move, you just push it and it will move. You know how, Christina.

Christina: But if you push it it has to go around (getting irritated).

Alanah: It *does* go around.

Christina: (angrily) *That's what I'm trying to figure out! If you push it the other way it might break! And how are we going to make the floor move?*

Alanah: (sweetly) I think that our door should look real pretty. Do you think we should decorate it or something?

Christina: *I just want to get building!*

Lynn: Would you girls be interested in one more trip across the street to the revolving door to try to look carefully at how that door works? Would that help you to feel better?

Christina and Alanah: Yea!!!

After this heated debate, I wondered if the engineering was too difficult a concept. This was hard work; they weren't just thinking about how the door "looked" anymore. Now they were trying to understand something much deeper—how the door "worked." But they stuck with the problem and hurried off with their clipboards and a student teacher on another reconnaissance mission. About twenty minutes later, they came rushing into the studio yelling, "Its not the floor that moves, it's the door!" And with that piece of wisdom to guide them, they set about drawing new and improved plans. Together we chose our best interpretation of the door. Then we did some measuring of the space. Spinning around with the measuring tape to get the width of the door figured out, Alanah and Christina created a human revolving door and learned about teamwork and spatial relationships at the same time.

When the plan was finally complete, we met with the carpenter friend who had helped us with the rabbit playground the year before; we discussed our hopes and dreams for this door. We gave him our plan, and he promised to bring us a "kit" with all pieces cut to proportion and ready to be assembled by our community.

When the day arrived for the assembling of the door, we had quite a turnout. Parents and grandparents had been keeping up with the project by means of our documentation, through conversations, and from the enthusiastic comments of their children.

Christina's Mother Comments on Projects

I think that this project gave Christina an opportunity to show what her interests were. By going to the studio and choosing materials and planning, she was given a sense of empowerment, and she was finally able to take charge of a portion of her life. And I think that the other kids, in seeing that, were drawn into the project too, and that helped her form some of the friendships that developed.

She loved the planning and the creating and the use of unusual materials, and that seemed to help her bridge that gap from being an observer to being a little more in control and having some of the other kids take an interest in being involved with her. The whole experience was a blessing for Christina and for her family, and we'll never forget it.

On another note, I've taken notice of how the school respectfully documents the process of exploration and investigation, and I've adopted this atti-

Assembling the door.

tude for myself. The revolving door project has a special chapter of its own in our family albums.

Assembling the Door

It took two days to assemble the entire door. The main pole had to be erected and attached to the ceiling and the floor. Christina and Alanah crawled up a ladder to remove a ceiling tile in order to determine a way to fasten the door to a secure anchor. The Plexiglas door panels had to be screwed into the main pole, and handles had to be painted and attached to the doors. The children used drills, hammers, wire, paint and a lot of perseverance and determination. We were all busy and excited because we could see our dream coming true before our very eyes. And finally we stood back and took a look at what we had accomplished together. The greatest satisfaction was not that we had a pretty impressive "real revolving door" in our hallway, but that Christina and Alanah together had managed to circumnavigate an emotional challenge. We were convinced that project work had greatly contributed to the development of all the children.

Enjoying the fruits of our labor!

SUMMARY

Benefits of Project Work: Social Constructivist Theory in Action

1. During the course of a project, teachers continually question their motives, their biases, and their abilities. In this way, a project requires an enormous amount of reflection and consequent action.
2. Projects allow children to identify their interests and their areas of expertise and give them opportunities to practice and refine the skills in the company of a supportive learning community.

3. Projects help families become involved and come to value the benefit of the process. They allow families the opportunity to make suggestions and meaningful contributions to the life in the school.

4. Projects can bring in outside community resources that make a school more visible in the community.

5. The early work of observing, collecting, analyzing, and reflecting on the work of the children ensures that no child is missed in the educational process.

CHRISTINA'S STORY CAN TEACH US

■ The importance of social and emotional security in a school: Until this most basic of needs is provided for, it is difficult to learn and grow.

■ That the quieter, less obvious children in the classroom can be important and powerful protagonists when given the opportunity.

■ That our schools need to rethink some policies and procedures and ensure that they are both developmentally appropriate and family-friendly.

■ The true meaning of a learning community.

A community is a safe place for learning and growing, a space that welcomes you fully, that sees you for who you are, that invites your participation, and that holds you gently while you explore."
Mara Sapon-Shevin (1995)

GETTING STARTED ACTIVITIES

1. What are the current interests of the children in your classroom?

2. Which ones have the potential for longevity, community, and learning?

3. Call a small-group meeting (a committee) to discuss the possibilities of the project.

4. Have the committee make a report to the larger group.

5. Keep all forms of documentation and make it available to the children, families, and school community.

RESOURCES

On the Web
www.ecrp.uiuc.edu/v3n2/index.html
    A site that offers early childhood research publications. A good site for publishing action research.
www.Erikson.edu
    A site that includes articles and resources related to early childhood education.
PROJECTS-L@LISTSERV.UIUC.EDU
    Project Approach web site
REGGIO-L@LISTSERV.UIUC.EDU
    Reggio Emilia web site

Books and Chapters on Caring, Community Research, and Learning in the Classroom

Alexander, T. M. (1987). *John Dewey's theory of art, experience, and nature: The horizons of feeling.* Albany: State University of New York Press.

Berk, L., & Winsler, A. (1995). *Scaffolding children's learning: Vygotsky and early childhood education.* Washington, DC: NAEYC.

Forman, G., & Fyfe, B. (1998). Negotiated learning through design, documentation and discourse. In C. Edwards, L. Gandini, & G. Forman (Eds.), *The hundred languages of children—advanced reflections.* Greenwich, CT. Ablex.

Mardell, B. (1999). *From basketball to the Beatles: In search of compelling early childhood curriculum.* Portsmouth, NH: Heinemann.

Noddings, N., & Witherell, C. (1991). *Stories lives tell: Narrative and dialogue in education.* New York: Teachers College Press.

Paley, V. (1990). *The boy who would be a helicopter: The uses of storytelling in the classroom.* Cambridge, MA: Harvard University Press.

Palmer, P. (1998). *The courage to teach: Exploring the inner landscape of a teacher's life.* San Francisco: Jossey-Bass.

Palsha, S. (2002). An outstanding education for all children: Learning from Reggio Emilia's approach to inclusion. In V. Fu, A. Stremmel, & L. Hill (Eds.), *Teaching and learning: Collaborative exploration of the Reggio Emilia approach.* Upper Saddle River, NJ: Merrill/Prentice-Hall.

Shafer, A. (2002). Ordinary moments, extraordinary possibilities. In V. Fu, A. Stremmel, & L. Hill (Eds.), *Teaching and learning: Collaborative exploration of the Reggio Emilia approach.* Upper Saddle River, NJ: Merrill/Prentice-Hall.

REFERENCES

Cadwell, L. (1997). *Bringing Reggio Emilia home: An innovative approach to early childhood education.* New York: Teachers College Press.

Commune di Reggio Emilia. (1987). *To make a portrait of a lion.* Reggio Emilia, Italy: Centro Documentazione Ricerca Educativa Nidi e Scuole dell'Infanzia.

Edwards, C., Gandini, L., & Forman, G. (Eds.). (1998). *The hundred languages of children: The Reggio Emilia approach—advanced reflections.* Greenwich, CT: Ablex.

Forman, G. (1994). Different media, different languages. In L. Katz & B. Cesarone (Eds.), *Reflections on the Reggio Emilia approach.* Urbana, IL: ERIC Clearinghouse.

Forman, G., & Gandini, L. (Prods.). (1994). *The amusement park for birds.* Amherst, MA: Performantics Press.

Gandini, L. (1997). Forward. In L. Cadwell, *Bringing Reggio Emilia Home* (p. x). NY: Teachers College Press.

Goldhaber, J., Smith, D., & Sortino, S. (1997) Observing, recording, understanding: The role of documentation in early childhood teacher education. In J. Hendricks (Ed.), *First steps to teaching the Reggio way.* Upper Saddle River, NJ: Merrill/Prentice-Hall.

Katz, L., & Chard, S. (1996). *The contribution of documentation to the quality of early childhood education.* Urbana, IL: ERIC Clearinghouse.

Malaguzzi, L., Castagnetti, M., & Vecchi, V. (1997). *Shoe and meter.* Reggio Emilia, Italy: Reggio Children.

Mayesky, M. (1995). *Creative activities for young children.* New York: Delmar.

Oken-Wright, P., & Gravett, M. (2002). Big ideas and the essence of intent. In V. Fu, A. Stremmel, & L. Hill (Eds), *Teaching and learning: Collaborative exploration of the Reggio Emilia approach.* Upper Saddle River, NJ: Merrill/Prentice-Hall.

Piaget, J. (1973). *To understand is to invent: The future of education.* NY: Grossman.

Rinaldi, C. (1998). Projected curriculum constructed through documentation—progettazione. An interview with Lella Gandini. In C. Edwards, L. Gandini, & G. Forman (Eds.), *The hundred languages of children: The Reggio Emilia approach—advanced reflections*. Greenwich, CT: Ablex.

Sapon-Shevin, M. (1995). Building a safe community for learning. In W. Ayers (Ed.), *To become a teacher: Making a difference in children's lives* (pp. 99–112). NY: Teachers College Press.

Sergiovanni, T. (1992). *Moral leadership: Getting to the heart of school improvement*. San Francisco: Jossey-Bass.

Topal, C., & Gandini, L. (1999). *Beautiful stuff*. Worcester, MA: Davis.

Vygotsky, L. S. (1978). *Mind in society: The development of higher psychological processes*. Cambridge, MA: Harvard University Press.

CHAPTER 10

THE USE OF DOCUMENTATION IN AN INQUIRY-BASED CLASSROOM

"Documentation is key to a practice which genuinely unites thought with action, belief with ritual, philosophy with pedagogy, and perhaps aesthetics with the mundane."

Lauren Lawson, 2000

I will never forget my first visit to the schools of Reggio Emilia, Italy. I was one of those very lucky early visitors who was a member of a twenty-person delegation led by Carlina Rinaldi. As I think back on that unforgettable experience, one thing stands out most profoundly. I was simply blown away by the documentation of the experiences of the children I saw in the schools and in the Hundred Languages of Children exhibit that was making its grand reopening during our visit to the city. As a future teacher-atelierista, I was enthralled by the content, aesthetics, and respect so evident in each piece of documentation I viewed. I began to cry as I realized that I had finally found what had been missing for me in early childhood education in the United States—a way to share the experiences from the school in a beautiful, thoughtful, and meaningful way with the members of the larger community. This chapter expands on those emotional and intellectual moments that happened for us in Reggio Emilia and how I and others have found ways to interpret this information in a U.S. context.

For many visitors to the schools in Reggio Emilia, one of the most evident differences from U.S. schools is the astonishing respect for capturing the essence of the child's experience. This chapter will elaborate on this profound way of thinking and special way of learning.

- What is a socially constructed curriculum?
- What is the cycle of inquiry and what role does it play in an inquiry-based classroom?
- What role does documentation play in an inquiry-based classroom?
- What are some of the questions teachers can ask themselves during the observation and interpretation phases of the cycle of inquiry?
- What would you include in a child's assessment portfolio?
- How can you manage documentation in a busy classroom?
- How can older children use documentation as a learning tool?

As you read in the first section of this book, the concept of a socially constructed curriculum requires a high regard and respect for the intimate experience of teaching and learning. It takes a skill in listening, in watching, in reflecting, in doing, and in repeating the process again and again. A disposition and habit of mind that is one of great curiosity and interest in what is possible to do together is essential, as is trust in the child to lead the way. When this process of working alongside a child to coconstruct knowledge and to participate in coresearch in the classroom occurs, then intersubjectivity can be achieved. Intersubjectivity allows the teacher and child to operate within the bubble of the zone of proximal development, where the challenge to learn and grow and transform is supported and exciting.

Achieving this intimate and necessary stance between teacher and child takes a strong commitment to the process. One tool that can assist in building the critical intersubjectivity is *documentation*. Viewed as "an act of love" (Rinaldi, 1997) and "an act of courage" (Goldhaber & Smith, 2001), documentation can be the supportive link to truly understanding the child's curiosities and to crafting a curriculum that is then meaningful and joyful. In this way, then, documentation can be seen as "a search for understanding" (Goldhaber & Smith, 2001). The process of coming to understand has been well described by Lella Gandini and Jeanne Goldhaber (2001) as a *cycle of inquiry* (see Chapters 1 and 2 for additional details). The spiraling cycle of inquiry includes framing early questions, observing, recording and collecting artifacts, organizing and analyzing the data, making early interpretations, reframing the questions, and responding to the new understanding (see Figure 10.1). This ongoing process repeats itself with increasing fever and pitch as the experience takes on the personalities and curiosities of those involved and as teacher and child and program evolve. Documentation becomes the powerful element that allows for this transformation to take place.

T H I N K   A B O U T   I T

What role does documentation play in the process of a socially constructed, inquiry-based education?

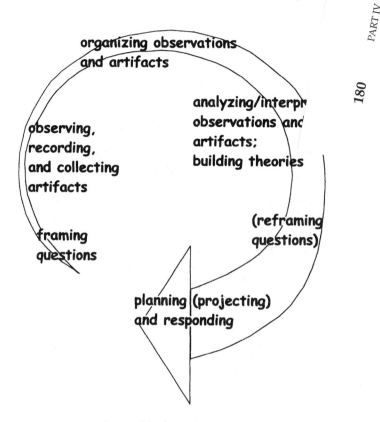

FIGURE 10.1   The Cycle of Inquiry

Source: Reprinted by permission of the publisher from Gandini, Lella and Carolyn Pope Edwards, *Bambini*, (New York: Teachers College Press, © 2001 by Teachers College, Columbia University. All rights reserved.), p. 135, figure 10.5.

FUELING THE PROGRAM AND EXTENDING THE CHILD'S INTERESTS

When children have the opportunity to review their processes in the company of supportive others in the community, the benefits are numerous. First of all, the learning process becomes visible and thus evident to the child. Children who can reflect on their own stages of learning are more in touch with *how* they are acquiring knowledge and information and can therefore be more present in their own educational process.

THINK ABOUT IT

How can documentation of an experience engender community contagion within a classroom?

Next, when artifacts from work in the school are made readily available for review by the children, the enthusiasm for the work remains high. Reflecting on the previous day's experiences allows the children to review the data and possibly to interpret the results in new ways. Reconstruction and transformation of ideas and of participants within process is a result. (See Chapters 9 and 11 for examples of the process of a project and the importance that documentation plays during its development.)

Master Teacher, Kelly Wells, Speaks

Our story began one beautiful fall day while on one of our many adventures to the duck pond. While making careful observations of her surroundings, Wendi discovered a stick in the shape of the letter *Y*. Soon the other children and teachers joined in her enthusiasm, and we all began to notice that many of the sticks we found on our adventures were shaped like a letter of the alphabet. Several days later Alicia found another stick, this one resembling the letter *A*. And so our journey to find or to create every letter in the alphabet began.

Keeping track of letters found and letters yet to be found on a large wall in our classroom kept the group project visible and exciting for our entire community. As each letter was added to the wall, the children would celebrate the new addition by adding a scanned version of the letter to a small book that was quickly growing. This documentation notebook soon became the class favorite and was the most requested book during group meetings and snuggly book corner reading.

Wendi begins a long-term project with her interest in the alphabet and her discovery of a twig shaped like a *Y*.

W came next. As we studied the worms underneath the wooden house on our playground, the children noticed that as the worms squiggled and squirmed, they formed letters.

Hannah noticed that the tire on the playground was the shape of the letter *O*. *X* came next and soon became our favorite letter. We first noticed the letter painted on the sewer covers located everywhere around campus. As we started to pay more attention, we noticed that you could find *X*'s everywhere if you looked carefully. We found them in the sky when trails left by the jets flying overhead crossed over one another. We found them in the cracks on the sidewalk and in the trees. We learned that we could use our fingers, our legs, and our entire bodies to form this letter. We noticed the many *X*'s in the exit signs located around our building. We know now that you can use just about any two straight-lined objects to make our favorite letter.

T is for our ongoing search for treasure, castles, princes, and princesses.

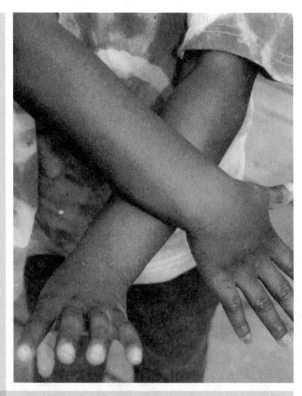

Mara joins in the alphabet hunt and proudly creates the letter *X* using her own body.

K is for the keys that will one day unlock the treasure. *K* is for Kelly and Karlin. Over the past two years, these girls have found many ways to create the letter *K*. "All you need is three straight lines!"

Emily and her mom designed our *J* one day in the classroom. After shopping together at the grocery store, they decided to use "jelly, junk food, and jelly beans" as their materials for creating this letter.

Cam carefully rolled a piece of blue clay into a "snake." He learned that if you curve the snake just right, you can make the letter *C*.

We all knew for several weeks that Steffen and Stephen would be in charge of the letter *S*. After careful thought and consideration, Steffen came running in to the classroom one morning exclaiming, "I have to make the *S*, I have to make the *S*, and I need some buttons!" After consulting with Stephen, the two agreed on the plan. Together they used buttons to form the letter on the scanner.

Darren chose dandelions to form his letter *D*. He developed his own supportive committee of friends to help him pick the flowers growing around the school.

Emily, Kelly, Hannah, and their teacher Jen worked collaboratively to use their bodies to form the letter *E*.

F is for the fish in our room that we cared for and nurtured over the past two years. Rachael Simion, our oldest fish, now lives in Cam's pond, located in his backyard.

G is for gack and all of its many possibilities.

Hannah made the *H* out of the grape hyacinths we found at the Horticulture Gardens.

Depending on your perspective, the leaf that Hunter found at the Horticulture Gardens can be an *H* or an *I*.

Kelly followed the beautiful scent of lilacs, just the perfect thing for the *L* in our alphabet.

Emily used the many beautiful materials from our classroom collection to create the letter *M*—the second letter in her own name and the first letter in Mara's.

N is for Naomi, who thought for several days about "three straight lines that were close to the same length." A pencil, a paintbrush, and a marker were chosen. When she noticed that the marker was a bit shorter than the other two items, she carefully made the proper adjustments and added a small block to the top of the marker.

P is for purple, *B* is for Bradford and for blue, and *R* is for red. Our class carefully and collectively sorted the materials to create these three letters.

Hunter soon realized that we still needed a *Q*. Always enthusiastic about collecting treasures on our walks together, one day he collected some materials that he knew he would use to create this letter. While working with this letter, he noticed that some of his treasured items also resembled the letter *U*.

After great collaboration and passion for the project, the children arranged their environmental alphabet into a beautiful poster.

Cam and Bradford, our resident LEGO experts and phenomenal collaborators, created our letter Z.

And last but not least came the letter *V*. You can find it in the word *love*, it's essential in learning how to draw a heart, and, if you look carefully, you can find a *V* in the branches of every tree.

For this classroom of coresearchers and investigators, the documentation of their shared experiences kept the group invigorated and intrinsically motivated along the way. Joyful learning was the happy result.

PROVIDING AN OPPORTUNITY FOR THE TRANSFORMATION OF TEACHERS

The professional development benefits of creating and reviewing documentation are numerous. First, when teachers take part in the process of collecting and organizing the artifacts from the classroom, they are practicing thoughtful discriminatory reflection on the work that has occurred to date. Capturing the moments and memories of the classroom must be an ongoing task to which the teacher is committed. Each day the child's work samples, the recorded conversations, and the visual images must be carefully reviewed. Sometimes the meaning of the documents is not immediately obvious. It may be some time before the "big ideas" (Oken-Wright, 2002) are apparent or before the developmental gains of an individual child are evident, but without multiple examples to review, authentic meaning and possibility may be missed. Therefore, this capturing process is crucial. Next, as teachers review the work samples in an attempt to understand, they begin to take part in a highly professional process. Meaning making requires teachers to collaborate and to share their individual expertise. This exchange of ideas among educators has not always been evident in our schools, where teachers have typically been isolated in single-teacher classrooms; therefore, it is often a difficult stage to achieve. However, with assistance and support from a committed administration, the time and skill necessary to collaborate can be accomplished. (See Chapter 9 on teacher collaboration for more elaboration.)

BRINGING FAMILIES INTO THE PROCESS

The benefits for the family of having the temporary documentation immediately available cannot be overstated. The attractive display of the artifacts invites others into the project. As with the children and teachers, the temporary documentation inspires communication between home and school and allows new levels of dialogue to be opened between all of the protagonists. When Christina's and Alanah's families (see Chapter 9) noticed the emerging interest in building together, they immediately offered to assist with the process. Recognizing the importance of a strong amiable relationship between the girls, the families began to arrange opportunities for them to see each other outside of school. Often the plans for drawing and conceptualizing Patch's new house were extended to their time together on the weekends, and they would happily bring new drawings and plans to school on Monday morning. Thanks to family participation, this project was able to achieve a greater depth of meaning for everyone. Likewise, parents are captured by this opportunity to take a closer, more intimate look at what their child is finding exciting. In turn, they feel more informed, and more enthused, by the whole school experience.

One Parent's Enthusiastic Response to the Power of Documentation

Finn's mother, Elizabeth Bloomer (an author from Chapter 12), was so enchanted by the documentation work she noticed happening in Finn's classroom that she decided to keep this running list of Finn's amazing words during the course of his fourth year. Because Elizabeth is also a writer and poet, she opted to document using her own major "language"—poetry. This poem was a treasured gift from Finn to his teachers at the end of the school year, and a meaningful addition to his personal portfolio.

FROM FINN AT FOUR

when i first went to school,
i think I was a little bit scared
because I didn't know how to
play and play with the dinosaur box
and shaving cream.

but let me tell you about the
costumes in the big box
by my cubby. sometimes i'm
your little brown bunny.
will you make me a brown bunny
costume this summer so
i can play with my friends?
you'd like the flower patches on
the knees. they look like our
old couch we gave away.

sometimes i'm a space man
when i'm not batman or
super hero guys. we have blasters
not guns because guns my
mom doesn't like but I like blasters.
blasters like buzz lightyear are
very very cool. I mean really, really.

i can also be the devil with
my red cape with black on the outside.
but don't worry. a devil is just a man
with horns and a pitchfork.

but I keep hitting my head
on the playground and getting
bumps. we chase and chase the other
kids and they tell us to stop but
sometimes we don't stop.
we run forever and ever.
feel my big muscles.
i am strong today.

to make an elephant
you need one and a half
inches of soil.

i'm going to build the technology
to go to the sky and go up and up
and grab your dead cat's spirit
and bring her back. And I'll
bring kinnakeet and spot.

to build a spaceship you just
need to put the ceiling fan on
top of the microwave, then
put the big wheel on the bottom
to steer it.

the toilets at school are
too small for a big boy like me.
they are for little mikayla.
there are lots of little toilets.
flush flush flush!

i'm concerned about strangers.
the teachers say to use your words
and have a conversation about it.

jenn i like because when i have the
spaceship guy and she has the racecar,
she vroomed with me. together . . .

see that boy over there? he is
my student. they are all my students.

chicka-chicka-boom-boom
chicka-chicka-room-room.
that's a rhyme, you know,
i mean, really, verklish.
i would be delighted to
drink out of a big-boy cup.

i like angie because she plays and
plays and plays and plays. she shows
me the new room and when i was very little
i sitted on her lap for looking at books.

i'm very concerned about this summer.
my best buddy is going to move away
and madeleine's dog is going to die today.
i'm having a very tired day.
i think eating gummy bears will help
my tummy feel better.

this summer i'm going to eat yogurt.
we'll watch the baby owls at nana's and ted's
let's plant fruit trees at their house and have
picnics. we can eat happy cow yogurt.
and we can learn how to read. together.

PROVIDING A MEANS FOR ASSESSING THE CHILD'S DEVELOPMENT OVER TIME

The compilation of daily observational notes and artifacts can be gathered together to craft an individual child's portfolio. The portfolio is a rich and authentic representation of the child when the teacher uses work samples, photographs, and meaningful captions to tell the story of the child's work and play in the school.

THINK ABOUT IT

Teachers who practice the fine art of observation can ask themselves these questions as they observe and then reflect on what they've noticed:

What are the children doing with the materials?

What seems fun or pleasurable?

How do they talk about it or represent it in their play?

What are the children inventing/investigating/understanding throug'

What new ideas, solutions, and answers are the children coming up as they play?

What can you conclude and summarize about what and how the c' are learning?

Consider these teacher reflections and the paired interpret ple of observational notes from the classroom: Remember that represents the very early stages in the cycle of inquiry.

OBSERVATION

Ian and Kareem were very involved in dinosaur play today. Each walked stealthily into the room, snarling. Matthew W. came up to them in his knight hat, pretending to combat them. However, Ian comes out of his dinosaur role and says, "No, you can't play. You're a knight. We are dinosaurs. You can't play with us. You need to go play somewhere else."

Sydney and Sofia are intently involved in building a train track. They work at putting the pieces together until there is no more space to place any pieces of the track. "What's this for?" Sofia asks, pulling out the revolving section of the track. "It's where the people go," says Sydney. "No, it's not," Sofia objects. "It's for trains, this is a train track." Later, Sydney reaches into the box that holds all the pieces and decides, "We need a building." However, Sofia objects saying, "NO, this is a TRAIN track."

Jordan worked very hard on our pinata bags today. She brought many different materials together in a collage in her creation. Then she began a construction paper creation. She folded the paper in half, glued it, and then taped four pipe cleaners to each corner. Then she taped two of the pipe cleaners together and put it around her neck, declaring that she had made a necklace. She removed the necklace and then continued her creation as if an idea became apparent to her. She also readily altered and didn't become frustrated when things didn't work as she had planned; rather she altered her plans to fit what the materials were doing

BEGINNING INTERPRETATION

Ian is very focused in his play. Only those who fit into his scheme are allowed to join in. Possibly somewhere in his experience with dinosaurs, he's learned that people didn't exist when the dinosaurs did. So a human knight does not fit into his imaginative scheme.

Sofia is very purposeful and definite in her play. She had decided that she was building a train track and she kept that goal fixed in her mind as she worked. She recognized what the objects were for and she stayed firm in her intent.

The first thing I noticed while watching Jordan today is that she works very symmetrically. What she would do to one side of her creation, she would do to other. She is also very versatile. For instance, her construction paper project went through an evolution based on her spontaneous ideas. A necklace can quickly change to a pocketbook if a step becomes obvious to her. She seems especially adept and interested in discovering materials and their abilities.

Capturing a child's sustained interest in and progression of an idea or an ability requires that the teacher consciously revisit the observation and early interpretations on a regular basis. A series of drawings by Matteo demonstrates his representational development and understanding. His teacher, Carla Liversedge, respectfully collects these drawings for his portfolio of learning. Sometimes a microanalysis of an "ordinary moment" (Shafer, 2002) gives insight into the developing skills, interests, and talents of a child.

The Development of a Dinosaur

Matteo has an interest in dinosaurs. He has been drawing them throughout the semester. This demonstrates his art development in the representational stage. Also, during these activities he is creatively expressing himself. We have been 'researching' dinosaurs through children's literature and other dinosaur art work. This is a series of Matteo's drawings that have changed over time. At the beginning, he drew dinosaurs similar to each other. Now, he does different kinds that he has seen in books or from home.

This dinosaur was from the beginning of the school year. He often calls this 'godzilla.'

This is another early dinosaur. This one shows the claws.

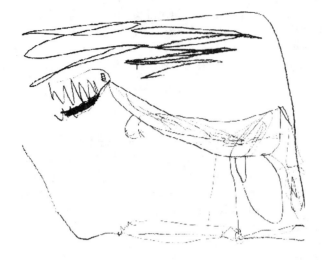

This dinosaur is one that Matteo saw in a toy store. We discussed the dinosaur's movable mouth. It is still inside the box.

These two drawings were done after looking at another artist's view of dinosaurs. Matteo includes details like stripes and background.

These dinosaurs show different positions that the dinosaurs are in. Matteo said of the middle one, "he is looking backwards." They also demonstrate that Matteo is considering different kinds of dinosaurs.

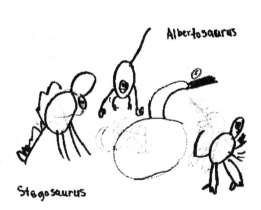

These most recent drawings depict all different kinds of dinosaurs in all different positions. And more than one on each page.

The teacher can also create an artifact that captures a child's achievement, as when student teacher Amanda James put together a photo and text to show the results of a morning spent in the computer loft; this artifact went into the portfolio of a four-year-old child. (For more details about the contents of a child's portfolio, see the Getting Started section at the end of this chapter.)

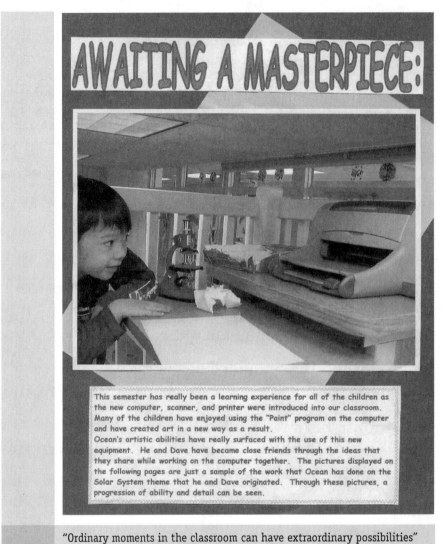

AWAITING A MASTERPIECE:

This semester has really been a learning experience for all of the children as the new computer, scanner, and printer were introduced into our classroom. Many of the children have enjoyed using the "Paint" program on the computer and have created art in a new way as a result.
Ocean's artistic abilities have really surfaced with the use of this new equipment. He and Dave have became close friends through the ideas that they share while working on the computer together. The pictures displayed on the following pages are just a sample of the work that Ocean has done on the Solar System theme that he and Dave originated. Through these pictures, a progression of ability and detail can be seen.

"Ordinary moments in the classroom can have extraordinary possibilities" (Shafer, 2002).

PROVIDING A MEANS FOR ASSESSING THE STRENGTHS AND WEAKNESSES OF A PROGRAM

It is not unusual for the documentation of the life in the classroom to reveal an unexpected insight. Embedded in the careful listening, observing, recording, and revisiting of the child's processes can be an essential key to a programmatic dilemma.

The documentation can bring these otherwise hidden problems to light so that action can be taken to strengthen the program for the entire community of learners.

In our own school, we have used documentation to substantiate the need to change several school practices and policies.

- Toys from home were considered a distraction to the children and a source of conflict in the classroom until the documentation on Christina (see Chapter 9) helped us understand the necessity of a transitional object for the comfort and security of the child.
- Snack was traditionally served in large groups in our school until we carefully documented and reviewed the entire process from the point of view of the child. This action research uncovered the discomfort that many children were experiencing when required to transition in large groups from play to snack and then back to play. Allowing children to choose their own snack time and to monitor their own hunger levels eliminated long waiting periods and empowered children by giving them the opportunity to self-discriminate between hunger and nonhunger.
- Our attempt to provide an intergenerational program for children and older adults was a source of pride and pleasure in our school; however, on careful review of the documentation, it became clear to us that the interactions between the participants was not as rich and intimate as we had hoped. Redesigning the intergenerational space to create a place where collaborative work and play could be the priority changed the experience for all of us.

PROVIDING AN ARCHIVE OR HISTORY
OF THE SCHOOL

Documentation can be used to create an archive of the school's history. This visual story-of-the-school can cement a community that feels a shared sense of pride and history. It can also be a means by which new families are incorporated into the school community.

In our school, we use our hallway as a museum and archive of the school's history. Families, children, teachers, and visitors can feel the essence of our shared time together by simply strolling down the hall and observing the choices we have made in our displays. Here you can feel the importance of time and relationships to the whole experience, as expressions of joy and care are everywhere. The celebration of each family that traditionally takes place each year as an offering of welcome from the studio can be seen in the treasure display, the collaborative weaving, and the family mosaic. The annual action research projects conducted by our teachers are also part of the "museum" and emphasize to the viewer our commitment to lifelong learning. The ritual of welcoming the ducks back to our playground each spring (see Chapter 11) is also evident in a prominent display that cites the history of the project and suggests the possibilities for more to come.

ADVOCATING FOR OUR PROFESSION

Documentation can be a tool by which our early childhood education profession is made visible to others. Policymakers, superintendents, teacher education personnel, community members, and others can all benefit from viewing carefully worded and aesthetically constructed documentation that brings to light the learning processes of children. The National Association for the Education of Young Children (NAEYC) has awarded grants to groups and organizations that can find creative and effective ways to advocate for our children. Margie Carter and Deb Curtis were awarded one of these grants for developing a system of creating and displaying documentation panels in churches, banks, community centers, malls, and other public arenas. Their book, *Spreading the News* (1996), details the process of creating an advocacy panel and finding community partners.

In a similar vein, an organization in support of quality programming for children was created in Burlington, Vermont. Burlington Children is a group of policymakers, teachers, professors, parents, and interested community members who are dedicated to supporting the lives of its youngest citizens. Their personal celebration of childhood means creating spaces for children in their town where they can play safely, ensuring health care for all children, reorganizing quality child care for the young, rethinking the teacher education systems in Vermont, and above all emphasizing the rights of children. Burlington Children uses documentation and display as a primary means of bringing the public's attention to its children (Gandini & Goldhaber, 2001).

> **THINK ABOUT IT**
>
> How can the process of documentation be managed in the classroom?

Managing documentation takes a concerted effort and an abiding commitment to the process. Although it can be seen by some as just another duty in the already overwhelming list of teacher responsibilities, a careful review of the benefits listed earlier ensures attention to the processes in the classroom. To manage the process, we suggest beginning the year with a collection of important data based on home visits and detailed communication with families. This is arguably the teacher's greatest source of understanding of the individual child. Understanding the child's perspective is the main component in ensuring an intersubjective stance between child and teacher. Collecting information on family experiences allows the teacher to begin to negotiate a curriculum based on the reality of the child's previous experiences.

Next, as the work in the classroom ebbs and flows, it is important to keep track of the sounds and rhythms in order to document the processes for all members of the community. Meaningful photographs that depict the important moments in the course of a project can be coupled with transcriptions of the children's conversations and debates, and when work samples are added, the result begins to represent the essence of the actual experiences. When these documents can be gathered and displayed almost immediately, this temporary documentation can be extremely beneficial to the community. Recent technological advances now make it quite possible to digitally photograph or videograph a classroom episode for almost immediate use by the community.

THINK ABOUT IT

How can the role of documenter be shared with older students?

What would be the benefits?

Meaning-making conferences with co-workers to review the data and make intentional decisions about next steps in the curriculum bring a collaborative element to the process and share the workload. Decisions about what's happening in the classroom, what it means, and where to go from here can be a more creative process when shared with colleagues. Two heads (or three or four) are certainly better than one in these cases and can often lead to much richer experiences for the children.

Once children have developed some basic literacy skills, it can be an incredible leap in learning to share the task of documenting with them. When children begin to pay closer and closer attention to their own processes of learning by means of the documentation, they are confirming their knowledge base and "owning" their own learning. When children take on the role of documenter, they are practicing the fine art of careful, discriminatory watching and listening to what is going on around them, and they are building dispositions of inquiry, wonder, data collection, and analysis that can last a lifetime.

Consider the project undertaken by student teacher Becca Rainey's fourth-grade classroom from Monte Vista Elementary School in the Albuquerque public school district. To meet school district requirements, all fourth-grade students were required to have an understanding of their immediate communities. Since the elementary school is located in a historic district of Albuquerque, Becca thought that it might be more significant for the children if they were to explore and document their own immediate environment. Using as a model the architectural photographs of Balthazar Korab in which he captures the twenty-six letters of the alphabet in architecture throughout the country in a book entitled *Archabet* (1992), she suggested a similar project to her students. Initially, she engaged the students by leading a sort of guessing game. She presented large copies of Korab's photographs in random order and asked the students to find letters in the structures. Many of the images could represent various letters, depending on the perspective, and each student was able to contribute to the enthusiastic search. Some of the photographs were taken at close range and others from unusual angles, which prompted a discussion on careful attention to detail. Next came a conversation about what constituted architecture. The students decided that architecture was more than just buildings and could include landscaping, sculpture, and other human-made things around buildings. Finally, a group decision was made to try to re-create Korab's work through their own investigation of their own local neighborhood. Daily walking trips, an opportunity to use the digital camera, and a chance to point out all of their houses and

Children in Becca Rainey's fourth-grade class create their own version of an "Archabet" (Korab, 1992). The role of documenter can easily be transferred to older children, with strong learning results.

apartments contributed to high enthusiasm on the children's part. It seemed that the students had a natural ability to look at architecture in a more abstract way than adults do. "We looked at architecture from up close, from far away, by squinting our eyes, and by standing on our heads," said Becca.

It proved a small leap for a porch railing to become a capital letter *S* or an archway to become an *M.* Once all of the letters were collected, the students studied the copies of the potential images to determine which were "book-worthy." Images were then downloaded and altered in Photoshop and placed into a format acceptable for a bound book. This draft was then taken to the school's district media resource center, where a copy of the book was made for each of the students. In the end, this project challenged the students to look at the structures they see in a new way, allowed the students to use their neighborhood as the foundation for exploration, and taught them the power of a group documentation project.

SUMMARY

In this case, as in the others detailed in this chapter, a dedication to the documentation process seems to have been the necessary fuel behind a responsive, caring, and inquiry-based classroom. And so the cycle renews itself. New questions are pondered. New responses are offered. And with a commitment to both head and heart, the community moves forward using its documentation in its search for understanding.

GETTING STARTED ACTIVITIES

1. In small groups of four students, observe the same half-hour play period in a classroom. Each student should use a different style of documenting what they have observed: audio, video, photographs, note-taking.

2. Share, compare, and reflect on the process and product of the experience.

3. Create four separate documentation displays using all four methods of data collection. Each documentation display should be aimed at a separate audience: student teachers, children, families, funding sources.

4. Compare, contrast, and reflect on this process. Are there benefits to one style of data collection? One style of documentation? How does the documentation differ depending on the audience for whom it is intended?

5. How could older children take part in this process? What would be the benefits of such an exercise?

6. Which items would be most authentic for inclusion in a child's portfolio? Preschool-age children? Elementary-age children?

RESOURCES

On the Web
www.ecrp.uiuc.edu/v5nl/hong.html
This site offers teachers a new form for reflecting on the experience in the classroom. The use of technology is explored as an important form of documentation.

Books on Documentation and Making Learning Visible

Carter, M., & Curtis, D. (1996). *Spreading the news: Sharing the stories of early childhood education.* St. Paul, MN: Redleaf Press.

Curtis, D., & Carter, M. (2000). *The art of awareness: How observation can transform your teaching.* St. Paul, MN: Redleaf Press.

Fyfe, B., & Rinaldi, C. (2002). Making learning visible: Adults as individual and group learners. *Innovations, 9*(4), 1–10.

Goldhaber, J. (2001). *The choices we make: Documentation as an act of courage.* Paper presented at the Recasting the Reggio Emilia Approach to Inform Teaching in the United States Conference, Virginia Tech, Blacksburg, VA.

Goldhaber, J., & Smith, D. (2002). The development of documentation to support teacher reflection, inquiry and collaboration. In V. R. Fu, A. J. Stremmel, & L. T. Hill (Eds.), *Teaching and learning: Collaborative exploration of the Reggio Emilia approach* (pp. 147–160). Upper Saddle River, NJ: Merrill/Prentice-Hall.

Himley, M., & Carini, P. (2000). *From another angle: Children's strengths and school standards. The Prospect Centers' descriptive review of the child.* New York: Teachers College Press.

Project Zero, Harvard Graduate School of Education, & Reggio Children. (2001). *Making learning visible: Children as individual and group learners.* Reggio Emilia, Italy: Reggio Children.

REFERENCES

Carter, M., & Curtis, D. (1996). *Spreading the news: Sharing stories of early childhood programs.* St.Paul, MN: Redleaf Press.

Gandini, L., & Goldhaber, J. (2001). Notable practices: Reflections about documentation. In L. Gandini & C. P. Edwards (Eds.), *Bambini: The Italian approach to infant/toddler care.* New York: Teachers College Press.

Goldhaber, J., & Smith, D. (2001). *The choices we make: Documentation as an act of courage.* Paper presented at the Recasting the Reggio Emilia Approach to Inform Teaching in the United States Conference, Virginia Tech, Blacksburg, VA.

Korab, B. (1992). *Archabet.* New York: John Wiley, & Sons.

Lawson, L. (2000). Personal communication. Burlington, VT: University of Vermont. In Hendrick, J. (Ed.), *Next steps toward teaching the Reggio way: accepting the challenge to change.* Columbus, OH: Merrill/Prentice-Hall.

Oken-Wright, P., & Gravett, M. (2002). *Big ideas and the essence of intent.* In V. Fu, A. Stremmel, & L. Hill (Eds.), *Teaching and learning: Collaborative exploration of the Reggio Emilia approach.* Upper Saddle River, NJ: Merrill/Prentice-Hall.

Rinaldi, C. (1997). *The fine art of listening.* Paper presented at the Second Annual Summer Institute, Columbus School for Girls, Columbus, OH.

Shafer, A. (2002). Ordinary moments, extraordinary possibilities. In V. Fu, A. Stremmel, & L. Hill (Eds.), *Teaching and learning: Collaborative exploration of the Reggio Emilia approach.* Upper Saddle River, NJ: Merrill/Prentice-Hall.

CHAPTER 11

PROJECTS AS A KEY TO COMMUNITY BUILDING

It seems important . . . that the projects are most meaningful when they involve others, when they touch others' lives.

Maxine Greene, *1995, p. 23*

Once upon a time there were two ducks that lived at the duck pond near the children's school. The children had named the ducks. The mama duck's name was Love and the daddy duck's name was Free. One day in the spring, Love and Free decided to hunt around for a place to build their nest. They searched and they searched all around the pond, but they didn't find quite the right spot, so they went up the hill and through the forest and across the street, through a parking lot and under a fence, until they found just the right place for their nest. And do you know where that place was? It was on the playground of the Virginia Tech Lab School! And the spot they had chosen for their nest was right in the middle of a tire that was right in the middle of the children's playground.

The children and the teachers were so excited when they discovered that Love and Free had built a nest on their playground, and they were determined to make certain that Love would be happy and safe in her new home. So they roped off a section of the playground and made signs that told people to stay away from that area. They also brought food and water to Love every day.

Meanwhile, Love was sitting on her nest . . . and she sat and she sat and she sat. One day when she got up to get a drink of water, the children counted the eggs and found that there were fifteen eggs! And every day the children would check on Love and every day they would see her sitting and sitting and waiting and waiting.

Finally, one day we looked out on the playground to find that the eggs had hatched and there were fifteen ducklings with Love. And right away Love decided that it was time for her babies to move back to the pond where Free was waiting for them. And so she led them under the fence and through a parking lot and across the street and through the forest until they came to the pond—and when they did, they all jumped in and took a long bath! And every year after that, Love and Free have come back to the children's school to search for a new nesting place.

This true story was offered as a provocation to the children, families, and teachers at our school for several years. The legend was so provocative that it led to the development of a shared, long-term, schoolwide project that we called Project Think Like a Duck. Read along now and discover how two small ducks helped to create an enormous community spirit, pride, and history that has carried over for years and has created many, many opportunities for learning.

Schools must function as viable, nurturing communities in order for all members to grow and learn. Building such communities is not easy, but is it essential. When a school shares a commitment to ensuring, as John Dewey (1938) said, that "each individual comes into full possession of his or her personal power," then that educational system is functioning well. Coming together around a shared project on behalf of learning and building a sense of personal power can build community pride and a sense of group accomplishment. When individuals have the opportunity to contribute to such a shared goal, they thrive. The fable of Love and Free is part of one community project that lifted its members up and made education an exciting and meaningful experience for everyone.

QUESTIONS TO BE CONSIDERED

- How does a teacher know when the kernel for a long-term project has appeared?
- What questions could a teacher ask in order to keep the enthusiasm for a project alive and viable in the classroom?
- How are the interests of all the children in the classroom attended to during project work?
- What are some of the multiple styles of teaching and learning evident throughout this project?

HOW CAN WE WELCOME BACK THE DUCKS?

The children in our school have become aware of several important parts of the culture of our school. First, they understand that amiability is one of the issues we all embrace and work toward achieving on a daily basis (see Chapter 8). Therefore, considering ways to welcome the ducks was similar in many ways to how we functioned as a community of learners. Next, they know that their ideas, theories, and

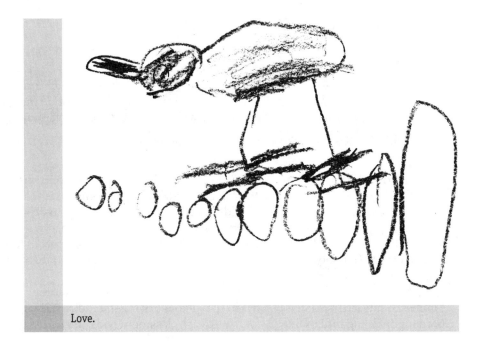

Love.

Free.

suggestions will be respectfully considered and listened to as a way to negotiate the curriculum (see Chapters 9 and 10). So when the question of how to welcome back the ducks was posed to the children, it was not surprising that they came up with several interesting suggestions:

"Make sure that they have plenty to eat and that they have friends."

"Make sure that they know how to get back to the pond once the ducklings hatch."

"Make sure that they have a safe and comfortable place to nest."

"Make sure that their return to the pond from the playground is safe from danger."

And with these ideas from the children, we began to work

THINK ABOUT IT

What is the big question here?

What do we really want the children to consider during the course of this project? The answer is complex, as you will see, but the first question we decided to ask was: "How can we welcome the ducks back to our playground this year?"

together to build a negotiated curriculum that would attend to the concerns voiced by the children. We met with our families to talk about the enthusiasm, concern, and care we had heard from the children and asked them to help us to think of ways to support these emotions and traits. Attending to one concern at a time seemed the way to go. So the parents opted to first assist with the effort to feed the ducks. Figure 11.1 shows the flyer that was sent out to every family advertising A FAMILY BUFFET FOR THE BIRDS.

And so on a cold and blustery day in February, hundreds of children and their families and teachers showed up at the school to work together to create a smorgasbord for duck and bird dining. Beforehand, each classroom had contributed to the ef-

It is with great enthusiasm that we, the Outdoor Committee, announce the kick-off of our next whole school adventure! Please join us on Saturday, February 17 for the first in a series of experiences that will launch

PROJECT THINK LIKE A DUCK!

As many of you know, each spring we are blessed with an annual visit from "Love Duck" and "her husband, Free" (the children named them in 1998) as they seek a safe shelter in which to build their nest. Each year we are thrilled to be a part of this ritual and have found many ways to take advantage of the learning opportunities that accompany this experience. This year, we thought that we would like to think ahead and be more planful for the upcoming event. We would like to offer the provocation of the inevitable return visit from our duck friends as the impetus for a shared project. Already many of the children have expressed enormous enthusiasm and interest in finding multiple ways to welcome them back to our playground.

The Outdoor Committee has scheduled
A Family Saturday: Buffet for the Birds
during which we hope to create a delightful smorgasbord for duck and bird dining.
Don't miss this opportunity to get down and quacky!

Catering for the Birds

Please review the attached flyer for more details. We will need lots of help with collecting, organizing, and assembling! We look forward to all the possibilities!

FIGURE 11.1   Buffet for the Birds

Families worked together to provide winter food for the birds and ducks.

fort by providing birdseed, pinecones, peanut butter, suet, cranberries, popcorn, and other yummy goodies for our feathered friends. All of the contributed goods were being displayed in the hallway for days ahead of time leading up to our big Saturday event, which seemed to engender community support and enthusiasm for the event. There was a great sense of collaboration and high humor that day as we all worked together to line our playground with the eclectic treats we had fashioned for the ducks and birds. Would the birds really enjoy this sort of offering, most of the adults seemed to ask? The children were always quick to respond from some intuitive knowledge base: YES!

And the children were absolutely right, because we came back to school one Monday morning to find that Love and Free had indeed found their way back to our playground and were happily munching on the buffet line created in their honor! Although enthusiasm for the project had been high before this point, the actual sighting of the ducks for the first time and the shared knowledge that they were "our" ducks who had returned to "our" playground was a heady experience for adults and children alike. We were all hooked now as the project began to take on a life all its own. We immediately reviewed the documentation from our previous meetings with the children and made a pact to assist them with each of their thoughts and concerns regarding their friends the ducks.

The school's playground was ringed with the bountiful feast.

Remembering that the children had initially suggested that we should concern ourselves with housing arrangements for the ducks, we launched into multiple possibilities for ensuring this most basic of needs. The children formed committees that investigated and studied various options. Each classroom created a prototype nest using materials and theories unique to the personalities of the children from that room. As with the bird buffet, we displayed all the nests through the ever-growing notebook of documentation in our hallway so that families and visitors to our school could keep abreast of the exciting happenings. And as we do in all of our inquiries and investigations, we continued to ask ourselves these crucial questions each day:

THINK ABOUT IT

How could we support the children in their efforts to ensure that the ducks had a safe and comfortable place to nest?

- What's happening here?
- What does it all mean?
- Where do we go from here?

Meanwhile, a couple of committees of children had preferred to work on a more permanent duck house built of wood. They began with some initial brain-

Love and Free enjoyed the smorgasbord provided for them.

storming and some sketches of ideal homes. These children met regularly in small groups to think together about their individual and collaborative ideas, and as they got closer to being able to articulate exactly what they wanted, we invited a couple of architecture students into our school to help us take the planning to another level.

About that time, one of the children voiced a concern: "If Love and Free decide to build their nest near our playground, then they will be far from the pond and all their friends." Bringing the problem back to the children, we ask them for a suggestion, a solution. "Well," said one child, "we could dress up like ducks and they would think that we were their friends!"

THINK ABOUT IT

How would you support the children with this suggestion?

Because the thinking behind the idea is not accurate, would you follow their lead, or inform the children of the truth of the situation?

This disequilibrium or problem stage that is inevitable in every project is the "good stuff." (See Chapter 9 for a discussion of the concept of project dissonance.) This moment is usually ripe with possibility and potential. These edgy times are the most crucial ones in teaching because it is exactly at this point that children are willing to allow themselves to be pushed just a bit further than before. And it is exactly at this point that the teacher must be ready to offer a provocation that is pitched at the perfect challenge point—not too high or too low. And so, if we were going to dress up like ducks, we needed to know an awful lot about them first. So we started with some baseline drawings to see what they might tell us. While these early drawings were quite simple in detail and design, they told us a lot about the children's current knowledge level and what they valued. We noted a sincere interest in, appreciation of, and care for ducks coming out in the children's artwork, dramatic play, and concept building. The children seemed especially captured by the concept of "the nest." We noted many repeated attempts to create and represent what they understood about this important piece of what we were now calling "duckness." Unprompted cir-

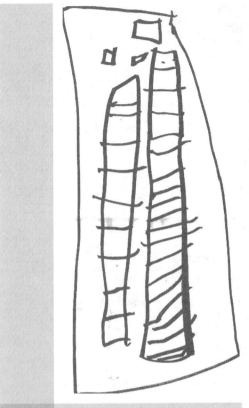

Early drawing of a house for the ducks.

Beginning-stage drawing of a duck.

Children spontaneously created nestlike images with a variety of materials.

cular icons appeared in their paintings, in their clay creations, and even in their outdoor playground play.

Another strong theme or "big idea" (Oken-Wright, 2002) that continued to emerge throughout this project was that of caregiving. This seemed to be an important element of what the children were coming to understand about duckness. They carefully attended to their own "eggs" in their dramatic reenactments of Love and Free's experience. And they attentively cared for the nesting mother in each of their pretend scenarios. As teachers we watched and wondered how we might continue to support this obvious interest and important learning opportunity.

With the help of our ever-growing extended parental community, we found a way to allow the children to experience legitimate costuming. One of our parents was a costume designer who had access to the design lab on campus. She graciously volunteered to invite a committee of interested children to learn the fine art of costume design in her laboratory. In this supported setting, the children sketched new ideas for duck costumes, made miniature practice versions that would fit on their models, and then finally created versions that could be worn in the classroom during their dramatic reenactments of the story of Love and Free.

"Caring for the ducks" was a recurring play theme.

Children learning draping and clothing techniques at the design lab.

MAPMAKING, MEANING MAKING

Next we tackled a new problem suggested by the children: How would the ducks find their way back to the pond? As always, we turned the problem back to them and asked for their ideas. They said:

- "We could make signs that only ducks could read."
- "We could make a trail of 'duck foot prints' for her to follow."
- "I think I'll just draw her a map." And then in the spirit of collaboration, "Does anyone want to help?"

Mapmaking began in two-dimensional form as the children sat together and thought about the duck pond. It was fascinating to note their sophisticated understanding of this place they had all visited many times before. They included details such as the handicapped parking lot, the small islands in the pond, the bridges, and the bike trail.

THINK ABOUT IT

How will Love know how to find her way back to the pond once the ducklings are hatched?

After another staff meeting at which all the current documentation of this ongoing project was reviewed, we

"I know, we'll make a map so that the ducks will know how to get back to the duck pond."

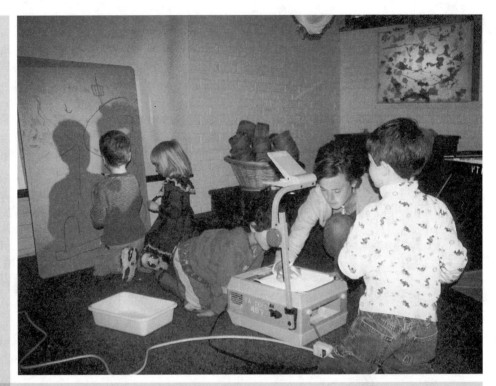

Using an overhead projector added another element and dimension to the maps.

considered the possibility of supporting the children in creating a three-dimensional map of the pond. This idea was pitched to the children during a group meeting and was met with enthusiastic acceptance. The overhead projector (which had been investigated thoroughly during earlier experiences in the classroom) was reintroduced as a tool for bringing their map to life. During this experience with a new tool, it became clear to the children that they needed more firsthand experience with the site in order to properly represent it. They took yet another trip to the pond to capture additional details. During this outing, we discovered that there are three islands in the pond, not two, as we had previously assumed. We also made careful note of all the trash containers and the bridge designs. The children carefully sketched their new ideas while at the pond and then brought them back to the school for inclusion in our new and improved map of the pond.

This stage of our project took several weeks as we worked together to represent all of what we knew about our beloved pond. The children made lots of choices during this time, including paint color selections and the best choices for representing concepts such as ponds and bridges. Also during this period, George Forman's (1994) concept of "affordances" was introduced to our teachers and was embraced as another means of supporting learning.

Back to the pond for more "research."

The three-dimensional map takes on exciting new details.

THINK ABOUT IT

How can children be introduced to the abilities they are capable of achieving with a variety of materials?

Here is a brief summary of George Forman's concept of affordances:

> Children learn more deeply when they represent the same concept in different media. Each medium has different affordances. Each affordance provokes a special orientation to the problem to be solved. Children learn to make compromises with what the medium does not easily afford. Children should be encouraged to revise earlier representations because of discoveries made with more recent representation. (Forman, 1994)

More detailed descriptions with examples can be found in Chapter 9.

COMMITTEE WORK

Meanwhile, the housing committee was still hard at work. Their initial drawings and ideas had been shared with the architecture students, who had diligently worked them into viable building plans, which they then enthusiastically shared with the children. The children reviewed these plans, made suggestions for alterations, and chose a final plan. The architecture students (who were quickly becoming members of our school community) promised to build the shell of the new duck house and to deliver it to the children as soon as possible. The children still planned to paint the house and to situate it in "the perfect location" for Love and Free for the current nesting year.

Architecture students volunteered to help the children with their building plans.

One day in late March as the children filed out of the school for a fire drill, they were surprised to hear a loud quacking sound coming from a nearby bush. On careful examination, the children discovered that Love had built her nest in these bushes and had already laid one precious egg.

Although enthusiasm skyrocketed among the school community, one question begged to be answered. Again and again the children wondered: Why is there only one egg in the nest? As is our negotiated style of teaching, once again we turned the problem back to the children, and immediately the problem prompted a new direction for our project. The children's shared theory (which we captured on tape recorder as it evolved) was that a bank robber had stolen all of the other eggs. Though this theory was highly unlikely, we chose to support the children in their enthusiastic conviction. They believed there was significant evidence to support their robber theory because in further investigation of the nesting site, they had located several "clues." The children had gathered gum wrappers, cigarette butts, and a bank deposit slip from the vicinity. In their shared version of events, it was evident to them that bank robbers who littered and smoked had come along and taken the remaining eggs from the nest. Their new direction for the project was obvious to them! They would need to create decoys for the robbers that would fool them when they came back to collect the rest of the eggs. The children enthusiastically launched into this new but related experience and began to create decoys using matches (as the robbers obviously smoked), and gum (as the robbers obviously chewed gum and then carelessly disposed of their wrappers) and "fool eggs" (that would trick the robbers into taking the wrong eggs).

> **THINK   ABOUT   IT**
>
> What does a teacher do when an unexpected turn of events takes the curricular plan in a new direction?

This was a moment of disequilibrium for the adults in our community. Should we support the children in their robber fantasy? Would we be reinforcing inappropriate ideas if we did? What would happen to all the rest of our plans for the project, including the effort, which we had already channeled much energy, to create housing?

Although we as teachers were admittedly concerned that the emphasis had shifted significantly, in the end we chose to support the children in their new endeavors and to allow the project to unfold on its own. "Trust in the children; trust in the project" became our new mantra as we threw caution to the wind and waited patiently to see what would unfold. With the coming days the children would note that additional eggs were appearing in the nest. This new observation would contribute to their ever-growing understanding of the life cycle of the duck. They now knew that eggs were laid one at a time. But even with this new knowledge base, the children opted to keep the excitement of their robber theory alive and to continue to play it out. We watched in wonder and respect at the group's tenacity and emphasis on keeping the project alive at all costs. As we noted during previous projects, the children seemed to naturally divide themselves into committees based on their greatest interest and expertise. This time we noticed a housing committee, a costume committee, a migration committee, and others evolve.

> *The exterior committee:* We were pleasantly surprised to note that the children did not lose their enthusiasm for the work they had already begun. In fact, the spirit of the project had taken on a new energy. Now that the children suspected that bad guys were on the loose, they seemed to feel more compelled than ever to take care of Love's nest and the babies that would soon hatch from it.
>
> *The interior committee:* The interior committee crafted special sleeping bags for baby ducks that they decided would be placed in the decoy house.

The location committee: And the location committee continued to observe the ducks in order to choose the perfect location for the decoy house that would soon be delivered to them.

> ### THINK ABOUT IT
>
> How might committees best be used in a classroom of diverse learners? Note that children eagerly volunteered for the committees of their own choosing. This style of working together in small groups to accomplish a shared goal has been a successful way for children to express themselves in their most appropriate language.

One beautiful spring morning, the decoy house arrived at our school. Our entire community was giddy with the results. The architecture students had paid close attention to the children's design ideas. The house boasted a retractable roof, "for when the babies needed to fly out of the house." It also had a comfortable ramp for easy access by ducks. And it included lots of doors and windows so "the babies can see outside." The children chose paint colors and quickly set to work to beautify the new duck house.

Preparing the duck house for occupancy.

Love and Free explore their new home.

And in keeping with our tendency as a community to celebrate momentous occasions, we gathered together for a ribbon-cutting ceremony (with lots and lots of ribbon and many, many pairs of scissors). Spontaneous speeches were made by parents, teachers, and children as we reveled in the excitement of our culminating experience together. And within a few days, just as the children had predicted all along, Love and Free were spotted checking out their new home.

Based on the current community expertise and always on the interests expressed by the children, the school project took several exciting new directions in the following year. With the assistance of a parent who taught creative writing, the oldest children in the school opted to write a play about the now famous ducks, Love and Free. With the help of their teachers, they wrote the play, designed a set, chose parts, practiced, and filmed their version of Love and Free's love story. One child who had a strong propensity for music even wrote an original song. By the end of the school year, his song was being hummed and sung by the entire school community.

THINK ABOUT IT

How does a school achieve a sense of ritual and shared knowledge?

What impact does this have on the community of learners?

PAUL'S SONG
Two Mallard ducks that we once knew,
Love and Free their love was true.
Those two Mallard ducks with their feathers on their back,
Waddled to the Lab School with a Quack, Quack, Quack
Quack, Quack, Quack   Quack, Quack, Quack
Waddled to the Lab School with a Quack,

Over to the playground they did go,
Wibble, wobble, wibble, wobble, to and fro.
And those two Mallard ducks with the feathers on their backs
Waddled to the playground with a Quack, Quack, Quack
Quack, Quack, Quack   Quack, Quack, Quack
Waddled to the playground with a Quack, Quack, Quack

Free and Love knew what to do,
They laid their eggs in a tire or two.
And those two Mallard ducks with the feathers on their back
Had baby ducklings with a Quack, Quack, Quack
Quack, Quack, Quack   Quack, Quack, Quack
Had baby ducklings with a Quack, Quack, Quack

Over to the duck pond they did go
Free and Love their babies in tow.
And the family of ducks with the feathers on their backs
Were happy ever after with a Quack, Quack, Quack
Quack, Quack, Quack   Quack, Quack, Quack

AN EMPHASIS ON MIGRATION SHOWS
PROMISING POSSIBILITIES FOR CURRICULAR FUEL

Yet another group of children became very interested in the migration of the duck-lings back to the pond. Again and again they watched the video that had been captured a few years earlier of Love's return trek to the pond. They were quick to note the dangers that were apparent for both mama and baby ducks, and they decided they needed to do something to protect them. Particular fears surrounded the necessity for the ducks to cross several roads and parking lots on their way back to the pond. In the children's minds, this was simply not safe and not acceptable. Their attitude was one of strong empathy, care for others, and a determination to make a difference. After all, the ducks had *chosen* the playground as a nesting location every year; wasn't it therefore our *responsibility* to take care of them? With this motto in mind, the children launched into an avid sign-building subproject.

Signs were designed using a multitude of materials. Computers, paint, clay, wire, and chalk were some of the mediums the children adopted in their efforts to come up with signs that would warn cars to take care while driving the duck route.

The children paid special and careful attention to the words on the signs and to the pictures that would represent their concerns.

As the interest and effort surrounding the signs grew in the school, the teachers began to concoct a plan. Might it be possible to use the children's ideas to create legitimate campus signs to protect the ducks? Phone calls were made to officials from Building and Grounds on campus and then to the university architects' offices. The story of Love and Free was shared across the campus, and with each retelling of the story, new enthusiasm grew for the project. The officials in charge of signage for the university were invited to the school one morning to view the children's ideas and early attempts to design their own signs. During the presentation, the children clearly articulated their concern and their ideas for ensuring duck safety on campus. The university officials were enchanted and impressed by the work the children had accomplished, and much to our delight they agreed to take the children's ideas and fashion them into "real-life signs" (Finn, age four) that would be strategically hung on campus.

STANDARDS OF LEARNING ADDRESSED IN PROJECT: THINK LIKE A DUCK

Mathematics

Children participated in authentic learning experiences to use the concept of one-to-one correspondence; to count by number of items orally; to understand the ordinal position of items from left to right, right to left, top to bottom, and bottom to top; to investigate and recognize patterns; to compute and estimate by adding and subtracting whole numbers; to investigate measurement by identifying instruments used to measure length, weight, time, calendar, and temperature, and to make direct comparisons by attributes such as length, height, weight, temperature. They investigated and experienced geometric figures including circles, triangles, squares, and rectangles. They sorted, classified, and ordered according to similar attributes such as size, shape, and color and were able to identify, describe, and extend a repeated pattern found in common objects. (All of these standards are from the Virginia State Standards of Learning, 2002).

Science

The children conducted investigations in which basic properties of objects were identified by direct observation. Observations were made from multiple positions to achieve different perspectives. Children developed questions from one or more observations and were able to describe objects both pictorially and verbally. The children investigated and discovered that objects could be described in terms of their physical properties including the key concepts of color, shape, texture, size, weight, and position. They came to understand that water has properties that can be observed and tested (different forms of water, water flow, and the float and sink concept).

The children understand life processes of living things—that they change and grow and need food, water, and air to survive and that offspring of animals are similar but not identical to their parents and to one another. They experienced the concept of cycle and change in earth patterns and know that change occurs over time and that rates may be fast or slow. They understand that materials can be recycled, reused, and conserved.

THINK ABOUT IT

How does this negotiated brand of curriculum meet the standards of learning required in most public schools?

They were able to investigate and understand that animals have life needs and specific physical characteristics and can be classified by certain characteristics such as life needs, physical characteristics, and others. They took note of seasonal changes and weather and its impact on the activities of life processes (for both plants and animals). They learned about animal behaviors including migration, body covering and habitat, camouflage, adaptation, and dormancy. They understood that habitats change over time due to many influences.

English

Children demonstrated growth in the use of oral language including listening to a variety of literary forms, participating in choral speaking, reciting, and singing songs with repeated patterns. They participated in creative dramatics and understood words in a rhyming pattern. They built oral communication skills. They understood how print is organized and began to follow words from left to right to demonstrate that the printed word has meaning and to comprehend stories, characterizations, and the alphabet. They became adept at printing their own names and at exploring available technology for reading and writing. They understood how to write to communicate their ideas and to use descriptive words in expressing themselves. They became adept at sharing stories and information orally with an audience and at participating as a contributor and as a leader within a group. They came to understand how to record information from print and nonprint resources including dictionaries, encyclopedias, and web sites.

THINK ABOUT IT

How do you bring a project to a close in a respectful and meaningful way?

History and Social Sciences

The children were able to compare and contrast the relative location of people, places, and things. They used simple maps, globes, and other three-dimensional models to locate areas referenced within the project. They could identify symbols such as street signs and map legends. They were able to match simple descriptions of work that people do and the names of those jobs. They could identify the differ-

Child-created signs that were hung on campus.

ence between basic needs and wants. They became good citizens of our community by demonstrating an understanding of civics, including taking turns, completing their classroom responsibilities, and identifying rules and the consequences of breaking them. They could create a simple map of a familiar area and could describe how climate, location, and physical surroundings affect the way people and animals live.

Celebrating the official hanging of the signs.

SUMMARY: WHAT HAVE WE LEARNED ABOUT COMMUNITY PROJECTS?

Participation in a community project can help a community define itself. Throughout the process of this project, our community needed to ask itself some tough yet important questions. Who are we in the lives of these children? What do we value? What form of presentation do we want our values to take in our school? How will families and school work together to contribute to our shared ideals?

Participation in a community project celebrates both the individual contributors and the group as a whole. We found that within a long-term, inclusive project there is room for each individual to make a strong and meaningful contribution. Celebrating all the styles of thinking and learning in a community is what made this project so powerful. Appreciation for diversity and uniqueness within the community is one of the important end results.

Participation in a community project allows for learning to take place at multiple levels. The individual comes away with a strong sense of accomplishment, participation, membership and affiliation, self-esteem, power and control, support for ideas, and the joy of participating in the process of bringing an idea to life.

Hundreds of specific instances of learning occur when a topic is approached holistically, as opposed to the out-of-context learning that is more typical of traditional learning settings. Incidents related to reading, mathematics, geography, science, and social relationships were evident within this one project.

Successful community projects should always address the interests of the community. Be ready to be spontaneous. Trust in the children to lead the way. Trust in the power of the project to take on a life of its own. Be ready, as a responsive community, to negotiate all the potentialities and possibilities that exist when learning is treated as joyful.

ACKNOWLEDGMENTS

This community project was conducted over several years at the Virginia Tech Child Development Lab School. Special thanks go to the wonderful teachers who shared their documentation of the project for this chapter: Kelly Wells, Carla Lockwood, Angi Primavera, Sonia Mehta, Nicki Nichols, and Miguel Martin. More thanks go to the parents who supported, sweated over, and strengthened our project, especially Christine McCartney, Jennifer Brugh, Cathy Woerner, Lissa Bloomer, and Patrice Hart-Schuber. And then a huge thanks to community members who embraced the possibilities and understood the importance of supporting children in their learning processes: Karen Leichtenstein (university sign architect), Jason Neal and Scott Simpkins (architect students), and staff at the VA Tech Design Laboratory.

GETTING STARTED ACTIVITIES

1. Brainstorm several ways to welcome families into your school at the beginning of the school year.

2. Consider adopting a whole-school project with many spin-off subprojects. What would this project be? How would you find a way to involve everyone in your community?

3. How would you justify your use of projects as learning opportunities?

RESOURCES

On the Web
www.ecrp.uiuc.edu/v4n2/bullard.html
   This site will lead you to a review of an online course about Reggio Emilia and its projects.

Books and Articles on Projects and Community Building
Berk, L., & Winsler, A. (1995). *Scaffolding children's learning; Vygotsky and early childhood.* Washington, DC: NAEYC.
Goldhaber, J. (1998, July). Oh, Miss Jones where did you get that beautiful butterfly? *Young Children, 53*(4), 60–63.

Hill, L. T. (2003). Growing a community of place, friendship and mind. *Innovations, 10*(1), 7–14.

Katz, L. G., & Chard, S. (1989). *Engaging children's minds: The project approach*. Norwood, NJ: Ablex.

Stremmel, A. (2002). Teacher research. Nurturing professional and personal growth through inquiry. *Young Children, 57*(5), 62–70.

REFERENCES

Ayers, W. (1995). Interview with Maxine Greene. *Qualitative Studies in Education, 8*(4), 319–328.

Dewey, J. (1938) *Experience and education*. Toronto, Ontario: Macmillan.

Forman, G. (1994). Different media, different languages. In L. Katz & B. Cesarone (Eds.), *Reflections on the Reggio Emilia Approach* (pp. 41–55). Urbana, IL: ERIC Clearinghouse.

Oken-Wright, P., & Gravett, M. (2002). Big ideas and the essence of intent. In V. Fu, A. Stremmel, & L. Hill (Eds.), *Teaching and learning: Collaborative exploration of the Reggio Emilia approach* (pp. 197–220). (2002). Upper Saddle River, NJ: Merrill/Prentice-Hall.

Virginia State Standards of Learning. Available from www.pen.k12.va.usa/VDOE/Superintendent/Sols/home.shtml.

CHAPTER 12

LIFE IN THE CLASSROOM
Teachers Speak Out about Inquiry-Based Teaching and Learning

The style of teaching and learning we have professed in this book has often been associated with classrooms for our youngest learners. The schools of Reggio Emilia have thrived on their ability to promote and nurture joyful learning for children from infancy through age six. Although the concept of projects as a basis for learning can easily be justified for young children, those teachers and schools who have been employed to teach older children, whose progress will be monitored and charted according to their ability to successfully pass a series of assessment tests, have been less willing to take the risks of adopting this brand of education. Some teachers have even been concerned for their job safety should their students fail to thrive in this sometimes-controversial mode of teaching. It is because of these fears that we have been especially adamant about writing this book. Our teacher education philosophy at Virginia Tech is committed to embracing the negotiated and exciting styles of teaching and learning that you have read about in the previous chapters, and we believe strongly in the positive results we have documented in these pages.

As you read in Chapter 11, Becca Rainey was especially successful in articulating the learning that took place in her fourth-grade classroom when she offered her students the opportunity to learn in a more joyful and hands-on way. Chapter 12 gives the reader the chance to hear from four additional teachers, all of whom work in public school systems with older children. We have designed the chapter in an interview style so that you can hear the actual words from each of the teachers as they describe the enthusiasm, the hardships, and the rewards of working in this way with their students.   Let us introduce you now to four more teachers who have bravely taken the risk to teach in this exciting and enticing way:

Cindy Clemons Dowdy, First-Grade Teacher
Carla Liversedge, Second-Grade Teacher
Gretchen Distler, Sixth-Grade Teacher
Elizabeth Bloomer, College Instructor, First-Year English

CINDY DOWDY: FIRST-GRADE TEACHER, PUBLIC SCHOOL

Demographics

Thirty years old; six years of teaching; B.S. in early childhood education, Virginia Tech; M.S. in child development, Virginia Tech.

Teaching Philosophy

For as long as I can remember, I have wanted to be a teacher. It was a calling for me, and it was a dream come true when I got my first teaching job. It is my honest belief that *all* children can learn and that *all* children are special in their own way. It is my job to figure out how to reach each individual child and help them be all that they can be. I also believe that children learn best through active, hands-on learning experiences. I want my children to be able to get involved with their learning and try out their ideas. By doing this, they learn more and have a more worthwhile experience. Children learn best by "doing," not by "watching."

How Does Your Teaching Philosophy Mesh with Who You Are as an Individual?

I think that my philosophy of teaching goes hand in hand with who I am as a person. I really enjoy being with people and learning more about them. I also try to look for the good in all individuals and focus on their strengths. I believe that you have to do this with your students also. It may take some studying to find a child's strengths and to figure out how to capitalize on them, but it is well worth the effort. All people deserve to be looked at in a positive light, and I try to do this in my personal life and as a classroom teacher.

Describe Your Approach to Covering the Required Curriculum, Assessing the Learning That Is Occurring in Your Classroom, and Keeping Schooling a Joyful Experience

In my classroom, the children are the primary focus and they drive everything that takes place throughout the school year. At the beginning of the school year, I have the children brainstorm things they would like to learn about. Then, I try to find ways to include those items in their learning experiences throughout the year. I have discovered that it is very simple to cover the required curriculum by doing this. During the course of the year, I go back and look at the required curriculum elements and make a note of those that I have covered. By doing this, I can make sure that the children will leave my classroom with an understanding of the required curriculum. My children learn the skills they are supposed to learn, they do it through experiences they have selected. This makes the entire learning experience more enjoyable and exciting for the students. When they are learning about things they have chosen themselves, they have incredible ownership. They are more motivated to participate and much more eager to learn. By allowing the children to lead the way, the first-grade experience is more joyful for them and for me. Assessment takes place in many different ways in my classroom. The children can show their understanding through discussion, drawings, written material, and required standardized testing. Different children with different learning styles use different methods. I try to make sure that I provide opportunities for all of the learning styles in my activities.

How Do You Determine What Has Been Learned and How, in a Classroom with Wide Variety of Learning Styles?

Throughout the year, my students and I do a lot of talking about things. I love to hear their ideas and have them share their thoughts on what we are learning. This is one of the ways I find out what they are learning and how it is connecting with things they already know. It is amazing what first graders can tell you if you give them the opportunity. My conversations with them allow me to see not only what they know but also what they are still unsure of. Our discussions help me to plan what comes next and the activities I should do. I also like to listen to the conversations that take place between the students. I give my children many opportunities to work with a partner or in a small group. During these times, I try to walk around and eavesdrop on what they are saying. It is great to hear a student explaining something to another child or to hear several students struggling with and debating an issue they still aren't very clear on. I learn so much from what they say. I also have my children do written activities to help me get an understanding of what they have learned. I keep a portfolio for the year with these pieces of documentation inside. The portfolio is a super way to show growth from one month to the next and over the entire school year. It is a valuable tool for me and for the parents.

How Do You Keep Interest and Motivation Alive and Strong in Your Classroom?

I truly believe that one of the reasons my children stay so motivated is that their ideas are the basis for the learning, and it is all very real to them. Children need to be connected to what they are learning or it is not going to stick with them. I try to use situations and things they know from their prior experiences and everyday life. For example, when we are doing math activities with money, I take them on a pretend shopping trip to Walmart. The local Walmart is about three miles from our school, and it is the one store that *all* of my children have been to. It is real to them and it is a part of their daily lives. This makes the math lesson come alive, and they get so excited about it.

How Does Your Brand of Teaching and Learning Coincide or Conflict with That of the Other Faculty in Your School? If There Are Conflicts, How Do You Handle the Dissonance?

When I first started teaching first grade at my school, I received some strange looks from the other teachers. They just weren't sure that they approved of how I was running my classroom because it was very different from what they were doing. I almost felt like I was in my own little world. There wasn't anyone else on the staff who really shared my teaching philosophy and who was trying things that I was trying. It was difficult and lonely at times. Since I was working in a small school, there was only one other teacher at my grade level. My teaching style was drastically different from hers and there was very little sharing taking place between us. She wasn't very interested in my methods and I disagreed with some of the things that she was doing. This was a tough situation, but I felt confident that what I was doing was good for the students and that they were learning a lot. Those beliefs were what kept me going. I knew that my students were learning and growing as individuals and that was the most important thing. After a couple of years, people became more accepting of the things I was doing in my classroom, and the funny looks started to fade. I began sharing some of my ideas and techniques a little at a time, and some teachers became interested and wanted to hear more about what I was doing. This sharing has continued between several of the teachers and myself, and it has made all of us better at what we do.

What Role Do Families Play in Your Classroom?

Families are the foundation of what I do as a teacher. Each family is the expert on their child, and I need them to help me learn about their child, teach him or her, and make him or her successful. Without the help of the family, my job is much more difficult. From the first day of school, I let my families know that I value their opinions and that it is crucial that we work together. Their child will make the most progress if it is a team effort between them and me. During the year, I send home a weekly journal. In the journal, I write a personal note home to each child's family. Underneath my note is a space for the family members to write back to me. This is an amazing way to communicate and to keep families involved. If it has been a rough week at school, I can let them know. If their child has had a great weekend at home, they can let me know. I have found this to be a super way to build relationships with the families of the children I teach. I also invite family members to come in my class at any time. They know that they are welcome to stop by and visit at any time during the year. The door is always open. I also send out invitations to the families when there are special events going on in the classroom. The children love having their families come to school, and it really makes them feel special.

Do You Have Discipline Problems in Your Classroom? If So, How Do You Handle These Behaviors?

When I first started teaching, most of the teachers at my school used a behavior plan based on Cantor and Cantor. The plan involved putting the children's names on the board when they did something wrong and adding check marks for each additional discipline problem throughout the day. The consequences included phone calls home, missed recess, and trips to the principal's office. I really did not feel comfortable with this system, so I chose not to use it. For the past six years, I have not had an established behavior plan, but I have found very effective ways to handle discipline problems within my classroom. At the beginning of the year, my students work together to brainstorm a set of class rules. Typically their ideas include a lot of statements that begin with "don't." After brainstorming, the students vote on the four rules that they feel are most important. It is interesting that they have always picked the four I would have chosen myself. At that point, we work together to come up with ways to restate the rules in a positive way. For example, instead of "Don't hit people," we might say, "Keep your body to yourself." After developing the rules themselves, the children have such ownership of them and are much more apt to follow them. The children remind their friends about the rules and let them know if they are breaking one of them. This decreases the discipline problems. I also encourage the children to handle as many of the problems on their own as they can. For example, if two children get into an argument on the playground, the first thing I have them do is sit down and share their side of the story with each other. Sometimes this is all it takes for them to see it was just a misunderstanding. Then, if someone has been hurt in the incident, I ask them to tell me what they feel a fair consequence would be. Most of they time they are harder on themselves than I would be. I believe that it is important to put as much of the situation in their hands as possible. There is not always going to be an adult around when they have a problem, and I want them to have the skills to handle situations on their own. My main goal is to teach the children the skills to solve their own problems and monitor their own behavior.

What Role Does Your Classroom Environment Play in the Learning Experience?

I believe that the classroom environment plays a big part in the learning experience. I try to make my classroom vibrant and visually pleasing without being overwhelming. I know that my surroundings determine my mood, and I think that children are affected in the same way. They need colorful things to look at during the day and they need an environment that is nurturing. In my classroom, I have posters and decorations on the walls and stuffed animals and pillows in various locations around the room. I also have areas of the room that are designated as quiet or cozy areas, for those times when a child needs to take a break from the action. The children need to know that they are in a safe place, and they need to know what is expected of them. Good planning of the environment can prevent discipline problems from even happening. I always make sure that I don't have any long, open spaces in my class that might look like a road and encourage running. I also arrange the materials in my room so that it is ready for several small groups (rather than one large group) so that there is less chance of an argument between the children. I have found that little environmental changes can change the entire mood of the classroom.

Describe the Benefits of Long-Term Projects

Long term projects are great within the classroom and really amazing to be involved with. So much learning takes place during one project, and it crosses into all academic subject areas. I think that is one of the biggest benefits of a long-term project. It touches on all subject areas and makes everything more meaningful for the children because it all ties together and they see the connections. When I was in elementary school, I remember having a certain time for math and a certain time for reading and a certain time for science. It never went together. By using projects, I can incorporate all of the subject areas together. The children get to see how it all blends together, just like it will in the real world. This past year we were doing a project about sea creatures. The children were very curious about the size of some of the sea creatures, so we pulled in our math skills and did some measuring. I sent the children off with yardsticks and rulers to map out the size of a sea creature they were curious about. They were fascinated by what they discovered when they could actually "see" how big it was. Not only were they learning about sea creatures, but they were also practicing their measurement skills. Projects provide learning moments like that all the time.

Describe the Use and Benefits of Documentation by You and the Students in Your Classroom

I am known at my school for keeping the walls covered with the children's work and documentation of what is taking place in my classroom. I am always putting out new things in the hall and usually looking for more room to display things. Documentation is crucial in the learning process. It reminds children of where they are and where they have been, and encourages them to think about where they might go next. I surround my children with displays about what we are working on and the things we have learned. It is great for them to be able to go back and look at something we discussed early on in the project and remember what happened and what we learned. It also allows them to make comparisons between things and learn even more. The children love seeing their work, their words, and their names up on the walls. It seems to give them even more ownership of the classroom and really makes them feel valued and special. I love to watch them walk up and proudly show another child something they have done that is on display. My students also document their own learning throughout the year, especially in science activities. When we do experiments, I often ask them to document what they saw and learned. It is fascinating to see eighteen children document the same experiment in eighteen different ways, but all have an understanding of what took place. It is extremely rewarding!

CARLA LIVERSEDGE: FIRST- AND SECOND-GRADE TEACHER, PARENT CO-OP

Demographics

Twenty-five years old; three years of teaching (one year at the preschool level); graduated from Virginia Tech with a B.S. in human development, with a concentration in early childhood education.

Teaching Philosophy

My teaching philosophy consists of three major components. The first and most important component is to know my students. The second is to create a comfortable and safe environment. The third important component is for me to be and feel a part of the school community.

I believe that to teach students I need to know them. I need to build a relationship with them. This is the foundation of my teaching philosophy. I am fortunate enough to be in a situation where I have my students for two years. Each year I do say good-bye to some students and meet new ones as well. No matter how long I have known the students, I am continually getting to know students better throughout the year, not just at the beginning of the year. I use my knowledge of the students to implement a curriculum based on the students' strengths and needs, to problem-solve social and behavioral issues, and to help determine the direction of the curriculum.

I believe in encouraging a noncompetitive, accepting academic and social environment. I want every child to have a voice and feel a part of the classroom community.

Not only do I want my students to participate in cooperative learning, but I also want to work well with the teachers in my school and learn from this. I think it is important for the students to see the teachers in their school working well together and see their teachers comfortable in their work environment.

How Does Your Philosophy of Teaching Mesh with Who You Are as a Person?

Each one of the components of my teaching philosophy correlates with my personality. The most important one is building relationships with my students. This is also important to me in my private life. My family is a priority. I enjoy continually getting to know friends and family and enjoy being there for important life events. School is not the only place that I want people to feel comfortable and safe.

I want everyone who comes into my home to feel welcome. I love having friends and family around me. I want to work well with others in my life outside of school.

Describe Your Approach to Covering the Required Curriculum, Assessing the Learning That Is Occurring in Your Classroom, and Keeping Schooling a Joyful Experience

Sometimes those things can feel like opposites, especially covering the required curriculum and keeping schooling a joyful experience. However, I am learning how to work with learning standards, not let them take over my curriculum, and I'm learning not to tense up anytime someone mentions them. They are a part of our curriculum, as are important community and school events and developing curriculum with children, parents, and teachers.

When I began teaching first and second grade, I planned for only one theme in advance. I realized from conversations with parents and teachers that knowing at least the next several themes would be appreciated. At first, I felt like I could not accommodate this. I felt that by planning several themes in advance I would stop listening for emerging curriculum. I can now plan in advance because of the information I have on my students from previous narrative evaluations, conversations, and observations, and because I allow myself to change the themes if needed. This plan allows for parents and school administration to have the information they need to feel confident or raise questions about the curriculum.

In the summer before the school year begins, I consider the next year's curriculum. Many theme ideas come from previous conversations with students and parents, evaluations from the previous teacher, and my previous knowledge of the students. I use these ideas and ideas from other teachers to formulate a long-term plan for theme topics. However, I allow myself to change the topics as other things emerge. After I have a preliminary schedule of themes, I sit down and correlate the themes with the state standards. I do not teach only the state standards, but I do see how they can fit into my plan. Since I teach a combined first- and second-grade classroom, I do not teach all the social studies and science standards for each grade each year. Instead, some standards from both grades and both science and social studies are correlated with our class's themes. Once the school year begins, I keep listening for emerging curriculum. This could mean some themes are cut and others are added, or we go in a different direction in that particular theme.

I believe that continually building relationships with students and building classroom community through academic and nonacademic activities is a way to keep school a joyful experience. This often happens naturally during reading and writing workshops. Reading stories aloud is extremely important. It fulfills standards for literacy and often touches on other subjects, but it also helps build community. Also, having a time when students are reading to themselves, incorporating a time to share their thoughts and feelings about books they have read, and carving out other times to share their work are ways we are continually learning from and about each other. Students are also learning to listen to each other. Not only am I working to keep school joyful during these times, but I am also assessing students.

I use other more formal assessments and plan for those. However, I don't feel that they take over our class time. I try to vary my assessment techniques, with less time spent on things like spelling tests and more on authentic assessment.

How Do You Determine What Has Been Learned and How, in a Classroom with a Wide Variety of Learning Styles?

A variety of assessment occurs in my classroom. In several subject areas, I keep records of anecdotal notes and class brainstorming sessions. Both formal and informal assessments are given to the students. I often record information into a checklist form, as well as keeping some work samples. Here are some specific examples of assessment in each subject area:

- *Writing Workshop:* writing sample analyses, running records of conferences
- *Word Study:* Formal Spelling Inventory, observations, inclusion of skills into writing and reading
- *Spelling:* spelling practice and tests
- *Reading Workshop:* running records of guided reading group, formal reading evaluations, projects and independent work related to readings
- *Math:* formal assessments from teacher- and publisher-created materials, application of skills into large-group lessons and discussions and small-group problem-solving skills, participation in group activities
- *Science/Social Studies:* observations, photographs, written assessments, projects, academic games

How Do You Keep Interest and Motivation Alive and Strong in Your Classroom?

Again, I think building and maintaining relationships with students is important. One part of that is listening to the students. I build listening to my students into the curriculum. During my student teaching, I discovered the importance of using K-W-L charts. I noticed the interest generated just asking the questions

"What do you *Know* about _____?"
"What do you *Want* to know about _____?"
"What have you *Learned* about _____?"

I think writing down what the students said showed them that what they had to say was important. Last year I asked my students, "What have you learned about ancient China?" Instead of recording their responses on a pad of paper, I asked them to create in cooperative groups a mural representing what they had learned. The murals hung in our room for most of the school year. I remember the excitement in their voices when they realized the next day that I had hung them up. If they know I'm listening to them, I think they feel that they have a voice in our classroom.

How Does Your Brand of Teaching and Learning Coincide or Conflict with That of the Other Faculty in Your School? If There Are Conflicts, How Do You Handle the Dissonance?

There are differences and similarities with our teaching methods. However, the differences don't feel like conflicts because of the open and respectful learning environment that is there for teachers as well as students. I am very fortunate to work with the teachers at my school. I feel a sense of real cooperation. Often, our lunch discussions are about what and how we are teaching. I go to the teachers to help me problem-solve various issues. We are all different, of course, and it is interesting to see how that plays out in our teaching. We all have respect for our students, each other, teaching, and learning. I think that because we respect each other's ideas and listen to each other, differences are allowed.

What Role Do Families Play in your Classroom?

Families play a big role in my classroom. Volunteers for field trips or for making special snacks for our classroom are always appreciated. Also, I have parent volunteers who have committed to being in-class assistants, and also I have an out-of-class assistant. These are yearlong positions. Often parents come in for students' birthdays. There have been several instances of a parent saying, "I'm here for a few minutes. I can read to them while you get ready." The cooperative environment of our school facilitates these kinds of interactions.

Do You Have Discipline Problems in Your Classroom? If So, How Do You Handle These Behaviors?

I think every classroom has some discipline issues. At the beginning of the year, my students and I create a classroom contract. We brainstorm rules and also consequences for breaking those rules. I help to guide my students in creating these because I want to keep the consequences as logical as possible. For specific issues that come up with individual students, I have used behavior contracts. Sometimes this has helped and sometimes it hasn't. I think that the process of identifying the specific problem behavior with the student is important. Also, the students think of positive consequences for completing the behavior contract. I think it is important that the parents are involved in this process as well. Usually I would not start a contract without having discussed the problem behavior with the parents and the possibility of using a contract. Parent involvement in solving issues is key.

What Role Does Your Classroom Environment Play in the Learning Experience?

There are some very important elements to my classroom environment: space, organization, and lighting. My students need space to learn. Each year that I rearrange the space, I try to maximize their space while considering my needs as well. The students sit at tables when they are working. Depending on the lesson, students are sitting at the tables or in a circle on the carpet. The carpet area is also used for literature read-aloud and during free time.

I think it is important that the classroom reflect not only the students' needs but also the needs of the teacher. I am a part of the classroom. The first year I was teaching first and second grade, I did not allow much of a workspace for myself because I wanted the students to have as much room as possible. I had projects and papers stacked up in my small space, and it felt very cluttered and unwelcoming. The second year I created a much larger space for myself. This helped me feel like I was part of the class community. Although it seems like a small thing, it made a big difference in the way I felt about being in the classroom. It took me a whole year to realize that and change it. I think it took so long partially because giving the students what they needed is a big part of my teaching philosophy, and I felt that I couldn't change that. I still believe in identifying the students' needs and trying to accommodate them, but now I include myself as well.

I think a classroom environment should be organized. I have many books, and my classroom would be in chaos without an organizational system for them. The students don't come in knowing how my books are organized, but after a few lessons they have a general idea, and we go from there.

I love natural and warm light, and I try to keep the windows unblocked. Last year my students often wanted me to turn off the fluorescent lights and use only the natural light and lamps. This creates a cozy and comfortable feeling in our room.

Describe the Benefits of Long-Term Projects

Last year we studied our ocean theme for almost two months. Over that time, the students were able to complete two at-home projects to share in a museum day, as well as spend time in class on learning about many different aspects of ocean life. Also, the art teacher was able to incorporate different projects into our ocean theme. Because we studied this so long, we covered many topics that had to do with the ocean. I noticed that all of our students were interested in at least one topic in that large theme. The students were very proud to display their projects during the museum day. I think another benefit was that this project became a community building event. Two of our classes were studying this topic, the whole school saw the students' work, as well as their parents, and we were able to take two field trips during this time. We could look back on that time and remember different things from it because there was so much to remember.

Describe the Use and Benefits of Documentation by You and the Students in Your Classroom

There are a few ways documentation occurs in my classroom. There are two major end-of-the-year documentation products. Throughout the year, I take photographs of different events. The past two years I have compiled them into portfolios with captions for my students. I like to include samples of their work in the portfolio or photographs of their work. These books are for the students, and they receive them on the last day of school. The students enjoy looking through these end-of-year gifts. I use my notes, checklists, and other forms of assessment to write the end-of-year evaluations. These narrative assessments are given to the parents before the last conference of the year. These act as "report cards," but give much more detail on the student's academic, social, and personal development.

I like to include class displays of learning as well. These include things like the ancient China murals, a mural representing the layers of the rain forest, and a labeled diagram of the ocean environment. I also like to document their individual work for others to see. Last year, families would often stop to read the display of autobiographies my students completed. These were accompanied by black-and-white headshots of the students that I took in class and a title that explained the purpose of our study. This use of documentation allows families to see what their children are doing in school, our school community to see what we have been learning, and my students to know that I value their work.

GRETCHEN DISTLER: SIXTH-GRADE TEACHER

Demographics

My name is Gretchen Distler. I am thirty-three years old. I have happily taught sixth-grade language arts and social studies at Blacksburg Middle School for the past nine years. I teach in a county that supports the idea of fully including children with disabilities in each classroom, so there is often more than one adult in the classroom. From kindergarten through third grade, I was a student at Blacksburg New School (a small, liberal, hippy dippy private school). From fourth to ninth grade, I went to public schools in Blacksburg, Virginia. I spent my sophomore year in Italy attending a tiny American school in Turin (there were six kids in my class). I returned to Blacksburg to finish eleventh and twelfth grades at Blacksburg High. After taking a year off, I went to New Orleans and spent six wild years at the University of New Orleans.

Teaching Philosophy

It's all about **RELATIONSHIPS**! Before I even begin thinking about curriculum, I make sure that I have developed some sort of rapport with each of my students. When I know where they are coming from and they know where I am coming from, it makes the teaching–learning experience a thousand times better.

How Does Your Philosophy of Teaching Mesh with Who You Are as a Person?

Hummmmmmmmmmmmmm. I thrive on interactions with people, so I guess there is not really a separation between my teaching philosophy and who I am as a person.

Describe Your Approach to Covering the Required Curriculum, Assessing the Learning That Is Occurring in Your Classroom, and Keeping Schooling a Joyful Experience

Kids are so curious; making sure the required curriculum is covered is rarely a problem. I chunk the material into large units and incorporate as many different teaching and learning tools as possible. The students ask a lot of questions, and most of the time they find the answers with just a little guidance from me. At the end of a large unit (one to two months), when I look at the state requirements, we have usually "covered" all of the requirements and much more. As far as assessment, it really depends on what we are doing at the time. I ask the students to "react" in their journals a lot. A reaction can be a number of things (a picture, a poem, a few paragraphs . . .). When I analyze their reactions, I can get a good feel for what they do and do not understand. If there are aspects the students didn't quite grasp, we revisit sections of the unit from a different angle. Keeping it joyful goes back to relationships. When I know my students well, I know what makes them tick, and I keep that in the forefront of our teaching–learning interactions. I also make sure that I am having a good time, and that contributes to the mood in our space.

How Do You Determine What Has Been Learned and How, in a Classroom with a Wide Variety of Learning Styles?

Luckily, there are so so so many ways to determine what a student has learned. I have not given a traditional test or quiz in over six years. During a unit, we may have a number of small learning check-ins. For example, I might ask the students to choose between writing a journal entry from the point of view of a character we are studying, or to make a map, or to design a web site (on paper). During this stage of evaluation, choice is absolutely essential. The more choices I offer, the more learning styles are satisfied. It seems that the best way to determine what a student has learned is to simply ask him or her. At the end of a unit or period of study, I ask the students to do a lot of reflection. I offer questions to be considered, such as, What did you like best about this unit? What was interesting? What was boring? What struggles did you encounter? What was new? What was review? What would you like to know more about? What are your overall thoughts? These questions are answered in their journals and are more process than product oriented. It is so much easier to really assess a child's learning and share with his or her parents doing it this way. When I used to give tests, I never really felt that I had a good idea about what was going on in my students' heads. Yes, I could see what they did not know, but I didn't see what was exciting them, or boring them, or, most important, really making them think.

How Do You Keep Interest and Motivation Alive and Strong in your Classroom?

It is a struggle to keep interest and motivation going strong for each child throughout the entire year! Mostly, I try to think of the individuals in our room. When I am pulling together materials, I try to make sure I have a little something for everyone. Sometimes, when the information is less than enthralling, we turn it into a different lesson. For example, when we study Christopher Columbus, I try to show them that history is written by those who are in power and that they can't always believe everything they read. We research as many accounts of Columbus as we can find (at least six), and then we compare and contrast the information we have gathered. It always turns out that no two sources tell the exact same story (and sometimes the stories are drastically different). That leads into discussions about primary and secondary sources and why history is written with a slant. So in a case where interest may be waning, I can sometimes get the kids fired up in other ways ("You mean they can write things that are not true in our history book?!").

How Does Your Brand of Teaching and Learning Coincide or Conflict with That of Other Faculty in Your School? If There Are Conflicts, How Do You Handle the Dissonance?

Those of us who share similar philosophies and are interested in collaboration seek each other out to bounce ideas around, offer support, and share ideas. There are other teachers who have very different philosophies, but obviously what they are doing works for them. I have never really experienced much conflict over methods. I guess we realize there are as many teaching styles as there are learning styles. That goes back to the relationship thing again.

What Role Do Families Play in Your Classroom?

The direct role the families play in our room is not as large as I would like it to be. Family involvement is something I put a lot of thought into, but I know that I have a long way to go. Again, in the beginning of the year I work really hard to establish a relationship with every family. Sometime during the first two weeks of school, my teammate and I have a potluck dinner for the families on our team. During the dinner, the students introduce their parents and siblings to the rest of the families. Then we try to meet with each family individually (either at school, at a coffee shop, or at their home) just to share thoughts and information. These meetings usually occur during the first six weeks of school. Most of our parents have e-mail addresses, so I write a general letter at the end of each week to share what we did during the week and what the following week might look like. I also use these letters to bring up issues (social, academic, emotional) that need to be addressed. For those parents who do not have e-mail, I print a hard copy and slide it into their child's homework assignment book. I also correspond with individual parents via e-mail throughout the week. We try to have family socials at least four times during the year. We also invite parents to come in and share stories or information about their jobs, their families, their past, an interesting trip. . . . We usually have a handful of parents with flexible schedules who join us on field trips, lead literature circles, or help out in other ways, but most of the parents work during the day and do not have flexible time. That is where I feel some conflict when trying to increase the interactions with families. I am a working mom and feel a good deal of guilt that I cannot be more active in my children's schools. At night I am tired and just want to have family time at home. Philosophically, I believe having many opportunities for families to be involved is important, but I also think about the parents who also do not have flexible schedules. I hate to be a factor in parents feeling badly about the amount of time they are or are not able to invest in their child's school. I know there is a perfect balance out there; hopefully I will find it before I retire.

What Discipline Problems Do You Have in Your Classroom? How Do You Handle These Behaviors?

Relationships, relationships, relationships! I am not saying that our room is in perfect harmony all the time—everyone has rough days—but I spend very little class time on "discipline." Once I know my students well, I can be proactive. If I notice one of the kids is a bit off, right away I try to get him or her involved in something I know he or she is interested in. I learned quickly that having a power struggle with a sixth grader is a lose–lose situation. Sometimes a child just needs to chill outside of the room, so I'll send him or her on an errand with a friend. I attempt to be as respectful as possible and add humor whenever I can. It really comes down to trying to understand what is going on with that person and addressing any problems on an individual basis. In years that my relationships with the students are very strong, I don't really have issues with discipline. We are a group of human beings, and when we treat each other with understanding and mutual respect, things run smoothly.

What Role Does Your Classroom Environment Play in the Learning Experience?

This is another area I am constantly thinking about and working on. I obviously use the space I have to document what we are working on as projects unfold. We put up examples of the students' work with written explanations to accompany the work. We take a lot of photographs and make sure they are always displayed. I try to create comfortable spaces with pillows, beanbags, and plants. I think that when a stranger enters our space, he or she can get some feel for what we are about. We try to make the room look and feel as welcoming as possible, but I am never completely happy with the environment. It always feels like I need more, or less, or something different.

Describe the Benefits of Long-Term Projects

The reason I love long-term projects is the infinite possibilities that accompany them. When we begin an investigation, I obviously have a desired outcome in mind, but the questions that arise and the direction the inquiries take always surprise me. Spur-of-the-moment discussions that can pop up challenge me and the students in ways a textbook never could. Even after nine years, I continue to be in awe of the eleven- and twelve-year-old people I work with. I feel that if we took a more traditional approach, we (the class and I) would not have the opportunity to see the brilliance buried deep within these kids. With long-term, multilayered projects, every student is involved in ways that are comfortable to him or her. Also, when some aspect of a project really blossoms, not only am I excited, but the students are too. After all, most of the issues and investigations stem from their questions and discussions. Long-term projects remind me how very lucky I am to work with these young people.

Describe the Use and Benefits of Documentation by You and the Students in Your Classroom

For me, documentation serves a number of important purposes. First and foremost, it reminds us where we have been. I try to keep documentation up for the entire year so we can revisit whenever we need to. It is also a fantastic visual for anyone who is curious about what goes on in the room. Finally, and least important, it validates what we are doing. If there are people who doubt the approach we are taking to teaching and learning, it is our "proof" that amazing things are happening within the four walls of our room.

ELIZABETH BLOOMER: COLLEGE INSTRUCTOR, FIRST-YEAR ENGLISH

Demographics

Thirty-six year old; fourteen years of teaching: twelve years as an instructor, plus two years as a graduate teaching assistant of college-age students (typically undergraduates). B.A. in English from Virginia Tech, an M.A. in English from Virginia Tech, and another M.A. in children's literature from Hollins University.

Philosophy of Teaching

"Come to the edge," he said.
They said, "We are afraid."
"Come to the edge," he said.
   They came.
  He pushed them
  And they flew
          Apollinaire

When my husband and I first enrolled our four-year-old into the wonderful preschool here at Virginia Tech, we discussed learning theories with the young teachers. What I recognized was a teaching philosophy I hoped to embody in my own collegiate classes: the Reggio Emilia approach of the award-winning Italian schools that practices the idea of "nothing without joy"—and also suggests that the role of the teacher is of one who "brings the students to the edge."

Of course, my students are much older, typically eighteen to twenty-one years of age, and have presumably chosen to engage in active learning and the joys of education. However, what I have found too often in my twelve years as an English instructor is that many of our students do not have a joy of reading and writing. Somewhere along the way many of them have lost or subdued their curiosity and intellectual inquiry. Too many of my students have written end-of-the-year letters to me that start with, "When I first thought of a college English class, I thought I was going to hate it." Thankfully, by the end of the semester, they ask for lists of good books and tell me they love writing—some even switch their majors to English!

My first challenge is to get my students hooked—to share my intense passion for reading others' ideas and convey enthusiasm for writing. I find that my students do their best when they really enjoy what they are reading. Therefore, I must choose literature that students will find themselves in—after all, something is more meaningful if we find reflections of ourselves in it. A connection grows between the reader and the story. In my 1106 Critical Literacy course, students favor Octavia Butler's novel *Kindred,* the triumphant plight of a young African American woman living in the 1970s who is pulled through the wall into the antebellum South, where she finds herself on her great-great-grandfather's plantation. This story of a young woman who crosses dangerous boundaries captivates the students; they take part in the story, and they are compelled to respond by writing their ideas as their own texts. They engage in the community of learners who are actively, carefully inquiring into our world. As they begin to unfold the story and their ideas, they participate in a socially constructed experience and collaborate in their learning environment. They are hooked.

And this is that amazing point I wait for—the point when I look out to see that my students are completely engrossed; so much so that I am no longer the one who is pulling and pushing. Instead, the students are the ones moving the class forward. This is when the students begin to take over; they make the joyful choice of becoming responsible for their own learning. They become active learners. Once the students have been hooked by a good book, once they rekindle the love of learning, everything else seems to fall into place. In creative writing courses, the philosophy is the same, though hooking the students is slightly different. While I certainly believe that a teacher can lecture and do a fine job, I tend to believe that active learning on the students' part is more effective—especially in a writing course. And I have found that learning is more powerful when humor and metaphor are used. For example, in the introduction to creative writing class, I have brought in slides of famous paintings; one in particular is by Picasso. Rather than lecture about *persona, antiheroic alter ego,* or *dramatic monologue,* I ask the students to write what the figure in the painting is thinking . . . to tell her story. What comes from such assignments is often amazingly poignant, sometimes humorous, and oftentimes a remarkable study of self. Afterwards, in discussing the prompt with the students, we talk about the theories of their stories and then begin to understand these writing techniques more clearly—because the students have actively engaged in them themselves. They are willing to try new ideas, see what others see, critique, and trust their inquiry.

My next challenge, after helping the students find the joy of learning again, is to bring my students to the edge. What this metaphor means to me is that I must help the students to see critically what they might not want to see, to move beyond the safety net. I must help the students celebrate the state of not knowing and show them that the state of confusion is good. I want to help them step out of the mold. To do this, I must help my students learn to play again—to take chances, investigate, and tell their stories. I help my students figure out the questions we can ask of any text, whether it be a Pepsi can, poem, advertisement, essay, or novel. Then, by asking such questions, we can begin to understand that text more deeply. In the beginning of each semester, my students and I begin making of list of the huge questions we have about life and our world: "Why are we here?"; "Is there a larger power?"; "What is our social responsibility? Our professional obligation?"; "What kind of government works the best?" Then, after each text we read, we go back and amend the list with more specific questions, questions such as, "What does this text have to do with community?"; "What does this text have to do with environment and ecology?" and "What does this text have to do with economy, class, and money?" By creating a toolbag list of such questions, the students begin to embark on critical literacy, even beginning to understand and use such theories as sociohistoricism, reader response, feminism, Marxism, ecological, and psychoanalytic.

When the students realize that they are engaging in a worldwide conversation of ideas, they feel a part of a larger whole, and realize that their ideas and voices matter. When I can help a student arrive here—to the point where she knows her voice matters, or his ideas are beautiful; when I see students realizing they are part of a larger context; when a student's letter to the editor is published, a student's poem is accepted into a journal, or another reads an essay to a large audience; when the students test their wings again—that is when teaching is the greatest profession there is.

How Does Your Philosophy of Teaching Mesh with Who You Are as a Person?

I suppose I teach in a way that is very much like who I am as a person. I shoot for joy all the time—which is evident in the fact that my office is filled with beautiful toys, illustrated books, pens imbued with mystical powers, crayons, music, and reams of paper. I am most often found in overalls so that I can sit on the ground outside with my students, but also so that I don't appear intimidating. I don't want to "dress for success," as they say; I want to "dress for play" so that my students and I can get down to business.

Describe Your Approach to Covering the Required Curriculum, Assessing the Learning That Is Occurring in Your Classroom, and Keeping Schooling a Joyful Experience

At the collegiate level, I am concerned with how often I hear from other faculty members that they "do not have the time to entertain their students, and that they don't have time for joyous activities." While I understand their feelings of pressure to cover certain material, what disturbs me is that faculty often assume that being happy in the classroom somehow reflects simplicity—that those who are joyful in their work must not be really doing work. I am not suggesting that to bring joy to the classroom we must amuse our students; amusement, after all, implies passiveness and an audience. Rather, I am suggesting that the students be motivated into bringing their joy to what we must learn. I have always found that shifting into joyful learning is not only rewarding to the students but profoundly enjoyable to me as well. For example, in first-year English, we must cover grammar. Instead of lecturing about it (which we now know is the least effective way to transfer information), I tell humorous stories with funny grammatical utterances and have the students teach the rest of the class one rule we need to cover. The students know (as we have discussed) the kinds of learning we remember: active learning involves storytelling, humor, and actually teaching the subject matter. The students make up skits or build sentences with blocks. I remember one group in particular had to explain run-on sentences. They painted an enormous road map, with sentences as roads. At each "intersection" were bridges between the sentences, illustrated with commas and coordinating conjunctions, semicolons, or periods that sent the "car" back to start to rewrite the road. It was creative, funny, and memorable.

To assess learning, I must assign grades at this university. If the students help us to remember in joyful, interesting, creative ways, then they have been successful and therefore receive high grades.

We do require essays and grading at my university—and while I know that this exchange promotes the strange hypocrisy of commodifying education, I think feedback is extremely important in the learning process. My feedback of the students' writing is a lengthy paragraph in which I write about their content, organization, cohesion, and clarity—accompanied by a letter grade. The students who have come to the table with insights—with questions, finds, confusions, and connections—are the students who are beginning to inquire again into their world. When a student writes, "I don't have the answers, but I have these questions, . . ." and when a student begins to engage in the joyous big questions, well, then I know that she has begun again on the path.

How Do You Keep Interest and Motivation Alive and Strong in Your Classroom?

I keep interest and motivation alive with these three things: First, I like to surprise my students. Not shock—surprise. For example, I might come into class and say, "Your in-class writing today is to define the difference between actuality and truth." Their eyes light up, they giggle, they raise their hands to ask me questions, and I simply say back, "Look, I don't have the answers—but you might begin to bring some neat stuff to the table. Write. Let's see what happens." On another day when I need to work with the students on, say, argument, I will begin class with a fun question like, "Cheesecake: Is it pie or cake?" What happens here is that students will begin to realize that opinions alone won't cut it (pun intended); instead, one student will usually say, "Well, we could consult a friend of mine who is a chef" or "Let's look it up in a culinary dictionary." Without me ever standing in front of them and defining argument, they have acted the process and discovered that arguing a position means research, questioning the opposition, and looking for off-the-wall possibilities through discussion with a wide range of backgrounds and beliefs. Second, I like to send the students out of the classroom to realize that learning happens everywhere and to provide some refreshing change. If I must "teach" comparison and contrast, then I'll take my students to the horticulture gardens here on campus and have them find two flowers, shrubs, or koi in the pond and write about the two—their differences and likenesses. And third, I try to allow for enough flexibility in my calendar for the serendipitous. Each class, even if it's the same course, will go in different places, and I believe that intellectual curiosity is furthered when we encourage time to meander. In one of my creative writing classes, for example, I had a student who loved rap music. He brought in a couple of CDs, and we played them for the class when we were discussing rythm and rhyme. I changed my next assignment to incorporate a rap; I brought in a painting of St. George and the dragon and asked the students to write what the dragon was thinking—as a rap. The poetry that came out of this assignment was simply amazing.

How Does Your Brand of Teaching and Learning Coincide or Conflict with That of Other Faculty in Your School? If There Are Conflicts, How Do You Handle the Dissonance?

Another faculty member said to me once that he didn't like all the "busywork" my students did. Being interested in words, I started thinking about what busywork really is. Strangely, I think I like busywork! I think my students like being busy! The best moments in my class occur when my students say to me in so many words, "Leave me alone, I'm busy!" So what's wrong with being busy? I think there are not necessarily conflicts between faculty at the university so much as there are misunderstandings or feelings of inadequacy. I know that while some other teachers might be concerned that their classroom is not joyous, others also feel that their work shouldn't be joyful: It's too serious! What I hope happens in our culture is that we shift from thinking that that which is serious is not fun or joyful. A good work ethic to me seems to be one where we find joy in our serious work.

What Role Do Families Play in Your Classroom?

While my students are older and not accompanied to school by their families, we do discuss our community here and at home. Certainly, my students who are comfortable with their families seem to be happier away at college. And I also see quite a lot of unhappiness in the students who feel forced into a certain major by their parents. Some students don't even want to be in college, but are doing what their parents wanted them to do. Unfortunately, many of these students fail on purpose, which is devastating to their sense of education and how they learn. What I find myself saying over and over again is "Do what you love" and, as Joseph Campbell says, "Follow your bliss." I hope these ideas sink in. I also see that students build a new kind of family here at college, a family of friends and faculty who are interested in the same kinds of learning. It is in this kind of family where I think students begin to really collaborate. I jokingly call each one of my classes a "little family where learning is based on us all together," and, since I come from Hawaii, that we are "ohana"—and, like Lilo and Stitch say, "Family stays together and no one gets left behind." Learning doesn't work in a vacuum. I think it happens in ohana.

What Discipline Problems Do You Have in Your Classroom? How Do You Handle These Behaviors?

In the college classroom, discipline is rarely an issue. More often, it's an attitude. I have several students a year who are angry that they are here, angry that they have to take an English class when they are not even English majors, and even angry that their crazy English teacher has the audacity to suggest that education should be joyful. After all, if their educational experience has been difficult and emotionally stressful, then suggesting that it should have been joyful means that I am exposing a fault in their lives. A lot of students come to class with pains that I might not ever grasp—pains from being severely abused, emotionally neglected, or teased when they tried to communicate a deepness. When they come into a safe space where they can let their guard down, sometimes the initial response is an outburst of anger. I try to handle such times with a bit of humor, or even better, let the other students suggest help—and nine out of ten times, they do. Another student will quip something funny, like "Hey, remember in here it's 'no joy, no gain.'"

What Role Does Your Classroom Environment Play in the Learning Experience?

My classroom environment is not my own at the university—I teach in all sorts of different places and different environments—and unfortunately most of the older classrooms are not what I'd call conducive to learning: seats bolted to the floor in a lecture format; no windows; a huge desk in front that divides me from them. We talk about this. We laugh. We go outside and sit in a circle. We lie on the floor and listen to each other read. We make do because we have to, but also because our environment in the writing classroom is really what we write. It's a space that we fill by our written communication—and it's usually pretty beautiful there.

Describe the Benefits of Long-Term Projects

In first-year composition classes (formerly known as freshman English), we have small projects like journal writing (working through such questions as the cheesecake one or the truth versus actuality one) that lead into the essays, which lead into the final writing project at the end of the second semester: a kind of research paper where the student defines his or her own line of interest and goes for it. The bene-fits are enormous: In this long-term writing project, we have seven weeks to re-search, discuss, change our minds, rewrite, flail, and "bring others to the table." In the end, the students have opened up a line of inquiry that allows for pondering the big questions—and, more important, illustrates by active learning the role of one's self in one's own education: We learn what we want to learn; we can teach ourselves anything; we are part of the big discussion; we matter.

Describe the Use and Benefits of Documentation by You and the Students in Your Classroom

In my classes, the students make the documentation—they write the journals, the letters, the essays; they videotape the interviews, the natural scenes, the environ-mental issues they want to write about. My documentation is in feedback by writ-ing to the students in each of their pieces. And finally, at the end of the semester, we put a book together of the students' best work so they have an artifact of the be-ginning of their journey.

INDEX